American
Conservative Thought
Since
World War II

Recent Titles in
Contributions in Political Science

The President and Civil Rights Policy: Leadership and Change
Steven A. Shull

Nominating Presidents: An Evaluation of Voters and Primaries
John G. Geer

A Right to Bear Arms: State and Federal Bills of Rights and Constitutional Guarantees
Stephen P. Halbrook

The Politics of Economic Adjustment: Pluralism, Corporatism, and Privatization
Richard E. Foglesong and Joel D. Wolfe, editors

Policy through Impact Assessment: Institutionalized Analysis as a Policy Strategy
Robert V. Bartlett, editor

Behind the Uprising: Israelis, Jordanians, and Palestinians
Yossi Melman and Dan Raviv

From Feudalism to Capitalism: Marxian Theories of Class Struggle and Social Change
Claudio Katz

The Challenge of the Exception: An Introduction to the Political Ideas of Carl Schmitt between 1921 and 1936, Second Edition
George Schwab

The Demobilization of American Voters: A Comprehensive Theory of Voter Turnout
Michael J. Avey

Iran: From Royal Dictatorship to Theocracy
Mohammed Amjad

Managing Fiscal Strain in Major American Cities: Understanding Retrenchment in the Public Sector
William J. Pammer, Jr.

The Latin American Narcotics Trade and U.S. National Security
Donald J. Mabry, editor

Public Policy and Transit System Management
George M. Guess, editor

American Conservative Thought Since World War II

THE CORE IDEAS

Melvin J. Thorne

CONTRIBUTIONS IN POLITICAL SCIENCE, NUMBER 251
Bernard K. Johnpoll, *Series Editor*

GREENWOOD PRESS
New York • Westport, Connecticut • London

Library of Congress Cataloging-in-Publication Data

Thorne, Melvin J.
American conservative thought since World War II : the core ideas
/ Melvin J. Thorne.
p. cm. — (Contributions in political science, ISSN 0147-1066
; no. 251)
Includes bibliographical references.
ISBN 0-313-26731-6 (lib. bdg. : alk. paper)
1. Conservatism—United States—History—20th century. I. Title.
II. Series.
JA84.U5T49 1990
320.5'2'0973—dc20 89-23303

British Library Cataloguing in Publication Data is available.

Library of Congress Catalog Card Number: 89-23303
ISBN: 0-313-26731-6
ISSN: 0147-1066

First published in 1990

Greenwood Press, Inc.
88 Post Road West, Westport, Connecticut 06881

Printed in the United States of America

The paper used in this book complies with the
Permanent Paper Standard issued by the National
Information Standards Organization (Z39.48-1984).

10 9 8 7 6 5 4 3 2 1

CONTENTS

Acknowledgments   *ix*

1. The Elusive Definition of Conservatism   1

2. Unchanging Human Nature   21

3. The Objective Moral Order   37

4. The Need for Authority   55

5. Freedom vs. Authority   77

6. Government and Economy   101

7. Community   137

8. Change and Tradition   163

   Bibliography   *183*

   Index   *193*

ACKNOWLEDGMENTS

Of the many people who have given me assistance and helpful criticism in this project, two deserve particular mention. I owe a great debt of gratitude, both personal and intellectual, to Clifford S. Griffin, for his encouragement and especially for his questions, which have made me think and rethink this material. I fear that I never answered a few of those questions to his satisfaction, and my conclusions about this material are often not the same as his. Yet my conclusions are much better for his scrutiny.

And for the unfailing support and penetrating criticism of my wife, Sandra, on this and on every worthwhile project I undertake, no thanks could ever be sufficient.

1

THE ELUSIVE DEFINITION
OF CONSERVATISM

A major problem hindering the understanding and evaluation of conservative thought in America is the lack of an adequate definition of conservatism. This is especially true of the contemporary period. Since World War II there has been a renaissance of self–styled conservative thinking and writing in the United States. Yet this significant intellectual movement remains largely misunderstood because no adequate definition of the conservatism propounded by these thinkers has been given. A number of scholarly works focus directly or indirectly on these thinkers, but most of these works do very little to elucidate the nature of the conservatism that these thinkers put forward. Some offer valuable information about individual thinkers or about the history and development of the contemporary American conservative movement, but they are not successful at making clear just what contemporary American conservative thought is—what defines it and distinguishes it from the ideas of thinkers of other persuasions.

Without such a definition, we cannot clearly and confidently distinguish contemporary American conservative thinkers from nonconservatives. An article in the *New York Times Magazine* illustrates the confusion over conservatism. The author, Steven R. Weisman, a White House reporter for the *New York Times,* asserts that it is almost impossible to define the unifying philosophical principles that underlie conservatism in America. He lists a number of people who he seems to feel can be labeled conservative because he says they have taken positions traditionally considered conservative: Jimmy Carter, because he advocates fiscal restraint and military strength; Lane Kirkland, because he appeals to Congress to rearm to meet a strategic Soviet threat; Gary Hart, because he favors fiscal restraint and limitations on environmental laws; Theodore H. White, because he opposes the use of quotas; Susan Brownmiller, because she advocates the censorship of pornography; and the Rev. Jesse Jackson, because he tells black teenagers to study hard, exercise self-discipline, and stay away from sex, pornography, and drugs.[1] One wonders how many people could not be considered conservatives on such grounds. Certainly the individuals mentioned by Weisman do not consider themselves conservatives and are not recognized as conservatives by contemporary American conservative thinkers.

The confusion over what is conservative is even more severe on the level of ideas than it is on the political level with which Weisman deals. It is not difficult to identify the most prominent conservative thinkers, mostly on the basis of their own self-identification, but there is little agreement, even among conservative thinkers themselves, as to what qualifies the ideas of those thinkers as conservative. Yet without an adequate definition, we cannot understand the nature of contemporary American conservative thought and its implications for American society. Without an understanding of the basic tenets of conservative thought, it is difficult to understand what conservative thinkers mean by what they say and write, and it is nearly impossible to evaluate their thinking properly. What do they mean by such terms as *authority, freedom, community,* and *tradition*? What would the world be like if conservative hopes and dreams were realized? What price would we have to pay to realize them? This study is an attempt to open the way to answers to these questions by providing a definition of contemporary American conservative thought, or at least a conceptual framework within which its nature and scope can be understood.

Conservative thinkers disagree among themselves about many things, sometimes vehemently. They have come to conservative positions from a number of different starting points—opposition to ethical relativism, love for tradition, concern for the fragility of freedom in the modern world, and anticommunism, among others. They therefore emphasize very different things. And a love of variety and individualism (almost to the point of eccentricity) seems to be inherent in much of contemporary American conservative thought. Not surprisingly, one of the issues these thinkers disagree about is the nature of conservatism itself. Contemporary American conservative thinkers have arrived at no agreed upon definition of conservatism. One of the most notable aspects of their writings is a quest for such a definition, a quest that has generated considerable argument among themselves.

Yet, whatever their differences, conservative thinkers feel that they are connected to each other in more than just practical ways—that they are engaged in a common endeavor to analyze contemporary American society from a conservative perspective and to prescribe conservative solutions to the problems they perceive. They feel a sense of intellectual unity, even though they have not to their own satisfaction described what ideas tie them together. From my reading of contemporary American conservative thinking, I believe they are right to feel that they share some important ideas, even if they cannot agree on what it is they share.[2]

PREVIOUS DEFINITIONS

This combination of diversity and unity, of disagreement and agreement, makes contemporary American conservative thought hard to define. It is precisely this combination of unity and diversity that previous definitions of conservatism cannot account for. These studies, whatever their other merits, have done little to answer questions about the fundamental nature of postwar American conservative thought.

Some scholars emphasize one or two ideas that they see as fundamental to American conservatism. If the ideas that they focus on could be shown to really be shared by all contemporary American conservative thinkers, those ideas could potentially account for the unity that exists in conservative thought. But these scholars have not successfully shown this. The ideas they focus on are not sufficient to account for that unity, and they certainly do not adequately account for the complexity and variety of conservative thought.

For example, probably the most frequently repeated definition of contemporary American conservatism is a situational definition, which sees conservatism as an attitude of resistance to change, a love of tradition, and a defense of the status quo. Most scholars at least mention this definition, and several focus directly on it.[3] Such an attitude toward change is clearly a prominent aspect of American conservative thought, but these studies do not show how the conservative attitude toward change leads to other aspects of conservative thought. In other words, if this attitude were the normative foundation of conservative thought, we would expect it to have some shaping influence on the rest of conservative thought. But little or no analysis is provided by these observers to demonstrate that this is the case, or even to hint at how an attitude toward change and the status quo could have generated the broader intellectual unity that seems to characterize postwar American conservative thought. Furthermore, this definition cannot account for the almost radical flavor conservative thought sometimes exhibits. At times conservative thinkers express the desire not to prevent but to foster change, not to preserve but to alter the status quo. How is this to be accounted for, given the definition of contemporary American conservatism simply as aversion to change?

In addition, there is little discussion in these works of how an aversion to change leads to variety within conservative thought—to differences in the thinking of various conservatives. An aversion to change certainly is a broad enough umbrella under which contemporary American conservative thinkers with conflicting ideas on other subjects could take shelter together. As a definition of conservatism, it *allows* for the diversity, but it does not explain or account for it (I will try to show that a better understanding of the normative core of conservative thought does explain this diversity). The conservative attitude toward change is certainly an important part of their thinking and must be accounted for by any adequate definition of conservative thought. But that attitude is not itself a defining characteristic adequate to explain the combination of coherence and complexity of contemporary American conservative thought, as chapter 8 will make clear.[4]

Works that focus on other apparently fundamental aspects of conservative thought fare no better. Whether the idea focused on is a defense of aristocracy,[5] a nostalgia for the past,[6] harmony,[7] or a tension between equality and freedom,[8] these analyses account for neither the unity nor the variety of conservative thinking in America.[9]

Other works attempt to describe the diversity within conservative thinking, but they fail to account for the intellectual coherence that seems to exist in conservative thought despite the diversity. These works generally rely upon lists of the tenets of conservatism to provide a definition. But these lists differ from one another, sometimes greatly. Some lists contain four or five tenets, and some contain many more, but the authors of these lists give little indication as to which tenets might be more important or fundamental than others, which might have helped us to reconcile the different lists. Nor have they provided much analysis of the degree to which these tenets are accepted by various conservative thinkers. The lists do contain ideas important to conservative thinkers, but some conservative thinkers reject some of the ideas listed and many conservatives disagree about how important many of those ideas are. These lists illustrate to some extent the variety and complexity of conservative thought, but they provide little help in understanding what ties various conservative positions and thinkers together and what justifies or explains the conservatives' regarding each other as fellow conservatives despite their differences. And they contain many elements not exclusive to conservatism, providing little help in distinguishing conservative thinkers from nonconservatives.[10]

Even worse than works that oversimplify by focusing on one idea or works that fail to analyze by merely relying on lists are works that dismiss conservatism on psychological or sociological grounds without considering the nature of conservative thought.[11] A good example is *The Authoritarian Personality* by Theodore W. Adorno, Else Frankel–Brunswick, Daniel J. Levinson, and R. Nevitt Sanford. The major thesis of this large sociopsychological study is that the political, economic, and social convictions of an individual often form a broad and coherent pattern as if bound together by a "mentality" or "spirit." This pattern is the expression of deep–lying trends in the individual's personality. The authors argue that the pattern of convictions of American conservatives is determined by an authoritarian personality structure that is clearly aberrant. Thus the authors are in effect arguing that conservatism (or what they call "pseudoconservatism") has little or no intellectual or rational basis and may be dismissed as the product of a defective personality structure. By pseudoconservatives they do not mean merely some sort of radical fringe. While they explicitly focus on "potential fascists" and not on intellectuals, their delineation of the pseudoconservative and his ideology plainly includes the conservative thinkers, and the only people they label "genuine" conservatives are people they describe as already having been driven by economic, social, and political changes into the liberal camp.[12]

Other studies follow the approach of *The Authoritarian Personality* by focusing on the supposed personality defects and motives of conservative thinkers and not on their ideas.[13] Even if these studies are correct in their depiction of conservatives' personalities and motives and in arguing that personality determines general ideological identification—and of that there is considerable doubt[14]—they tell us nothing about the nature of conservative ideas and the differences in emphasis among conservative thinkers. They do very little to help us understand what contemporary American conservative thought is.

Other works also tend to dismiss conservatism as an intellectual force in America, but on more reasoned grounds than on the basis of ad hominem psychologizing. Once again, however, they do little to help us define or understand conservative thought. These observers argue on historical grounds that conservatism is wholly or partially alien or irrelevant to America, that significant portions of the American tradition or condition exclude conservatism. Louis Hartz, for example, argued in 1955 that the American tradition is almost completely that of Lockean liberalism. America has had no feudal social structure and therefore has never had the ideology appropriate to feudalism, which is how he categorizes conservatism. Because of this, America has adopted wholesale the liberal principles of John Locke. He acknowledges a significant element of traditionalism and conservatism in the American mood but asserts that both the content of that tradition and the principles conserved are liberal. Any other conservatism is alien to America.[15]

The problem with this kind of approach is that it leads these observers to dismiss postwar American conservative thought without considering it on its own merits simply because it is called conservatism, and conservatism is, a priori, excluded by America's history. They do not examine what these self-styled contemporary American conservative thinkers believe conservatism to be, and thus they give us no help in understanding contemporary American conservative thinking.

The best historical work on postwar American conservatism was written by George H. Nash, who provides detailed information on a great variety of people who have been considered conservatives. He gives careful attention not only to a wide range of individuals, but provides some very useful classifications (most notably the classification of conservative thinkers into three groups—libertarian conservatives, traditionalist conservatives, and anticommunists—which I will use at various places in this study) and much intelligent description of the interactions of these people. His careful and extensive use of sources and his detailed and thorough analysis make his work the most useful one in print. However, Nash's careful analysis of individuals leaves us without an answer to the fundamental questions about the nature of conservatism. He avoids the question of what conservatism is, stating that he accepts as conservative for his study whoever claims to be a conservative or is so considered by others. That is an appropriate beginning point for deciding whom to study,[16] but Nash does not go much further than that, even in his conclusions. His analysis certainly helps us see the varieties of contemporary American conservative thought, but it tells us very little about what these conservative thinkers share beyond the practical level that could account for the coherence of their thought and that could justify giving them a common label and distinguishing them from others.[17]

THE CORE OF CONTEMPORARY CONSERVATIVE THOUGHT

An understanding of the normative core of contemporary American conservative thought helps explain both the unity and diversity of that thought. Despite their differences, all contemporary American conservative thinkers hold two fundamental ideas: a certain view of human nature and a certain conception of an objective moral order. They believe that human nature is unchanging and unalterable. They believe that this constant human nature is mixed of both good and evil. Neither the evil nor the good can ever be wholly eradicated. (See chapter 2.) Conservative thinkers also believe that there exists an objective moral order, independent of man's knowledge or perception of it. This reality includes standards and principles that are real, immutable, and eternal. (See chapter 3.) It is not the holding of either core idea separately that distinguishes a conservative thinker, but the holding of both together. Although closely related, the two ideas are logically separable, so that without contradiction a person may hold one but not the other. A number of nonconservatives do profess one or the other of these beliefs, but never both, while all conservatives hold both. It is this shared normative core that defines contemporary American conservative thought and that distinguishes conservative thinkers from nonconservatives. This core of ideas shared by all conservative thinkers gives to contemporary American conservative thought its intellectual unity.

This core also influences conservative thinking in all areas, as the following chapters will demonstrate. For example, conservatives conclude from their beliefs about the unchanging nature of man and the objective moral order of reality that freedom is a natural part of man's being and is necessary to his efforts to conform to the truths of the objective moral order. On the other hand, these same core ideas lead them to believe that authority must be exercised over men for their individual and collective good. (See chapters 4 and 5.) The core of contemporary American conservative thought also strongly influences conservatives' thinking about government. The core beliefs in an objective moral order and an unchanging human nature lead conservative thinkers to conclude that the chief problem of government is how to have a government that is strong enough to do the things that conservatives believe government should do, but not so strong that it endangers freedom or other values that they hold dear. Because of their core beliefs, they think there is no easy or permanent solution. And the solutions they are willing to consider are only those compatible with their core beliefs. (See chapter 6.)

Contemporary American conservative thought on the nature of society and the relationship between individuals and society is also shaped by the conservatives' core beliefs in an objective moral order and an unchanging human nature, and by the tension between authority and freedom that stems from the core. Conservative ideas in this area center on the notion of community. Conservative thinkers see community and the institutions that constitute it as part of the solution to the tension between freedom and authority. They also believe that the need for community arises from human nature. And they believe that community is necessary for giving expression to the truths of the objective moral order. (See chapter 7.) The core ideas also lead conservative thinkers to a complex attitude toward change and tradition. Their focus on an unchanging human nature and an unchanging moral order lead them to be suspicious of change. The weaknesses inherent in man's nature make a reliance on traditional ways and beliefs essential, as an approximation of the objective moral order. Yet all the constructs of fallible humans, including tradition, are necessarily fallible; this makes change inevitable to bring tradition more in line with the objective order. Nevertheless, change is always dangerous, given man's nature. (See chapter 8.)

In these and other ways the core ideas shape conservative thinking.[18] Yet the core composed of these two ideas is not in itself a comprehensive system of thought. It does not encompass all conservative thinking, nor is it capable of explaining in detail all of conservative thinking. Conservative thinkers hold many ideas that, while they do not contradict the core ideas, cannot be directly derived from the core. Yet this core does comprise the shared central premises around which the thinking of each contemporary American conservative is built.

There are two reasons why all of conservative thought cannot be mechanically deduced from the core. The first is that the core is not for all conservative thinkers the whole of the foundation of their thinking. It can be wedded to a number of other ideas, not shared by all conservatives, to form somewhat different starting points.[19] The result is diversity, but diversity within limits and based on shared premises. The second reason is that the two ideas held together in the core are general enough to allow for genuine differences in emphasis and interpretation. Yet the range of such interpretations is sufficiently limited to warrant viewing these two ideas as forming a normative core of shared premises. Again, the result is diversity of thinking based on a common core.

Whatever their differences, conservative thinkers do share a core of fundamental ideas and a number of concerns based on that core. It is because they do that we are justified in considering them members of an identifiable group. However diverse their interpretation and elaboration of these shared ideas, contemporary American conservative thinkers share what Russell Kirk correctly identifies as the foundation for the beliefs of thinking American conservatives: "belief in a transcendent order, in an unalterable human nature, and in a natural law."[20] They agree with Eric Voegelin that the ultimate goal of political philosophy is the discovery of the "unchanging order of the soul and the world."[21] Recognizing this shared core of ideas allows us to account for the unity that exists in conservative thinking without artificially excluding any of its rich diversity. Recognizing that core allows us to distinguish conservative thinkers from others. It gives us a tool to judge who is and who is not conservative, while doing justice to the diversity of positions within contemporary American conservative thought.

BRIEF HISTORICAL SKETCH

The remainder of this chapter will briefly sketch the history of this intellectual movement, mostly for the purpose of introducing the individuals whose ideas will be discussed in the following chapters. There have been three streams of intellectual conservatism in postwar America.[22] One consists of "libertarian conservatives," as they have been labeled by Nash.[23] They emphasize the threat that the ever–expanding State poses to liberty, private enterprise, and individualism. These libertarian conservatives were significantly influenced in the early years after the war by a revival of classical liberalism in Europe. Particularly important were two Austrian economists who emigrated to the United States, Ludwig von Mises and Friedrich A. Hayek. These two influenced and cooperated with a number of thinkers, such as the newspaper editor and college president Felix Morley and the journalist John Chamberlain, who were unreconciled to the New Deal and who were persuaded of the superiority of the free market by the West German economic "miracle" and by the failure of Stalinist Russia and Socialist Britain to live up to liberal expectations. William Henry Chamberlin, a journalist; Leonard Read, businessman and founder of the Foundation for Economic Education; Edmund Opitz, Unitarian minister and staff member of the Foundation for Economic Education; Frank S. Meyer, ex–Communist and essayist; M. Stanton Evans, newspaper editor; and Stephen J. Tonsor, historian, have also contributed significantly to the development of libertarian conservatism.

The second stream of this conservative revival is composed of individuals known as "traditionalist conservatives." Shocked by totalitarianism, total war, and the development of a secular, rootless, mass society, these traditionalist conservatives desire a return to the observance of traditional religious and ethical absolutes and a rejection of the relativism of the Left, which they feel is undermining the West. They explore three different sources for the tradition to which they feel America should return. Some, such as the sociologist Will Herberg, the philosopher Frederick Wilhelmsen, professor of history and French literature Thomas Molnar, and the lawyer L. Brent Bozell, focus mostly on Christian orthodoxy, especially on its lesson of original sin. Others advocate a return to classical political philosophy and its emphasis on natural law, virtue, and duties rather than rights. These include the political scientists Willmoore Kendall, John Hallowell, Eric Voegelin, Donald Atwell Zoll, Walter Berns, and Harry V. Jaffa; professor of English Richard M. Weaver; and the philosopher Eliseo Vivas. Others emphasize European conservatism, especially that of Burke. The most prominent individuals here are Russell Kirk, historian and essayist; Peter Viereck, poet and historian; Francis Wilson, political scientist; George F. Will, political scientist and columnist; and Robert Nisbet, sociologist.

The third group of postwar American conservatives consists of militant, evangelistic anticommunists. To a large extent, this group has overlapped both of the other two. It has received impetus from a number of ex–radicals, most notably the philosopher James Burnham and the journalist Whittaker Chambers, who brought to the conservative intellectual movement a profound conviction that the West was engaged in a struggle with an implacable foe—communism. Other prominent anticommunists include the political scientist Gerhart Niemeyer and the editor and essayist William F. Buckley, Jr.

There have been genuine differences between these groups of conservatives. While the libertarian conservatives have emphasized economic arguments against the State, traditionalists have been more concerned with the ethical and spiritual causes and consequences of Leviathan. And the anticommunist impulse has seemed to require strengthening the State, at least in part. The traditionalists have been fundamentally social and cultural critics; to them conservatism has meant the restoration of values, not the preservation of material gains. While libertarians have stressed primarily the right of the individual to be free, the traditionalists have emphasized the duties of the individual and the need to make him virtuous.

Yet there are important practical bonds that have linked the three groups together. All have opposed collectivism and the liberal welfare state; all have supported private property and a free economic system. All have appealed to the wisdom of the past in some way. They have claimed some common ancestors and some important conservatives, especially William Buckley, have seemed at home in more than one group.

By the middle fifties, perplexed by their continuing minority status and by their internal differences, these conservative thinkers felt the need for consolidation. The founding of the *National Review* in 1955 was important in bringing traditionalists, libertarians, and anticommunists together in a cooperative effort. Yet some conservative thinkers felt that there was still a need to generate greater intellectual unity out of these different viewpoints. One of the most significant efforts aimed at reconciling these differences has been the synthesis attempted by libertarian conservative Frank Meyer. Meyer has tried to show that the chief principle of the traditionalist conservatives, virtue, and the chief principle of the libertarian conservatives, freedom, are inextricably intertwined. Each implies the other and neither can truly exist without the other, in Meyer's view. Although the intellectual success of this attempt at fusion is questionable, and has been questioned repeatedly by figures in the conservative movement, it has had considerable practical success in fostering a large measure of cooperation among conservatives despite continuing diversity of ideas. Others who have attempted to extend and refine Meyer's efforts or have worked on parallel lines include M. Stanton Evans and Stephen Tonsor, both libertarian conservatives.

SUMMARY

Chapters 2 and 3 will describe the two core ideas, explaining their content and showing that they are in fact shared by all contemporary American conservative thinkers. Chapters 4 through 8 illustrate the influence of these core ideas on the rest of conservative thought by focusing on the topics of authority, virtue, freedom, government, economy, community, change, and tradition. With the partial exception of the topics of authority, virtue, and freedom (discussed in chapters 4 and 5), the conservative positions on these topics will not be discussed for their own sakes. Instead the focus will be on how conservative positions on these topics are influenced by the core ideas. The core ideas influence but do not determine the nature and range of positions on these topics. The purpose here is to show what influence they do have, not to discuss the variety and divergence of positions that conservative thinkers take on these topics, except when that variety is directly related to the core. Understanding the influence of the core is essential to a more complete understanding of conservative thinking on these topics, and conservative thinking on these and other topics is worth consideration on its own merits. But the focus here must

remain on the core ideas as a means of defining contemporary
American conservative thought. Only after that is understood
can a more detailed examination of conservative positions prove
genuinely fruitful. Chapters 4 and 5 consider in greater detail the
disagreements among conservative thinkers over the nature and
relationship between freedom on the one hand and authority and
virtue on the other because the disagreements here, more so than
the disagreements on other topics, are directly related to the core
ideas. The nature of these disagreements are directly the result
of the nature of the core ideas. And the positions that individual
conservative thinkers take on freedom and authority are the
clearest and most useful means of distinguishing the way that
contemporary American conservative thinkers are divided into
opposing, or at least separate, camps.

My approach is descriptive, not prescriptive. Therefore, in trying to show what conservative thinkers share that distinguishes
them from others, and in describing how the ideas they share
influence the rest of their thought, I have tried to let them speak
for themselves.[24] For this reason this study is not intended as a
critique of contemporary American conservative thought. What
is needed first is an understanding of these ideas so that criticism
becomes possible. This has been one of the chief problems in
the scholarly works on contemporary American conservative
thought. They criticize before fully understanding conservative
thought.

Because my approach is descriptive and because I am not a
conservative—not in terms of the definition that I put forward
here—I believe that this analysis is more objective than would be
the case if I felt compelled to defend a set of "true" conservative
ideas. When discussing each other's ideas, conservative thinkers
focus most of their attention on trying to propound what the
others should have said. For the most part they have not tried
to describe what they share with other conservatives as much
as they have tried to show where others have gone wrong. I
also have no axe to grind *against* these conservative thinkers
or their ideas. That is, I have enough sympathy for what these
thinkers are trying to do to believe that political, social, and
moral discourse in America would be enriched if those ideas
were considered more seriously. I am sympathetic enough to be

willing to try to understand conservative thought and not dismiss
it without considering it on its own terms, as many scholars have
dismissed it.

Finally, I have not tried to reconcile artificially all the diverse
aspects of conservative thought in America since World War II.
Instead, I am trying to describe what it is that these thinkers share
despite the diversity of their thought, a core of fundamental ideas
that shapes and limits that diversity but does not determine all
of conservative thinking, yet that does clearly distinguish conservative thinkers from others and gives us a better understanding
of what contemporary American conservative thought is really
all about.

NOTES

1. Weisman, "What Is a Conservative?" *New York Times Magazine* (31
August, 1980), p. 13.

2. To be fair, some conservative thinkers have described as fundamental the ideas that I will so describe. But they have also given the
same status to many other ideas, and those others differ from one conservative to another. The problem is not that they have overlooked these
core ideas, but that they have not appreciated their defining significance
apart from the other ideas that they cherish as much or more.

3. See, for example, Huntington, "Conservatism as an Ideology,"
American Political Science Review 52 (June 1957), pp. 454–73; Kronick,
"Conservatism: A Definition," *Southwestern Social Science Quarterly*
27 (September 1947), pp. 171–79; Auerbach, *The Conservative Illusion*
(New York, 1959); Newman, *The Futilitarian Society* (New York, 1961);
O'Sullivan, *Conservatism* (New York, 1976); Preece, "The Anglo–Saxon
Conservative Tradition," *Canadian Journal of Political Science* 13 (March
1980), pp. 3–32; Hall, "America's Conservative Revolution," *Antioch
Review* 15 (June 1955), pp. 204–16; Mark, *Modern Ideologies* (New
York, 1973); Murphy, *Modern Social and Political Philosophies: Burkean
Conservativism and Classical Liberalism* (Washington, D.C., 1982); and
Guttmann, *The Conservative Tradition in America* (New York, 1967).

4. A better effort in this direction has been made by O'Sullivan
(*Conservatism* [New York, 1976]). He, too, characterizes conservatism as
opposition to radical change, but the important contribution he makes
is to argue that this opposition was shaped by the historical fact that its
original enemy was the radical social change of the French Revolution.
Thus he argues that conservatism was shaped by the fact that it had to

fight the ideas of the French Revolution—that man and the world are malleable, that if social conditions are changed man can change, and that man has the rational ability to perceive and carry out the necessary changes. Therefore, conservative intellectuals had to show that there are limits to man's knowledge and limits to what can be achieved without destroying the stability of society. The result was what O'Sullivan calls a philosophy of imperfection. O'Sullivan apparently believes that American conservative thinkers share this philosophy of imperfection. O'Sullivan's explanation goes farther than the other attempts at showing how a conservative aversion to radical change leads not only to practical unity but to a certain intellectual cohesion as well. It accounts for the intellectual unity in contemporary American conservative thought better than similar attempts. But it fails to account for the variety within conservatism, and, like other situational definitions, it fails to explain the revolutionary character of some parts of contemporary American conservative thought.

5. For example, see Chapman, "The New Conservatism: Cultural Criticism versus Political Philosophy," *Political Science Quarterly* 75 (March 1957), pp. 17–34; Himmelfarb, "The Prophets of the New Conservatism," *Commentary* (January 1959), pp. 78–86; and Mills, "The Conservative Mood," *Dissent* (Winter 1954), pp. 22–31.

6. See for example Chase, "Neo–Conservatism and American Literature," *Commentary* (March 1957), pp. 254–65; Freund, "The New American Conservatism and European Conservatism," *Ethics* (October 1955), pp. 10–17; and Lewis, "The Metaphysics of Conservatism," *Western Political Quarterly* 6 (December 1953), pp. 728–41.

7. See for example Auerbach, *The Conservative Illusion*.

8. See Etzioni, "The Neoconservatives," *Partisan Review* 44 (1977), pp. 431–37. Etzioni's analysis is somewhat better than the others in that he tries to analyze conservative thought more objectively than most others in this category. But his analysis is too brief to give us any confidence that the conservative ideas that he focuses on are fundamental.

9. Better than the others in this group is the approach of British conservative Oakeshott ("On Being Conservative," in Oakeshott, *Rationalism in Politics and Other Essays* [London, 1962], pp. 168–96). To a degree, his explanation of conservatism belongs with the attempts to define postwar American intellectual conservatism as primarily the expression of certain psychological or emotional traits or dispositions. But he tries to show how a shared sentiment or disposition leads to shared principles and policy positions. Oakeshott argues that what is definitive of conservatism is what he calls a conservative disposition. This is a propensity to use and enjoy what is available and familiar

rather than wish for something else. He argues that this conservative disposition is especially appropriate toward tools, and in particular toward such tools as general rules of conduct. When this disposition toward tools is combined with the belief (which Oakeshott labels a hypothesis) that governing is the provision and custody of general rules of conduct, then a conservative disposition toward government is natural and appropriate. Oakeshott's argument succeeds in explaining how a minimum of intellectual cohesion, an approach to the nature and role of government, could arise from a nonintellectual disposition. But it can explain neither why there might be considerable variety with that cohesion nor why much contemporary American conservative thought has a revolutionary character—the desire not to preserve the status quo but to replace it with something else. Similar in approach to Oakeshott's analysis is an attempt at definition made by Doenecke ("Conservatism: The Impassioned Sentiment," *American Quarterly* 28 [Winter 1976], pp. 601–9). He too tries to explain conservatism as stemming from a common sentiment—a common antagonism to liberalism. He recognizes that, despite this common sentiment, conservative thinkers show considerable divergence in ideology, models for a better world, and heroes. He believes that they are unified more by what they oppose than by what they support. Sharing an antagonism to liberalism might account for conservative thinkers' practical unity and cooperation, but it does not explain their sense of intellectual unity. Conservative thinkers regard each other not just as allies against a common enemy but as fellow conservatives. They have other allies against liberalism that they do not regard as conservative, but they do regard each other as fellow conservative thinkers. That is, they believe they share some intellectual common ground. Doenecke's approach cannot account for that.

10. See for example Ketcham, "The Revival of Tradition and Conservatism in America," *Bulletin of the American Association of University Professors* 41 (Autumn 1955), pp. 425–43, especially pp. 425–27; Lief, ed. *The New Conservatives* (Indianapolis, 1967), especially p. 7; Guttmann, *The Conservative Tradition in America*, pp. 10–11, 165; Lora, *Conservative Minds in America* (Chicago, 1971); Harbour, *Foundations of Conservative Thought* (Notre Dame, Ind., 1982); Auerbach, *The Conservative Illusion*; and Fryer, *Recent Conservative Political Thought: American Perspectives* (Washington, D.C., 1979). A number of conservatives themselves take this approach to defining conservative thought. In principle it is a sound approach—it is essentially the approach that I take—but none have made it work, for the reasons discussed in the text.

11. These works have, however, been influential in shaping discourse about conservative thinkers.

12. Adorno, et al., *The Authoritarian Personality* (New York, 1950).

13. See, for example, Bell, "The Dispossessed," and "Interpretations of American Politics," in Bell, ed., *The Radical Right* (Garden City, N.Y., 1963), pp. 1–45 and 47–73; McClosky, "Conservatism and Personality," *American Political Science Review* 52 (March 1958), pp. 27–45; Coser and Howe, eds., *The New Conservatives: A Critique from the Left* (New York, 1976); Hofstadter, "The Pseudo–Conservative Revolt," and "Pseudo–Conservatism Revisited," in Bell, ed., *Radical Right*, pp. 75–95 and 97–103; Hofstadter, *The Paranoid Style in American Politics and Other Essays* (New York, 1966); Riesman and Glazer, "The Intellectuals and the Discontented Classes," in Bell, ed., *Radical Right*, pp. 105–35; Riesman, "The Intellectuals and the Discontented Classes: Some Further Reflections," in Bell, ed., *Radical Right*, pp. 137–59; Lipset, "The Sources of the 'Radical Right,' " and "Three Decades of the 'Radical Right': Coughlinites, McCarthyites, and Birchers," in Bell, ed., *Radical Right*, pp. 307–71 and 373–446; and Viereck, "The Revolt against the Elite," and "The Philosophical 'New Conservatism,'" in Bell, ed., *Radical Right*, pp. 161–83 and 185–207.

14. See for example Christie and Jahoda, eds., *Studies in the Scope and Method of "The Authoritarian Personality"* (Glencoe, Ill., 1954). This collection questions both the methods and conclusions of Adorno and his coauthors.

15. Hartz, *The Liberal Tradition in America* (New York, 1955). See also Schlesinger, Jr., *The Politics of Hope* (London, 1964); Rossiter, *Conservatism in America: The Thankless Persuasion* (New York, 1955); Crick, "The Strange Quest for an American Conservatism," *Review of Politics* 17 (July 1955), pp. 359–76; Guttmann, *The Conservative Tradition in America*; Viereck, in Bell, ed., *Radical Right*; Lora, *Conservative Minds in America*; Newman, *The Futilitarian Society*; and Auerbach, *The Conservative Illusion*.

16. I begin with an approach similar to Nash's. That is, the individuals here referred to as conservative are those thinkers who have identified themselves as such. This means of identifying conservative thinkers does not automatically identify a corresponding body of thought as conservatism and may therefore seem to place the cart before the horse—that is, it may seem that a proper approach would be to define a set of ideas as conservatism and then identify those who hold and expound these ideas as conservative thinkers. But the nature of my project will not allow that method—in fact, that is the major problem with many other studies of contemporary American conservative thought (Nash's work being the chief exception). They begin with a preconceived definition of what they believe conservatism

should be or what it has been. When contemporary American conservative thinkers do not measure up, they are dismissed without a careful consideration of what *they* think conservatism is. Whether these people who have claimed to be conservative have a rightful claim on that label is a question worth answering, but it is not the main issue here. Instead of examining the extent to which they operate within the tradition of Edmund Burke's conservatism, or European conservatism, or even an American conservatism (each of which has been identified by a number of commentators as the only true conservative tradition for Americans), I wish to focus on what these thinkers themselves believe conservatism to be. The question of what their ideas are must be answered before the question of whether their ideas deserve the label *conservative* can be addressed. For the present I will not attempt to criticize their appropriation of the label. Indeed, for this study I will use the words *conservative* and *conservatism* only for the ideas of these thinkers. Where this study goes beyond Nash's is to attempt to determine just what their conservatism is—the core they share that distinguishes them.

17. Nash, *The Conservative Intellectual Movement in America Since 1945* (New York, 1976); another good, although very brief, history of American conservative thought is contained in Nisbet, *Conservatism: Dream and Reality* (Milton Keynes, England, 1986); in the same work Nisbet also gives a good brief account of the sources of conservative thought.

18. Some analysts include these two core ideas, or something like them, on their lists of the tenets of conservative thought. However, they neither understand them well nor understand how central they are to conservative thought—how they shape conservative thinking. The person who comes closest to understanding the nature and influence of these core ideas is Harbour in *Foundations of Conservative Thought*. Among the other ideas on his list of the foundations of conservative thought are the conservative perspective on human nature and what he calls the conservatives' "Cosmological principle," which briefly stated is that God is at the center of all things and that there is an absolute moral order to the universe. However, he does not understand these conservative positions well; for example, he focuses on the negative aspects of the conservative view of human nature and largely misses the positive aspects, which later leads him to misunderstand the conservative position on human reason, individual responsibility, and the tension between freedom and authority. He also lacks an understanding of the significance of these ideas—how they influence the rest of conservative thinking. He does not see how other conservative ideas develop from this core, and therefore he misunderstands many of these other ideas.

19. In fact, conservative thinkers have not exhausted the possibilities.

There are other possible interpretations and systems of thought that could be built around that same core that would share much with the ideas of conservative thinkers but that would not be the same as the thought of any one conservative.

20. Kirk, *Beyond the Dreams of Avarice* (Chicago, 1956), p. 25.

21. Voegelin, *From Enlightenment to Revolution* (Durham, N.C., 1975), p. 277. Interestingly enough, a number of scholars make some reference to these core ideas in their studies. And a few even view them as fundamental: Aaron, "Conservatism, Old and New," *American Quarterly* 6 (Summer 1954), pp. 99–110; Brown, "Democracy, the New Conservatism, and the Liberal Tradition in America," *Ethics,* 56 (October 1955), pp. 1–9; Haiman, "A New Look at the New Conservatism," *Bulletin of the American Association of University Professors* 41 (Autumn 1955), pp. 444–53; MacDonald, "The Revival of Conservative Thought," *Journal of Politics* 19 (February 1957), pp. 66–80; and Spitz, "Freedom, Virtue, and the New Scholasticism," *Commentary* 28 (October 1959), pp. 313–21. I believe that they are right, but none of these writers thoroughly analyzes this core or attempts to show how this core influences the shape of conservative thought.

22. The focus here is on conservative thinkers, not politicians or organizations—on people who are serious about ideas and who have attempted to develop and expound more or less complete social, political, and moral philosophies that they label conservative. I have not attempted to consider in detail the writing of every thinker who considers himself or herself conservative. Instead I have focused on those individuals who have been most prominent in the movement, selecting thinkers across the range of positions held by contemporary American conservative thinkers. The selection is representative, not all inclusive.

23. Nash, *The Conservative Intellectual Movement,* p. xiii. Nash's analysis provides the basis for this brief description and classification of postwar American conservatives. It must be emphasized that the classifications are really by types of arguments and that the classification of individuals into groups according to these types of arguments is not very tidy. Individuals may at different times use different approaches or stress different ideas. Even so, the classification of individuals presented here seems to accord with the arguments most often made by particular thinkers, and it is the most useful classification that I have encountered.

24. At any one point in the following chapters I will, of course, quote only a representative sampling of statements made by conservative thinkers. That they are representative can be seen by examining conservatives' writings.

2

UNCHANGING HUMAN NATURE

One of the core ideas shared by all contemporary American conservative thinkers is the concept of an unchanging human nature. "Human nature is constant in spite of its unfolding in the history of mankind."[1] All contemporary American conservative thinkers would agree with this statement made by Eric Voegelin. As Russell Kirk puts it, the fact of "an unalterable human nature" is "one of the eternal verities."[2] Conservative thinkers believe that there are certain fundamental aspects of the human being that are unchanging and unalterable, regardless of time or place. And their thinking is marked not only by a belief that human nature is unchanging, but also by the specific attributes that they believe make up that nature. They believe that this constant human nature is neither wholly good nor wholly evil. As Kirk puts it, they believe that there has been "implanted in man a character of mingled good and evil."[3] Man is not naturally good, but neither is he incapable of doing good or attaining some measure of virtue.

INHERENT EVIL

Conservative thinkers see themselves as distinguished from liberals by having a less optimistic and more realistic view of man. Whether one examines the writings of traditionalist conservatives like Russell Kirk, Gerhart Niemeyer, John Hallowell, and Peter Viereck or of libertarian conservatives like John Chamberlain, M. Stanton Evans, William Henry Chamberlin, and Felix Morley, one finds the same theme repeated: liberals and radicals have been led astray by a too optimistic view of the nature of man, while conservatives see man in his full reality, both good and evil.[4]

James Burnham argues, for instance, that liberalism incorrectly sees human nature as plastic; "liberalism believes man's nature not to be fixed but changing, with an unlimited or at any rate indefinitely large potential for positive (good, favorable, progressive) development. This may be contrasted with the traditional belief . . . that human nature has a permanent, unchanging essence, and that man is partly corrupt as well as limited in his potential."[5]

Conservatives do not believe that the evil in man's nature is an accident of history or merely the product of environment. Viereck correctly states the conservative belief that "men are not born naturally free or good (assume conservatives) but naturally prone to anarchy, evil, mutual destruction."[6] Kirk speaks of human nature as being "irremediably flawed," Thomas Molnar describes man's "penchant for moral evil," and Robert Nisbet declares that there is in human nature "an ineradicable tendency toward mischief and even evil."[7] However they express it, the idea is the same.

For many conservatives, this inherent evil in man's nature is best expressed by the concept of original sin. Some literally accept the Christian idea of original sin, with its concomitant idea of a literal Fall, while others regard it as a metaphor for the nature of man. In either case, they find that the concept of original sin best expresses the *inherent* evil in man's nature—evil that must be accepted as a given and that is not due to any cause that human beings can remove. Richard Weaver states that "in my period of jejune optimism the concept of original sin seemed something archaically funny. Now, twenty years later and after the experience of a world war, there is no concept that I regard as expressing a deeper insight into the enigma that is man. Original sin is a parabolical expression of the immemorial tendency of man to do the wrong thing when he knows the right thing."[8]

Other conservatives of a less theological bent express this belief in other ways, but the meaning is the same. For example, Leonard Read, who speaks more optimistically about human potential than many other conservative thinkers, nevertheless believes that "man is imperfect by nature."[9] Conservatives all agree that there are limits inherent in the human condition that a concept like original sin attempts to describe. As Molnar puts it, "original sin explains aspects of man that are inexplicable without it."[10] Without a concept like original sin, conservatives warn, individuals and societies are unprepared to deal with what Will Herberg calls "the disruptive consequences of the sinful ego-centricity which characterizes man's 'fallen' nature."[11] Viereck recognizes the consensus on this point by calling conservatism "the political secularization of the doctrine of original sin."[12]

Because they believe that flaws and limits are inherent in human nature, conservatives do not believe that man is perfect-ible. As we have seen, they believe that "man is imperfect by nature; man can never do more than approximate perfection."[13] As Voegelin puts it, "there is a nature of man, a definite structure of existence that puts limits on perfectibility."[14] Conservative thinkers reject what they see as the illusion of liberals and radicals that man can create a new man, a new world, or a new society, either gradually or immediately. Donald Atwell Zoll observes correctly that there is a general acceptance among conservatives "of life and human nature as it appears to be, rather than the entertainment of utopian visions of human and social perfectibility."[15] Frank S. Meyer argues the same point. He states that conservative thought,

while it strives always for the improvement of human institutions and the human condition, . . . rejects absolutely the idea that society or men generally are perfectible. In particular, it is perennially suspicious of the utopian approach that attempts to *design* society and the lives of human beings, whether in the light of abstract rationalist ideas or operational engineering concepts. It therefore rejects the entire Liberal *mystique* of 'Planning,' which, no matter how humanitarian the motives of the planners, perforce treats human beings as faceless units to be arranged and disposed according to a design conceived by the planner.[16]

Therefore, conservative thinkers believe that leftist views are fundamentally wrong because, as Burnham puts it, they hold that, "innately and essentially, human nature is neither pure nor corrupt, neither good nor bad . . . [but is] 'plastic.' "[17] This leads liberals and other leftists to believe in what John P. East calls "the earthly perfection of the human condition through gradual 'reform.' "[18] Or as Vivas puts it, liberalism "amounts to a shallow, optimistic belief in social meliorism if we trust the welfare state, a vague and not too well informed belief in political action addressed to strengthening the welfare state, and a bland belief in the unqualified power of science to solve all problems (all based on an uncritical belief in the unlimited perfectibility of man)."[19] Conservatives, by contrast, believe that human nature is fixed, not plastic, and that it contains both good and evil rather than being neutral. As Kirk correctly tells us, the conservative knows "that man is not a perfect nor a perfectible being and that the prudent politician will endeavor to make life tolerable, not impossibly perfect."[20]

Read argues along similar lines: "Man is just as incapable of designing or creating a good society as he is of designing or creating life itself. . . . Only God can make a good society. . . . Imperfect men cannot manipulate imperfect men into a perfect society. The perfection of any society can be approached only as imperfections are overcome by its members, a project of infinite proportions, for man is imperfect by nature."[21] Even progress short of perfection is seen as problematic by conservatives. Progress and improvement cannot be taken for granted or assumed to take place regularly and without setback, even with the best human efforts. George Will, for example, criticizes what he calls "the therapeutic ethic"—the notion that social problems can be solved and society steadily improved by removing the social causes of antisocial behavior. "That idea seems fundamentally mistaken to [people] who take seriously man's fallen condition," as conservative thinkers do.[22] The institutions that have developed to help man curb the evil parts of his nature and strengthen the good can help him live a better life, but they cannot perfect him or change his nature.[23] The problems are innate in human nature, not the result of changeable social structures. "We are not constituted for perfect happiness," says Kirk; "we are meant to struggle;

we are Suffering Servants. The world always is full of genuine reasons for serious anxiety among thinking men. Our hope, and the mission of the man of letters . . . and the ethical philosopher, is not to sweep away that anxiety . . . but to keep anxiety from usurping the whole of life."[24]

IMPERFECT REASON

One of the chief flaws that conservatives believe prevents human perfectibility is man's limited rationality. As Kirk puts it, the conservative "is a highly reasonable person, although he looks with deep suspicion on the cult of Reason—the worship of an abstract rationality which asserts that mundane planning is able to solve all our difficulties of spirit and community."[25] Conservative thinkers believe that there is an essential role for human reason, by which they refer to people's intellectual powers, including their ability to comprehend the world in orderly, rational ways. But they think that in the modern world reason has been overvalued, with dangerous results. For instance they think that liberals have made a serious error in believing, as Burnham says, that "reason is man's essence, and in a practical sense his chief and ultimately controlling characteristic."[26] Conservatives believe that this has led to hubris, failed social programs, and social unrest caused by falsely raised expectations. Reason is just not capable of achieving the ends liberals call upon it to accomplish. "Man's slight, budding ability to reason," as Read puts it, is "an ability still linked to abysmal ignorance." Man "doesn't know enough to plan or mastermind all things or even the life of a single human being."[27]

Frederick Wilhelmsen argues that much of the world, including much of human relations and societies, is beyond human comprehension.

A traditional society does not permit dissection into the categories of contemporary academicism. Reality is fused into too tight a cultural unity for rational analysis: like existence itself, such communities defy conceptualization. . . . It is only a rationalist mentality, enamored of books and degrees, ignorant of history and innocent of the mystery of life, that insists on judging such [traditional] communities in the light of an abstract company of essences inhabiting a ghostly republic of ideals foreign to the rhythm of being and becoming.[28]

Better then to rely upon traditional checks on human behavior than indulge in the dangerous fantasy that man knows enough to discard those traditions and engineer his own utopia.

Conservative thinkers believe that some people do better than others at cultivating the power of reason, and as we shall see in chapter 6, they see an important role for such people in society. As William F. Buckley says, "the world would probably be better off, not worse, if many people who are currently hard at work thinking should desist from doing so, and spend their time, instead, cultivating the elevated thoughts of others."[29] But conservatives believe that even the wisest cannot live by reason alone. "Pure arrogant reason," Kirk warns, "denying the claims of conscience, leads to a wasteland of withered hopes and crying loneliness."[30]

Conservatives also believe that other aspects of man's nature are often at war with his reason, and that reason does not regularly win. In Kirk's words, "conservatives know man to be governed more by emotion than by reason."[31] Or as Buckley observes, "reason is *not* king."[32] They recognize that the human race has accomplished much through the power of reason, but they believe that those achievements are primarily the result of the efforts of a very few. One of those achievements has not been gaining control over emotions. As Morley points out, man has achieved "mastery both over the atom and over the force of gravity—though not, unfortunately, over his own passion and prejudice."[33] The result, says Weaver, is that although conservatives must pay "sufficient tribute to reason," they must also insist "that the area of its profitable operation is an island in a sea of prerational sentiment."[34]

Conservatives do not believe that human reason is powerless to achieve any good; but they do insist that while man must not turn his back on reason altogether, he must recognize the limits of reason, what Meyer calls "the finite bounds of the purview of any one man or any one generation."[35] He must respect the wisdom of his ancestors and place "only a limited trust in the power of human reason," for, as Kirk argues, conservatives know "that our future depends in considerable part on Providence, or chance, or that infinite combination of tiny causes which we call chance."[36]

SELF–INTEREST

Another flaw in man's nature that conservatives emphasize as an insurmountable barrier to the perfection of man or society is man's inherent self–interestedness. Conservative thinkers believe that man's appetites are voracious, his impulses anarchic.[37] His attempts to satisfy those appetites and express those impulses put him frequently at odds with his fellows, and he tends to resolve such differences in his own favor. Inside every man lies "brutality," argues traditionalist philosopher Eliseo Vivas, a "natural tendency" to "define values in terms of his own interests."[38] Libertarian conservative M. Stanton Evans agrees, stating that "man is hampered by a fallible intellect and a vagrant will."[39] Viereck puts the case even more strongly, arguing that "every human being is by nature barbarous, capable of every insanity and atrocity."[40] Conservatives do not argue that man has no positive or noble urges, just that they cannot be counted on to win out over his negative urges. "Man is frail," Molnar asserts, "and thus a battlefield of contending forces."[41] While conservative thinkers hope that the best in people can be cultivated, and as we shall see later they believe that one function of government and a chief function of other institutions is to foster the best aspects of human nature (and suppress the worst), they do not believe that the evil in man is merely accidental or temporary.

POSITIVE ASPECTS OF HUMAN NATURE

Although conservatives believe that man is not naturally good and that conservatism must reflect a distrust of human nature, they also believe that man is not entirely evil and that conservatism must express a sense of man's dignity and potential. Man is a *mixture* of good and evil, neither wholly one nor the other.

Just as many conservative thinkers find the best expression of man's innate evil tendencies to be the Christian doctrine of original sin, these same thinkers see the clearest expression of man's inherent dignity and potential for good in the Christian doctrine of the immortal soul. The same conservatives who believe that man is irremediably flawed also believe in Christianity's teachings about the infinite value of the human soul. The same thinkers who distrust man's nature believe, as Voegelin puts it, that man finds "his true nature through finding his true relation to God."[42] Erik von Kuehnelt–Leddihn asserts that according to conservatives, man is "even after the Fall a creature unlike the beasts—a transcendent creature called upon to rise above himself. . . . Man's existence is basically tied to God."[43] Kirk argues that "in its immediate influence upon culture, perhaps the most important aspect of Christianity is its account of the human personality: its doctrine of the immortal soul, the unique character of every person, the concept of human dignity, the insistence upon personal responsibility." These are essential beliefs for a conservative.[44] Without understanding this "moral nature of man," as Chamberlain describes it, one cannot have a true picture of human nature.[45]

This feeling for the dignity of man is not always expressed in religious terms, but it is an understanding "rooted in the Christian vision of the nature and destiny of man," as Meyer points out,[46] and even its secular expressions are compatible with that vision. Note the similarity in tone and content between the previous quotations and Viereck's expression of the same concept: "The core and fire–center of conservatism, its emotional élan, is a humanist reverence for the dignity of the individual."[47]

Viereck's comment also illustrates another conservative emphasis. Just as conservatives criticize liberals and radicals for holding a falsely optimistic view of man's innate goodness, so they condemn them for tending to view men as so many interchangeable units to be manipulated and transformed. Conservative thinkers believe that the liberal view of man is too narrow and ultimately demeaning. "The so–called humanist conception of man is a mean and shriveled conception," argues Eliseo Vivas, "lacking the components of heroism and tragedy that are essential to the realization of man in his full dimension."[48] Conservative thinkers believe that radicals, in their rush toward utopia, and liberals, in their reformist schemes for a more gradual approach to utopia, both lose sight of the uniqueness and dignity of the individual. Donald Zoll, a traditionalist conservative, believes that the conservative concept of the person is always "at variance with views of the Left in that it assumes some variety of an innate, irreducible dignity of the person."[49] John Chamberlain, a libertarian conservative, similarly believes that communists and others on the Left hold a false view of human nature, deriding "the Western, or Christian, view of life that was based on the inviolable nature of the human soul."[50] By contrast, asserts Meyer, for all conservatives "the human person is the necessary center of political and social thought. Whether their stress is upon his freedom and his rights [the libertarian conservatives] or upon his responsibilities and his duties [traditionalist conservatives], it is in terms of the individual person that they think and write."[51] According to Viereck, their reverence for the dignity of the individual "is incompatible with fascist or Stalinist collectivism; incompatible with a purely mechanistic view of man; incompatible with a purely economic view of history."[52] Kirk says that "a conservative society enables men to be truly human persons, not mere specks in a tapioca–society; it respects their dignity as persons."[53]

Thus conservative thinkers believe that they see man in his full reality, both good and evil. They take issue with liberals for being too optimistic about the possibility of improving people, while at the same time criticizing them for overlooking man's dignity despite his failings. As Vivas puts it, conservatives believe that liberals overlook both the "heroism and tragedy that are essential to the realization of man in his full dimension."[54]

THE POWER OF REASON

The conservatives' insistence on man's God–given dignity tempers some of the more negative aspects of their views of human nature. For example, the negative emphasis on the limits of man's reason is coupled with the more positive belief that

man's reason is a gift from God or an innate capacity of the
human being and must therefore be respected. If reason does not
rule absolutely, neither is it absolutely ruled. It does not always
control appetites and passions, but neither is it always controlled
by them. Conservatives argue that social philosophies that reduce
men to animals responding predictably to instinct or measurable
stimuli are just as false and dangerous as those that exalt man's
rationality as supreme. Neither approach stems from what conservative thinkers believe is a realistic view of man, a view that
takes into account both the good and the evil in man's constant
nature. John Hallowell, for example, argues that man's reason is
a reflection of the image of God. Man is "a creature made in the
image and likeness of God. . . . God's image in man is reflected
in the capacity of human beings to reason, and the disparagement
of that capacity can lead only to the denial of man's uniqueness."
Denying the capacity to reason and individual uniqueness leads
to dictatorship and totalitarianism.[55]

This capacity to reason "enables him, at least dimly," Hallowell
continues, "to grasp the meaning of . . . reality."[56] "The primary
mode of achieving understanding," according to libertarian conservative Frank Meyer, is "reason deriving extended conclusions
from simple apprehensions" of the nature of man and the
truths of the objective moral order.[57] Traditionalist Frederick
Wilhelmsen agrees, asserting the "conformity of the mind of
man to things as they are."[58] In other words, apprehension of
the good, true, just, and right is natural, although not easy.[59]
The good of society depends in part on "the exercise of right
reason by the leaders of . . . society," argues Kirk; "wise men in
our age must reconcile exigency and enduring standards."[60] The
conservative knows, according to Viereck, that "reason is only
a feeble flicker in a Stygian universe. But instead of joining the
stampede to abdicate it, [he] labors patiently to extend its San
Marino–like frontiers against the night."[61]

But conservative thinkers believe that man's reasoning capacity does not exist in isolation. It is one part of a constant human
nature; it is not autonomous. According to Hallowell, belief in
man's reason must be coupled with other truths; "that sentiment
plays an even larger role in social life than reason, that 'naked
reason' unmotivated by the love of what is good and abstracted

from the totality of human experience is likely to be turned not only against the good but against reason itself."[62] If it is to bring real understanding, reason must be directed by God, its author, through revelation, religion, and tradition.

INDIVIDUAL IMPROVEMENT

This vision of the innate dignity and potential of human beings also leads conservatives away from concluding that no individual can improve or be improved. Included in man's constant nature is the potential for individual improvement. Leonard Read believes that an integral aspect of man's nature is the ability "to grow and to emerge in consciousness."[63] Because such an ability to grow is part of his nature, man can temper his passions and appetites, although he cannot ultimately extirpate them. One chief responsibility of society and its institutions, in Viereck's view, is "to limit [man's] instincts and behavior by unbreakable ethical habits;"[64] or as Will puts it, to achieve "the steady emancipation of the individual through the education of his passions."[65]

According to conservatives, not only is man able to improve, he has a duty to do so. Man's "nature requires him to strive for his own perfection," says Willmoore Kendall; he "has a *duty* to subordinate himself to justice, to the principles of right and wrong, to the law,"[66] even if perfection is ultimately unattainable. Conservatives believe that one of the reasons for man's existence is to strive for virtue.[67] "Men are put into this world," explains Kirk, "to struggle, to suffer, to contend against the evil that is in their neighbors and in themselves, and to aspire toward the triumph of Love."[68] Therefore, according to Evans, "man's purpose is to shape his life to divine patterns of order."[69]

To help people achieve this virtue, God has placed in all people what Wilhelmsen calls "the in–built dynamic push towards perfection."[70] Conservatives believe, therefore, that they must attempt to aid men in this struggle toward virtue. They must be concerned, as Vivas says, with trying to bring men "face to face with the truth about their evil selves and, through self–knowledge, point to their ethical salvation."[71]

SUMMARY

Conservatives believe that from the fixed nature of man come certain principles that should guide individual and social life. As Niemeyer puts it, "human nature [is] the philosophical yardstick for what pertains to the good life."[72] Or as Wilhelmsen says in discussing the nature of law and the society it sustains, "the measure here is nothing more than man's very own nature."[73] On the one hand, traditionalist Russell Kirk emphasizes norms and responsibilities: "A norm is an enduring standard. It is a law of our nature, which we ignore at our peril. It is a rule of human conduct and a measure of public virtue."[74] Libertarian conservative Frank Meyer, on the other hand, emphasizes man's freedom: "Innate freedom is of the essence of his being." It is "the aspect of the nature of men which political institutions exist to serve" and "the decisive criterion of good polity."[75] What is common to both emphases is the belief that principles are derived from the nature of man which are used to judge individual behavior *and* social and political arrangements. In Willmoore Kendall's words, "The best regime is that which is best for the nature of man."[76]

The last few quotations taken from the works of Kirk, Meyer, and Kendall indicate the close connection that conservatives see between their view of man's unchanging nature and the second core idea, a concept of an objective moral order, which is the subject of the next chapter.

NOTES

1. Voegelin, *Order and History*, Vol. 2, *The World of the Polis* (Baton Rouge, 1957), p. 5.

2. Kirk, *Beyond*, p. 25. See also Wilhelmsen, *Christianity and Political Philosophy* (Athens, Ga., 1978), pp. 12–14; Molnar, *Authority and Its Enemies* (New Rochelle, N.Y., 1976), p. 132; and Weaver, *The Ethics of Rhetoric* (Chicago, 1953), p. 87.

3. Kirk, *A Program for Conservatives* (Chicago, 1962), p. 41. See also Vivas, *Relativism and Its Paradoxes and Pitfalls* (Philadelphia, 1962), p. 2; and Burnham, *The Suicide of the West* (New Rochelle, N.Y., 1964), p. 134.

4. See Kirk, *Beyond*, pp. 21–25; Niemeyer, "Conservatism and the New Political Theory," *Modern Age* 23 (Spring 1979), p. 121; Hallowell,

Main Currents in Modern Political Thought (New York, 1950), p. 84; Viereck, *Conservatism Revisited: The Revolt Against Revolt* (New York, 1949), p. xiv; John Chamberlain, "Ignore Human Nature?" *The Freeman* 14 (February 1964), p. 59; Evans, "A Conservative Case for Freedom," in Meyer, ed. *What Is Conservatism?* pp. 73–75; William Chamberlin, "Conservatism in Evolution," *Modern Age* 7 (Summer 1963), pp. 252–54; and Morley, *Freedom and Federalism* (Chicago, 1959), p. 29.

5. Burnham, *Suicide*, pp. 49–50.

6. Viereck, *Conservatism: From John Adams to Churchill* (Princeton, N.J., 1956), p. 14. See also Molnar, *Authority*, p. 132; Hallowell, "Modern Liberalism: An Invitation to Suicide," *South Atlantic Quarterly* 46 (October 1947), p. 454; and Weaver, *Ethics of Rhetoric*, p. 89.

7. Kirk, "Prescription, Authority, and Ordered Freedom," in Meyer, ed., *What Is Conservatism?* (New York, 1964) p. 24; Molnar, *Authority*, p. 21; and Nisbet, *The Twilight of Authority* (New York, 1975), p. 76.

8. Weaver, "Up from Liberalism," *Modern Age* 3 (Winter 1958–59), pp. 28–29.

9. Read, "Blessing," p. 48.

10. Molnar, *Authority*, p. 41.

11. Herberg, "The Presuppositions of Democracy," *Commonweal* 62 (3 June 1955), p. 235.

12. Viereck, *Conservatism Revisited*, p. 30. See also Will, "Who Put Morality in Politics?" *Newsweek* (15 September 1980), p. 108; Hallowell, "Modern Liberalism," p. 462; Kuehnelt–Leddihn, "The Portland Declaration," *National Review* (16 October 1981), p. 1188; Buckley, Jr., *The Jeweler's Eye: A Book of Irresistible Political Reflections* (New York, 1958), p. 20; Kirk, *Program*, p. 14; and Weaver, *The Southern Tradition at Bay: A History of Postbellum Thought*, eds. Core and Bradford (New Rochelle, N.Y., 1968), p. 33.

13. Read, "Blessing," p. 48.

14. Voegelin, "On Classical Studies," *Modern Age* 17 (1973), p. 3.

15. Zoll, "The Philosophical Foundations of the American Political Right," *Modern Age* 15 (Spring 1971), p. 115. See also Niemeyer, "Conservatism," p. 121; Will, "Onward and Upward," *Newsweek* (8 June 1981), p. 108; and Weaver, "Up from Liberalism," pp. 28–29.

16. Meyer, "Conservatism," in Goldwin, ed., *Left, Right and Center: Essays on Liberalism and Conservatism in the United States* (Chicago, 1965), pp. 6–7.

17. Burnham, *Suicide*, p. 50.

18. East, "Eric Voegelin and American Conservative Thought," *Modern Age* 22 (Spring 1978), p. 115.

19. Vivas, *Moral Life*, p. 2.

20. Kirk, *Beyond*, p. 23.

21. Read, "Blessing," p. 48. See also Kirk, *Program*, p. 4; Niemeyer, "Conservatism," p. 121; Viereck, *Conservatism Revisited*, p. 27; and Kuehnelt–Leddihn, "Portland Declaration," pp. 1188–89.

22. Will, "Who Put?" p. 108. See also Wilhelmsen, "The Conservative Vision," *Commonweal* 62 (24 June 1955), pp. 296–97; and Viereck, *Conservatism*, p. 12.

23. See chapters 6 and 7.

24. Kirk, *Enemies of the Permanent Things* (New Rochelle, N.Y., 1969), p. 26.

25. Kirk, *Program*, p. 6.

26. Burnham, *Suicide*, p. 53. See also Vivas, *Moral Life*, p. 113.

27. Read, "On Freedom and Order," *The Freeman* 15 (January 1965), p. 36; and in *The Freeman* 15 (September 1965), p. 64.

28. See Wilhelmsen, "The Conservative Vision," pp. 297–98; see also Burnham, *Congress and the American Tradition* (Chicago, 1959), p. 6.

29. Buckley, ed., *Did You Ever See a Dream Walking? American Conservative Thought in the Twentieth Century* (Indianapolis, 1970), p. xxxv. One must remember Buckley's penchant for the exaggerated and dramatic; yet even so this is a strong statement.

30. Kirk, *The Conservative Mind: From Burke to Eliot* (4th ed. rev.; Chicago, 1968), pp. 48–49.

31. Kirk, *Conservative Mind*, p. 18. See also Burnham, *Suicide*, p. 115; and Hallowell, *The Moral Foundation of Democracy* (Chicago, 1956), p. 86.

32. Buckley, *Jeweler's Eye*, p. 21.

33. Morley, *Freedom and Federalism*, p. xxi.

34. Weaver, *Ideas Have Consequences* (Chicago, 1948), p. 182.

35. Meyer, "Freedom, Tradition, Conservatism," in Meyer, ed., *What Is Conservatism?* p. 11.

36. Kirk, *Program*, p. 12.

37. See for example Kirk, *Conservative Mind*, p. 51.

38. Vivas, *Moral Life*, p. 133.

39. Evans, "Techniques and Circumstances," *National Review* (30 January, 1962), p. 58.

40. Viereck, *Conservatism Revisited*, p. 29.

41. Molnar, *Authority*, p. 40.

42. Voegelin, *The New Science of Politics* (Chicago, 1952), p. 68.

43. Kuehnelt–Leddihn, "Portland Declaration," pp. 1188–89.

44. Kirk, *Enemies*, p. 31.

45. John Chamberlain, *The Roots of Capitalism* (Princeton, N.J., 1959), p. 10. See also Will, *Statecraft as Soulcraft: What Government Does* (New York, 1983), pp. 25–26; Viereck, *Conservatism Revisited*, pp. 26–27; Buckley,

Dream, p. xxxii; Hallowell, *Moral Foundation*, p. 83; and Vivas, *Moral Life*, p. 39.

46. Meyer, "Why Freedom?" *National Review* (25 September 1962), p. 225.

47. Viereck, *Conservatism Revisited*, p. 6. See also Read, "Blessing," p. 49; and Will, "The Case for Automakers," *Newsweek* (7 March 1981), p. 88.

48. Vivas, *Moral Life*, p. 2.

49. Zoll, "Philosophical Foundations," p. 115.

50. John Chamberlain, "Ignore Human Nature?" p. 60.

51. Meyer, *What Is Conservatism?* p. 230.

52. Viereck, *Conservatism Revisited*, p. 6.

53. Kirk, *Program*, p. 40.

54. Vivas, *Moral Life*, p. 2. See also Berns, "The Need for Public Authority," *Modern Age* 24 (Winter 1980), pp. 16–20; Kuehnelt–Leddihn, "Portland Declaration," p. 1189; and Meyer, *In Defense of Freedom: A Conservative Credo* (Chicago, 1962), pp. 26–27.

55. Hallowell, *Moral Foundation*, p. 81.

56. Ibid., p. 25.

57. Meyer, *In Defense*, p. 23.

58. Wilhelmsen, *Christianity and Political Philosophy*, p. 202.

59. See, for example, Will, *Statecraft*, p. 30; and Kendall, *The Conservative Affirmation* (Chicago, 1963), p. 91.

60. Kirk, "Prescription," p. 31. See also Weaver, *Southern Tradition*, pp. 389–90; Meyer, "Freedom, Tradition, and Conservatism," p. 17; and Meyer, *In Defense*, p. 41.

61. Viereck, *Conservatism Revisited*, p. 28.

62. Hallowell, *Moral Foundation*, p. 86.

63. Read, "On Freedom and Order," p. 36.

64. Viereck, *Conservatism Revisited*, p. 10.

65. Will, *Statecraft*, p. 27.

66. Kendall, *Affirmation*, p. 91.

67. See chapter 4 for more on what conservative thinkers have to say about virtue.

68. Kirk, *Program*, p. 19.

69. Evans, "Technique," p. 58.

70. Wilhelmsen, *Christianity and Political Philosophy*, p. 33.

71. Vivas, *Moral Life*, pp. 8–9.

72. Niemeyer, *Foreign Policy and Morality* (London, 1979), p. 1.

73. Wilhelmsen, *Christianity and Political Philosophy*, p. 14.

74. Kirk, "Prescription," p. 29.

75. Meyer, *In Defense*, pp. 4, 23, 64.

76. Kendall, *Affirmation*, p. 91. See also Voegelin, *New Science*, pp. 61–63; and John Chamberlain, "John Randolph of Roanoke," *The Freeman* 15 (July 1965), p. 58.

3

THE OBJECTIVE
MORAL ORDER

The second core idea that all contemporary American conservative thinkers share is the concept of an objective moral order.
All conservatives are opposed to what they perceive as liberal
relativism. They believe that there exists an objective reality,
independent of man's knowledge or perception of it. This reality
includes standards and principles that are real, immutable, and
eternal--truths that men should live by and by which human
conduct and social and political organization should be judged.

This is what Frank Meyer means when he asserts that "conservatism assumes the existence of an objective moral order
based upon ontological foundations. . . . The conservative looks
at political and social questions with the assumption that there
are objective standards for human conduct and criteria for the
judgment of theories and institutions."[1] It is what Eric Voegelin
expresses when he refers to the "unchangeable order of the soul
and the world"[2] and to "the constitution of being" or "the order
of being."[3] "The constitution of being is what it is, and cannot be
affected by human fancies. . . . The will to transform reality into
something which by essence it is not is the rebellion against the
nature of things as ordained by God."[4] Eliseo Vivas expresses the
same thing when he asserts that "values are real and antecedent
to our discovery of them."[5]

According to John Hallowell, this premise held by all conservatives "might be summarized in this way. There exists a meaningful reality whose existence does not depend upon our knowledge of it. . . . The world in which we live is an orderly universe—a cosmos, not a chaos."[6] Russell Kirk means the same thing when says that conservatism necessarily includes "a belief in an order that is more than Human." He asserts that we must "confess that there are enduring standards superior to our petty personal private stock of rationality."[7]

In a lighter mood, William F. Buckley relates how he deals with people who press him for a one-sentence definition of conservatism, and in so doing reveals his acceptance of this core idea: "Those who are obstinate I punish by giving, with a straight face, Professor Richard Weaver's definition of conservatism as 'the paradigm of essences toward which the phenomenology of the world is in continuing approximation.' "[8] Weaver has indeed asserted that "the true conservative is one who sees the universe" as such an approximation, but he also explains what he means: "to put this another way, [the true conservative] sees [the universe] as a set of definitions which are struggling to get themselves defined in the real world."[9] William Henry Chamberlin is more concise when he says that "the conservative is the opposite of the nihilist."[10] But however this idea is expressed, the meaning is the same. All conservative thinkers believe that there is an objective moral order. Donald Atwell Zoll is correct, at least about contemporary American conservative thinkers, when he concludes that "twentieth century conservatives have *invariably* supported the objectivity and immutability of value."[11]

Most conservative thinkers believe that this objective moral order has its origin in a divine creation. As a result, says M. Stanton Evans, the conservative believes that "ours is a God-centered, and therefore an ordered, universe."[12] Conservative thinkers believe that God is the author of reality and rules it still. "The Hebraic–Greek Christian tradition teaches us," argues John Hallowell, "that the ultimate reality behind nature and history is a creative, rational, moral, loving Will and that man, since he is created in the image and likeness of God, achieves the perfection of his being in willing submission to the Reason and Will of Him that governs the universe."[13] In the same vein, Russell

Kirk lists as the first canon of conservative thought the "belief that a divine intent rules society as well as conscience, forging an eternal chain of right and duty which links great and obscure, living and dead. Political problems, at bottom, are religious and moral problems."[14]

God is not, for these conservatives, " 'The Totally Other,' " as Frederick Wilhelmsen puts it, who has "retreated to the lonely splendor of His transcendent majesty."[15] God's will still rules the universe, and he is concerned that his will be obeyed. As Thomas Molnar puts it, "society is not the final judge in these matters, and . . . there is a moral authority transcending society which ought to be consulted."[16]

Man's "natural rights are held to be gifts from the Creator," Felix Morley asserts.[17] As Kirk explains, conservatives believe that "the theory of 'natural rights' depends upon the premise of an unalterable human nature bestowed upon man by God. Only acceptance of a divine order can give enduring freedom to a society; for this lacking, there is no reason why the strong and the clever, the dominant majority or the successful oligarch, should respect the liberties of anyone else."[18] Therefore, as Leonard Read points out, conservatives are "totally or extremely at odds with the statists who hold the state to be the endower of man's rights."[19] Having received these rights from God, man has correlative duties to use those rights properly—that is, as God wishes—and to work to create and sustain social and political arrangements in which those rights are protected.

"Can you be a conservative and believe in God?" asks William F. Buckley. "Obviously. Can you be a conservative and not believe in God? This is an empirical essay, and so the answer is, as obviously, yes. Can you be a conservative and despise God and feel contempt for those who believe in Him? I would say no. . . . If one dismisses religion as intellectually contemptible, it becomes difficult to identify oneself wholly with a movement in which religion plays a vital role."[20]

Buckley is correct that some expressions of this conservative position are not avowedly theistic. Many conservative thinkers do not directly refer to God when discussing the source of these absolute standards and principles that they believe are contained in the objective moral order. They describe this moral order as stemming from the nature of things, "the constitution of being." They hold with Read that "order consists of what is in harmony with a thing's nature,"[21] so that the moral order for man, or the "enduring principles of order, justice, and freedom," as Kirk puts it, "may be discerned through a study of man's nature and man's history."[22] Such principles are laws of man's nature. They have an objective existence. John Hallowell's belief in the existence of an independent reality is much the same. It includes belief in an unchanging human nature from which, since "through knowledge of what we are, we obtain knowledge of what we ought to do," derive universally applicable principles that are embodied in the law of nature or the moral law.[23] Will Herberg, a traditionalist conservative, describes such belief in a higher law as "the very cornerstone" of conservative philosophy.[24]

Typically, however, the appeal to the constitution of being as the source of the moral order is not strictly divorced from a theistic position. Almost all conservative thinkers ultimately believe that this order of reality was created by God, although for one reason or another, or at one time or another, some choose to place their emphasis on this independent reality and consider its nature without reference to its divine origins. For example, Weaver at one point concludes a discussion of the objective moral order by saying, "I have tried, as far as possible, to express the thought of this essay in secular language, but there are points where it has proved impossible to dispense with appeal to religion. And I think this term must be invoked to describe the strongest sustaining power in a life which is from limited points of view 'solitary, poor, nasty, brutish, and short.' "[25] Willmoore Kendall makes the same case even more forcefully: "no society can survive—or should survive—without foundations driven deep in religious belief."[26]

Conservatives appeal to a number of authoritative sources for knowledge of the moral absolute and for standards that men should obey. Since most conservatives believe that God is ultimately the source of the order of reality, they naturally view revelation from God as a primary source of knowledge of that order. Scripture contains the revealed word of God, and more, as Kirk explains. Referring to the absolutes of the objective moral order as norms, he states that "one cannot draw up a catalogue of norms like an inventory of goods. . . . Most perceive these norms clearly only when they are part and parcel of the life of a human being. Aristotle made norms recognizable by describing his 'great–souled man,' the upright person and citizen. For the Christian, the norm is made flesh in the person of Christ."[27]

But conservatives do not believe that revelation can be expected to cover all aspects of social and political life. Even Kirk observes that "divine inspiration certainly will not suffice for the ordinary courses of life: one cannot expect the supernatural universe to manage the routine concerns of the natural universe."[28] Therefore, while revelation is the source of man's knowledge of some of the most important standards and principles, it is not a sufficient guide to the application of those principles to men's lives. Thus a further source of knowledge about the absolute is needed.

After asserting that there is an objective reality, Hallowell states his belief that it is knowable. "Man is endowed with a faculty which enables him, at least dimly, to grasp the meaning of that reality. . . . Knowledge does not involve the making or constructing of anything, but rather the discovery of what already exists."[29] All conservative thinkers agree. Most describe this faculty as reason and believe that it is here that man's reason finds one of its most appropriate roles: understanding the principles given through revelation, adding further perception of these principles through close study of the order of reality, and applying these principles to actions and institutions. Weaver argues that conservatism contains "the assumption that the world is intelligible and that man is free." Furthermore, he says, "Belief in universals and principles is inseparable from the life of reason. And to make rational choices in those areas where reason rightly applies is a moral duty."[30] Conservative thinkers are quick to point out that this role for reason is one of discovery and not construction. But they do believe that discovering absolute truths through study of the world and its inhabitants is a crucial task for human reason. As Wilhelmsen puts it, "Men do not 'think up these finalities': they are already there and simply need to be discovered by rational inquiry into the structure of human nature."[31] Kirk means the same thing when he says, "enduring principles of order, justice, and freedom may be discerned through a study of man's nature and man's history."[32]

But we have also seen the prevailing doubt among all conservative thinkers about the efficacy of human reason. Some conservative thinkers, therefore, talk about a somewhat different human capacity for apprehending truth instead of or in addition to reason: a nonrational or prerational intuitive perception. Wilhelmsen, for instance, believes that although these truths, which he refers to as the natural law, can be discovered by reason, "most men are incapable of achieving knowledge of the natural law. Yet they need it; therefore God revealed the content of natural law to all men," so that "men, left to themselves, follow the road of their own natures spontaneously because that is the way men are," although the road of their own natures contains evil as well as good, and the ability to read the road map is not spontaneous.[33] Other conservative thinkers make similar references, sometimes to common sense, other times to some sort of direct perception not mediated by reasoning. Kirk for instance says, "No, norms cannot be invented. All that we can do is to reawaken our consciousness to the existence of norms: to confess that there are enduring standards superior to our petty personal private stock of rationality."[34] And Molnar speaks of "man's naturally moral thinking."[35]

Whether rational or nonrational, the human capacity to perceive the truths of the objective moral order, "however dimly," as Hallowell puts it, is very important to conservative thinking. But, like revelation, it is not sufficient. As Wilhelmsen states, conservative thinkers find themselves confronted with a "tension and paradox: as natural, the law can be understood by reason, but we cannot trust just anybody's reason to do the job: we need an authority."[36] Reason, even reason applied to divinely revealed truth, will not suffice. It needs authoritative guidance.

Chapter 4 discusses the sources and the nature of the authority that conservative thinkers look to, but one source of knowledge about the objective moral order that they believe is authoritative is tradition. Tradition consists of the accumulated experience and wisdom of generation after generation and of numerous societies. This is what Kirk is referring to when he says that "the essence of social conservatism is preservation of the ancient moral traditions of humanity. Conservatives respect the wisdom of their ancestors."[37] Conservatives do not view tradition as opposed to revelation or reason as a means of gaining knowledge of the order of being and the principles and standards flowing from it. They view tradition as encompassing both revelation and reason. Tradition is largely the accumulated wisdom gained through revelation and reason by countless individuals and groups and tested in their experience. As Meyer puts it, the "moral and intellectual order, based on the constitution of being, [is] grasped and interpreted by generation upon generation"; "standards of virtue are the hard–won prize of millenia of civilization."[38]

But tradition *is* opposed to the reasoning of an individual who scorns the inheritance of the past and attempts to construct out of his own mind the perfect social and political order. Kirk expresses this clearly: "by trial and error, by revelation, by insights of men of genius, mankind has acquired, slowly and painfully, over thousands of years, a knowledge of human nature and of the civil social order which no individual can supplant by private rationality."[39] Meyer advocates a careful blending of reason and tradition:

What is required of us is a *conscious* conservatism, a clearly prin-cipled restatement in new circumstances of philosophical and political truth. . . . The conservative today, like the conscious conservative of all revolutionary eras, cannot escape the necessity and duty to bring reason to bear upon the problems that confront him. . . . He has the responsibility of establishing in new circumstances forms of thought and institutional arrangements which will express the truth of the great tradition of the West. Respectful though he is of the wisdom of the past and reverent towards precedent and prescription, the tasks he faces can only be carried out with the aid of reason, the faculty which enables us to distinguish principle and thus to separate the true from the false.[40]

Kirk makes the same point when he argues that conservatives must "seek, reasonably and prudently, to reconcile the best in the wisdom of our ancestors with the change which is essential to a vigorous civil social existence."[41]

No one source is seen by conservative thinkers as sufficient by itself to give knowledge of the objective moral order. All sources must be integrated to give a more complete understanding. But no combination of sources can give imperfect man a perfect understanding. Weaver, for instance, acknowledges that "there is a difference between knowing an absolute and knowing an absolute absolutely . . . .To know an absolute absolutely is something that is not given to men, unless there be such a thing as special revelation. As long as we inhabit this house of mortal clay we are none of us absolutists in this sense. This is but a recognition of our human condition."[42]

However, conservatives do not think that the necessary limit on man's grasp of absolute truths justifies him in failing to seek knowledge of them or in ignoring them and refusing to live by what he does understand. As Weaver continues, "This is not the same, however, as saying that there are no absolutes. The absolute is something that we apprehend without knowing fully, that we have fleeting intimations of, that we recognize as necessary to give validity to our intellectual and moral principles."[43] There *is* an objective moral order, conservative thinkers insist, and it matters. As Vivas asserts,

in spite of the difficulties which one encounters when one tries to formulate a hierarchy of values as they exist independently of human actualization, such a hierarchy does, in fact, exist. . . . We may not be able to say that courage, without qualification and considered by itself, is higher or lower than saintliness, but we are able to say that courage and saintliness and wisdom are higher than the values which a technological civilization pursues, those which contribute to bodily comfort. . . . Our partial ignorance of the true order of rank among values is not ground for moral cynicism or subjective relativism.[44]

Conservative thinkers oppose what they see as the modern, and especially liberal, abandonment of belief in an objective moral order in favor of philosophical and ethical relativism. Richard Weaver, for instance, believes that the cause of modern disintegration "was a change that overtook the dominant philosophical thinking of the West in the fourteenth century, when the reality of transcendentals was first seriously challenged." This was the "crucial event in the history of Western culture," because it has led to the abandonment of belief in transcendental values or universals. "The issue ultimately involved is whether there is a source of truth higher than, and independent of, man; and the answer to the question is decisive for one's view of the nature and destiny of humankind." From this abandonment of belief in universals "flowed those acts which issue now in modern decadence. . . . The denial of universals carries with it . . . the denial of truth . . . inevitably. . . . With the denial of objective truth there is no escape from the relativism of 'man is the measure of all things.' "[45]

One of the conservatives' main criticisms of liberalism is that it is relativistic. As Meyer puts it, the fatal flaw in the philosophical underpinnings of liberalism is that it "denied the validity of moral ends firmly based on the constitution of being."[46] Speaking of what he calls the disease of modernity, Vivas expresses a position parallel to Meyer's: he believes that at the bottom "of the liberal syndrome, one of a number of interrelated attitudes that are symptomatic of a complex illness at present pandemic in our academic society and possessing the virulence of a plague . . . is the staphylococcus of relativism."[47] Conservative thinkers put forward a wide variety of reasons for the growth of such relativism in modern times, but there is one common thread in this part of the conservative analysis that is pertinent here. The rejection of the objective moral order has resulted from some of the defects of human nature, such as the desire to do evil and be free of the restraints implied in the existence of objective truth, or the hubris that stems from intellectual attainment and scientific and technological advancement and that leads to the false belief that man has no need for the crutch of beliefs in absolutes. Conservatives do not believe that relativism is unique to modern times, but they do believe that it is particularly widespread and therefore particularly dangerous.

Conservative thinkers are so outspoken in their criticism of liberal relativism that Kendall says that relativism is the ultimate issue between liberals and conservatives.[48] Kendall overstates the case, of course; there is not *one* ultimate issue between liberals and conservatives. But it is on this issue of relativism that conservative thinkers voice some of their sharpest criticisms of liberalism.[49]

From the conservative perspective, relativism involves an abdication of the human responsibility to attempt to obtain truth, and it has terrible consequences, both personal and public. It leaves the individual bereft of the knowledge of values and contributes to what Vivas calls a "general erosion of the values of our society."[50] "Another effect of relativism that introduces a great deal of confusion into current ways of thinking and living," argues Weaver, "[is] supposing that no values are incompatible."[51] The result is a permissive culture that conservative thinkers regard as vile: "liberalism can do nothing to cleanse or halt this Augean wave; can only, in fact, smooth its advance," argues Burnham. "The secular relativism and permissiveness to which liberalism is committed provides no metaphysical foothold on which a stand might be taken. The logic of the liberal interpretation of free speech and the other civil rights not only cannot net the immoralist, but must on his demand successfully remove the checks and obstacles by which, over millennia, society has restricted his field of operation."[52]

Conservative thinkers believe that relativism also has evil political effects. One of the greatest injuries, according to Weaver, "that the idea of relativism has done to political thinking—and organization—lies in the encouragement it gives to middle–of–the–roadism."[53] Compromise for its own sake, mere expediency, denial of principle—conservative thinkers believe that these result from relativism and are inimical to the true purposes of government. Furthermore, conservative thinkers believe that relativism threatens the stability of government. Weaver states that "for four centuries every man has been not only his own priest but his own professor of ethics, and the consequence is an anarchy which threatens even that minimum consensus of value necessary to the political state."[54] Without a minimum consensus to bind people to government, only force remains. Vivas argues that "relativism leaves society no way to enforce behavior according to its norms except force—no moral force or power."[55] Weaver agrees: "there is a very direct connection between the belief in principle . . . and the preservation of freedom. I am entirely convinced that relativism as a doctrine must eventually lead to a regime of force. The relativist has no outside authority, no constraining transcendent idea to appeal to or be deterred by. . . . This is the way that leads to the rule of appetite."[56] Evans means the same thing when he says that "the loss of moral value feeds statism."[57]

Part of the problem, according to Burnham, is that a relativistic approach to government "recognizes only reason and individual conscience informed by reason" as guides in lieu of moral authority, so that the claim of society on a person can only be utilitarian. "But when once I see through the utilitarian fraud and realize that there is no necessary coincidence between my individual search for happiness and the greatest happiness of the greatest number, existing society has no further moral claim on me, granted the metaphysical premises" of relativism.[58]

The point is not that conservatives believe in values, moral standards, and God, and that they think that liberals and other nonconservatives do not. It is not just a matter of personal belief, as far as conservative thinkers are concerned. The significant point is that conservatives hold that there are objective and irrefutable grounds for this belief in an objective moral order[59] and that conservatives see a public role for these standards and principles, believing that in some way public policy must reflect and support this concern for God and for moral absolutes.

Rejecting relativism, conservative thinkers believe that the truths of the objective moral order must find application in the lives of individuals. It is only through compliance with these truths that people can find happiness and peace. As Kirk puts it, the conservative "knows that order in personality and order in society are possible only through an observance of norms. What the intelligent conservative is trying to conserve is the norms of private and public life: the ancient principles that keep man truly human."[60] John Hallowell makes the same point when he says that "being and goodness belong together. Through knowledge of what we are, we obtain knowledge of what we ought to do. The knowledge of what man should do to fulfill his human nature is embodied in what has traditionally been called the 'law of nature' or the 'moral law.' This law, though requiring positive laws to meet changing circumstances, provides universally applicable principles in terms of which we can guide our individual and social life toward the perfection of that which is distinctively human."[61]

These truths are so important to the worth of the individual's life, according to Buckley, that the individual must consider them "more important than the individual's own life."[62] They are so

important, in fact, that if they did not exist they would have to
be created or believed in anyway. Peter Viereck argues that even
if it could be proven that moral absolutes do not exist—which
he believes is impossible because they do exist—men would still
need to believe in them. "Sad experience would teach us that
man can only maintain his existence through guiding it by the
nonexistent: by the moral absolutes of the spirit. If this sounds
paradoxical, it is of such paradoxes that human truth is made."[63]

As some of the statements just quoted indicate, conservative
thinkers believe that the truths of the moral order apply not only
to individuals but also to society. They believe that there is no
essential opposition between what is ultimately good for the
individual and the common good—both are dictated by objective
reality. As Hallowell puts it, "the restraints that are necessary for
the development of a good man are identical with the restraints
that make life in society possible."[64] The truths of the objective
moral order are not, for conservative thinkers, of merely private
concern. They matter in public life.

Some of the ways that conservative thinkers believe that they
matter are discussed in the following chapters. Chapters 4 and
5 discuss how the core ideas influence conservative thinking
on the nature of freedom, the need for authority, and the
conflict between freedom and authority. Chapters 6, 7, and 8
discuss how the core ideas influence contemporary American
conservative thought in some other areas that are important to
conservatives: government and the economy, community, and
change and tradition. The emphasis in these five chapters is not
on conservative thinking on these topics for its own sake, but on
how conservative thought in these areas is shaped by the core
ideas—to show what conservative thinkers share because of the
nature of their core beliefs.

SUMMARY

To conclude the discussion of the core ideas in this and the
previous chapter, it will be useful to review a few statements
by conservative thinkers that express these two ideas together.
Some conservatives describe the core ideas as the foundation
of conservative thought. Others clearly include both in their

thinking without positing them as fundamental. But whether or not these two ideas are explicitly recognized as the core of conservative thought, they are present in the thinking of all contemporary American conservatives.

M. Stanton Evans: "If we view conservatism as a philosophy, rather than as an immutable catalogue of tastes and foibles, I think we can attribute to it certain primary and constant affirmations. The conservative believes ours is a God–centered, and therefore an ordered, universe; that man's purpose is to shape his life to the patterns of order proceeding from the Divine center of life; and that, in seeking this objective, man is hampered by a fallible intellect and vagrant will."[65]

Russell Kirk explains:

My present purpose is to suggest that such principles as Professor Voegelin expounds are the principles which increasingly are being recognized by thinking American conservatives as the foundation of their beliefs. . . . Conservative views [are] founded upon belief in a transcendent order, in an unalterable human nature, and in a natural law. . . . Recognition of a transcendent order in the universe does not make the statesman into a dreamer, but into a realist. Knowing his theology and his history, he takes it for granted that man is not a perfect nor a perfectible being, and that the prudent politician will endeavor to make life tolerable, not impossibly perfect.[66]

John P. East agrees with Eric Voegelin that "The ultimate goal of political philosophy . . . is the discovery of the 'unchangeable order of the soul and the world.' " He also believes that

the unifying and controlling theme [of conservative thought] is that of 'the great tradition' of Western thought. . . . The great tradition of Western political thinking has two principal components: one is classical in origin, the other is biblical. With classical thought . . . there is an insatiable quest for truth concerning the genuine nature of things. . . . In addition, there is a quest for the higher moral law, for those premises in the ethical realm that are transcendent, enduring, and permanent. . . . With the biblical component of the great tradition . . . there is a profound apprehension of the creatureness of the human condition, that is, man as creature and not as creator. The individual's life is frail and finite. . . . The human predicament is marred by evil, tragedy, and sorrow, which inhere in the nature of things. Life individually and collectively is imperfectible. . . . Is the biblical view wholly direful and pessimistic? The answer is categorically No, for there is the Incarnation and the Pauline trilogy of faith, hope, and love, and ultimately there is the promise of eternal life.[67]

Donald Atwell Zoll says that there are only two ways that it makes sense to distinguish between Left and Right (by which he means approximately what I have here referred to as conservatism): "1. political and social theory identified with the Right invariably displays a concept of the person at variance with views of the Left in that it assumes some variety of an innate, irreducible dignity of the person, coupled, at the same time, with a commitment to the legitimacy of some criterion for ascertaining relative standards of human worth; 2. a general acceptance by the Right of life and human nature as it appears to be, rather that the entertainment of utopian visions of human and social perfectibility."[68]

Will Herberg states: "The moral foundation of democracy consists of two convictions: (1) the conviction that beyond all earthly majesties, even the majesty of society and the State, there is a higher majesty and a higher law; and (2) the conviction that no man, or group of men, no matter how good or wise they may be, possess the wisdom or virtue to be entrusted with unrestricted and irresponsible power over others."[69]

Frank S. Meyer maintains: "Conservatives insist upon an eternal order of being and a fixed goal of freedom." "The Christian understanding of the nature and destiny of man, which is the foundation of Western civilization, is always and everywhere what conservatives strive to conserve. That understanding accepts the existence of absolute truth and good and at the same time recognizes that men are created with the free will to accept or reject that truth and good."[70]

John Hallowell argues:

Being and goodness belong together. Through knowledge of what we are, we obtain knowledge of what we ought to do. The knowledge of what man should do to fulfill his human nature is embodied in what has traditionally been called the 'law of nature' or the 'moral law.' This law, though requiring positive laws to meet changing circumstances, provides universally applicable principles in terms of which we can guide our individual and social life toward the perfection of that which is distinctively human. . . . Man is endowed with a faculty which enables him, at least dimly, to grasp the meaning of that reality. . . . Knowledge does not involve the making or constructing of anything, but rather the discovery of what already exists.[71]

NOTES

1. Meyer, "Conservatism," in Goldwin, ed., *Left, Right and Center: Essays on Liberalism and Conservatism in the United States* (Chicago, 1965), p. 5.

2. Voegelin, *From Enlightenment to Revolution* (Durham, N.C., 1975), p. 177.

3. These are terms that Voegelin uses in many of his works, most especially in the several volumes of *Order and History*.

4. Voegelin, *Order and History*, Vol. 1, *Israel and Revelation* (Baton Rouge, 1956), p. 453.

5. Vivas, *The Moral Life and the Ethical Life* (Chicago, 1950), p. vii.

6. Hallowell, *Moral Foundation*, p. 24.

7. Kirk, *Program*, p. 41; and "Norms, Conventions, and the South," *Modern Age* 2 (Fall 1958), p. 338.

8. Buckley, ed., *Did You Ever See a Dream Walking?* p. xvii.

9. Weaver, *The Ethics of Rhetoric* (Chicago, 1953), p. 112.

10. William Chamberlin, "Conservatism in Evolution," *Modern Age* 7 (Summer 1963), p. 253.

11. Zoll, *Twentieth Century Political Philosophy* (Englewood Cliffs, N.J., 1974), p. 124. See, for example, Evans, "A Conservative," p. 75; Kendall, *Affirmation* p. 99; East, "Eric Voegelin," p. 115; Carson, "Cutting Loose from Reality," *The Freeman* 15 (January 1965), pp. 45–46; Molnar, *Authority*, p. 83; Viereck, "But—I'm a Conservative!" *Atlantic Monthly* (April 1940), p. 539; and Wilhelmsen, *Christianity and Political Philosophy*, p. 17.

12. Evans, "Techniques and Circumstances," p. 58.

13. Hallowell, *Moral Foundation*, p. 102. See also Read, "Blessing," p. 49; Kuehnelt–Leddihn, "Portland Declaration," pp. 1188–89; and Jaffa, "Another Look at the Declaration," *National Review* (11 July 1980), p. 837.

14. Kirk, *Conservative Mind*, p. 17.

15. Wilhelmsen, "The Conservative Vision," p. 298.

16. Molnar, *Authority*, p. 30. See also Kirk, *Program*, p. 166; and Kendall, "Three on the Line," *National Review* (31 August 1957), p. 181.

17. Morley, *Freedom and Federalism* (Chicago, 1959), p. 27.

18. Kirk, *Beyond*, p. 171.

19. Read, "Blessing," p. 49.

20. Buckley, ed., *Did You Ever See A Dream Walking?* pp. xxix–xxx. See also Kendall, *Affirmation*, p. 4; Kirk, *Conservative Mind*, p. 10; and Kuehnelt–Leddihn, "Portland Declaration," p. 1188.

21. Read, "On Freedom and Order," p. 33.

22. Kirk, "Prospects for a Conservative Bent in the Human Sciences," *Social Research* 35 (Winter 1968), p. 581.

23. Hallowell, *Moral Foundation*, pp. 24–26.

24. Herberg, "Conservatives, Liberals and the Natural Law, II," *National Review* (19 June 1962), p. 458. See also Nisbet, *Twilight of Authority* (New York, 1975), pp. 94–97; Molnar, *Authority*, p. 48; and Weaver, *Ethics of Rhetoric*, p. 113.

25. Weaver, *Ideas Have Consequences*, p. 185.

26. Kendall, "Three," p. 181; See also Hallowell, *Moral Foundation*, pp. 112–15; and Meyer, *In Defense*, pp. 60–61.

27. Kirk, "Norms," p. 340.

28. Kirk, *Conservative Mind*, p. 45.

29. Hallowell, *Moral Foundation*, p. 25.

30. Weaver, *Ideas Have Consequences*, p. 1; and *Relativism and the Crisis of Our Times*, p. 12.

31. Wilhelmsen, *Christianity and Political Philosophy*, p. 14.

32. Kirk, "Prospects," p. 581. See also Kendall, *Affirmation*, p. 91; Carson, "Reality," p. 46; Weaver, *Ethics of Rhetoric*, p. 113; and Vivas, *Moral Life*, p. viii.

33. Wilhelmsen, *Christianity and Political Philosophy*, pp. 15–16.

34. Kirk, "Norms," p. 338.

35. Molnar, *Authority*, p. 30.

36. Wilhelmsen, *Christianity and Political Philosophy*, p. 181. See also Hallowell, *Moral Foundation*, p. 183; Vivas, *Moral Life*, p. 217; Meyer, "Freedom, Tradition, Conservatism," p. 17; and Kirk, *Conservative Mind*, p. 18.

37. Kirk, *Conservative Mind*, p. 17.

38. Meyer, *In Defense*, pp. 163, 166. For more on what conservative thinkers mean by tradition, see chapter 8.

39. Kirk, "Prescription," p. 28.

40. Meyer, "Freedom, Tradition, Conservatism," pp. 12–13.

41. Kirk, *Program*, p. 6. See chapter 8 for more on the relation between tradition and change in contemporary American conservative thought.

42. Weaver, *Relativism and the Crisis of Our Times* (Philadelphia, 1961), p. 11.

43. Ibid.

44. Vivas, *Moral Life*, p. 216.

45. Weaver, *Ideas Have Consequences*, pp. v (from 1959 Forward), 2–4.

46. Meyer, *In Defense*, pp. 1–2.

47. Vivas, *Relativism and Its Paradoxes and Pitfalls* (Philadelphia, 1962), pp. 4–5.

48. See Kendall, *Affirmation*, p. 99.

49. See, for example, Molnar, *Authority*, p. 47; Burnham, *Suicide*, pp. 74–75; Buckley, *Jeweler's Eye*, pp. 38, 101; Nisbet, *Twilight*, p. 111; and Weaver, *Ethics*, pp. 56–58.

50. Vivas, *Relativism*, p. 1.

51. Weaver, *Relativism*, p. 9. See also Will, *The Pursuit of Virtue and Other Tory Notions* (New York, 1982), p. 113.

52. Burnham, "Notes on Authority, Morality, Power," *National Review* 22 (1 December 1970), p. 1284.

53. Weaver, *Relativism*, pp. 5–6.

54. Weaver, *Ideas Have Consequences*, p. 2; see chapter 4 for more on the minimum consensus that conservative thinkers see as necessary for governmental and social order.

55. Vivas, *Relativism*, p. 6.

56. Weaver, *Relativism*, p. 12.

57. Evans, "Conservative Case," p. 71.

58. Burnham, "Notes," p. 1287.

59. See, for example, Weaver, *Ethics of Rhetoric*, p. 17; Vivas, *Moral Life*, pp. 38–39, 62ff; and Hallowell, *Moral Foundation*, p. 39.

60. Kirk, "Norms," p. 343.

61. Hallowell, *Moral Foundation*, p. 25. See also Meyer, *In Defense*, p. 48; Weaver, *Ideas Have Consequences*, p. 130; Wilhelmsen, *Christianity and Political Philosophy*, p. 186.

62. Buckley, *Jeweler's Eye*, p. 111.

63. Viereck, *Conservatism Revisited: The Revolt Against Revolt* (New York, 1949), p. 10.

64. Hallowell, *Moral Foundation*, p. 26.

65. Evans, "Techniques," p. 58.

66. Kirk, *Beyond*, pp. 23, 25.

67. East, "Eric Voegelin," p. 115.

68. Zoll, *Twentieth Century Political Philosophy*, p. 115.

69. Herberg, "The Presuppositions of Democracy," *Commonweal* 62 (3 June 1955), p. 236.

70. Meyer, *The Conservative Mainstream* (New Rochelle, N.Y., 1969), p. 57; and "The Separation of Powers," *National Review* (30 January 1962), p. 59.

71. Hallowell, *Moral Foundation*, p. 25.

4

THE NEED FOR AUTHORITY

An excellent example of the way that the two core ideas shared by all contemporary American conservative thinkers influence the rest of conservative thought can be found in conservative views on freedom and authority. On the one hand, conservatives conclude from their beliefs about the unchanging nature of man and the objective moral order of reality that freedom is a natural part of man's being and is necessary to his efforts to conform to the truths of the objective moral order. On the other hand, these same core ideas lead them to believe that authority must be exercised over men for their individual and collective good. This tension between the need for freedom and the need for authority is perhaps the most fundamental in conservative thinking.

Some conservatives believe, indeed, that it is this tension that distinguishes conservatism from other positions. Stephen Tonsor asserts that "conservatism is a synthesis of contradictory principles, the principle of authority and the principle of freedom. These principles are ever held in precarious balance . . . their synthesis is never complete."[1] Tonsor is correct that the balance is precarious and that the attempted synthesis of these two principles is basic to much of conservative thought. What Tonsor does not point out is that these two contradictory principles, in their conservative formulation, can be held together in tension and are balanced in the manner and to the extent that they are, only because they derive from the same core ideas. Frank S. Meyer, the most active of those conservatives who have sought to resolve this tension, does recognize this fact. He believes that freedom and authority "are fundamentally in accord" because "they are grounded both in the nature of men and in the very constitution of being."[2] Meyer is too optimistic, perhaps, about how easily freedom and authority can be reconciled or balanced, but he is correct in thinking that the reason the possibility of reconciliation exists is that for conservatives both ideas stem from a common core of ideas.

Conservatives are not, of course, the only people who believe that both authority and freedom are necessary and must somehow be balanced. What distinguishes them, however, is the origin of their concern—the fact that this tension results from their core ideas and therefore takes its shape from them. Conservative thinkers view this tension from a perspective different from that of others. Consequently they mean significantly different things when they speak of freedom and authority than do nonconservatives, and the ways in which they propose to resolve the tension between the two involve very different policies and institutional arrangements, all because of the influence of the core. It is the task of this chapter and the next to show what conservative thinkers mean by freedom and authority, how they attempt to resolve the tension between the two, and how their ideas are shaped by the core.

This task is complicated, here more than in any other area of conservative thinking, by disagreement among conservative thinkers on the nature of these two ideas and on the appropriate ways to balance them. That conservatives disagree more extensively and more obviously at this point than at any other is reflected in the fact that the major division of contemporary American conservative thinkers is between those who lean more heavily toward freedom in this tension (generally called libertarian conservatives) and those who tend to emphasize authority (the traditionalist conservatives).

In addition, because the core leads directly to this tension between freedom and authority and because conservatives disagree so strongly about the nature of this tension and of its resolution, a single conservative philosophy cannot be built deductively from the core. Yet even here, at the point of greatest divergence, it is possible to describe the limits within which these disagreements take place, limits that are established by the core and that distinguish the conservative position, diverse as it is, from any other.

AUTHORITY

The beliefs at the core of conservative thought dictate a firm commitment to authority. Conservatives believe that people cannot live together successfully without authority. Given the weaknesses inherent in man's unchanging nature, authority must be exercised over him, both for his individual good and for the good of others. Given the existence of the truths of the objective moral order, coupled with man's inability or unwillingness to understand or obey those truths, authority is required to teach and give force to those truths in human affairs. Conservative thinkers differ among themselves on how this authority should be exercised, on what institutions are most suited to exercise it, and on the extent to which authority can be exercised without jeopardizing freedom. Yet they are united in the belief that neither the individual nor society can prosper or even survive without authority.

By authority conservative thinkers generally mean the power, regarded as legitimate for the most part by the people over whom it is exercised, to influence behavior and thought. This includes the coercive power of the state as well as authority that stems from recognized expertise, from willing assent, or from any other source that leads one person to obey or be influenced by another. As I will discuss, conservative thinkers believe that the best authority is that which is willingly obeyed because it is perceived as right. But they argue that people need more than just the authority to which they are willing to assent, that to some degree they need to be coerced for their own good and the good of others. This conservative definition of authority, as I have formulated it here, is necessarily general because it must cover the thinking of conservatives who stress very different aspects of authority. Their thinking should be elucidated by the following discussion.

Authority is necessary, conservatives believe, to protect and assist the individual. For one thing, protecting the rights of individuals from invasion by others requires authority. Since man by nature tends to be selfish, passionate, and irrational, he also tends not to respect the rights of others in pursuing his own self–interest. Without some authoritative sanction against imposing one's will or desires upon another, no one would be free; no one would be safe from the power of the strongest.

As Frank Meyer argues,

that problem arises out of the dilemma of virtue and freedom, and out of the corollary contradiction that one man's freedom can be used to inhibit another man's freedom. The refusal by some persons to accept their duties, to obey the moral law, means that the rights of others have no protection from these predators unless they are restrained by force—that is to say, unless *their* freedom is interfered with and *their* rights limited. But since no man is perfect and no one can be depended upon absolutely to fulfill the whole duty of man in letter and spirit, prudential considerations require what the pure philosophical concept of rights cannot brook: that the absolute ideal of the rights of the person must be and will be modified in actual historical existence to the degree necessary to reach the closest possible approximation to that ideal for each individual person.[3]

From their view of human nature, conservatives conclude that authority is necessary to coerce people to respect the rights of others.

In addition, conservatives believe that authority must support individual rights by supporting belief in the truths of the objective moral order. As Russell Kirk puts it, "only acceptance of a divine order can give enduring freedom to a society; for this lacking, there is no reason why the strong and clever should respect the liberties of anyone else. Freedom without the theory of natural rights becomes simply the freedom of those who hold power to do as they like with the lives of those whose interests conflict with theirs."[4] Unless authority is used to teach and to coerce men to respect the rights of others, there can be no such rights. Therefore, as Frank Meyer argues, the conservative "cannot posit freedom as an absolute end nor can he, considering the condition of man, deny the role of the state as an institution necessary to protect the freedom of individual persons from molestation, whether through domestic or foreign force. . . . He knows that power exists in the world and that it must be controlled, not ignored with wishful utopian thinking."[5]

Another, broader way that conservative thinkers believe authority helps the individual is to foster virtue. Reason is a poor guide to the truths of the objective moral order. "Most men cannot govern their lives according to the scanty stock of private reason which is theirs," argues Kirk.[6] Yet man must order his individual and collective life on those truths—that is, he must work toward virtue—if he is to have a measure of happiness and security, and if he is to approach individual perfection and collective harmony.[7]

Thus authority assists man in discovering and understanding the truths of his existence. Within many institutions—the family, religion, social class, and also the State—conservatives believe authority is exercised to teach and convince people of these truths. Even the law, as George Will notes, "has an expressive function, expressing and thereby sustaining certain values."[8] The law teaches as well as commands. Customs and laws articulate the community's consensus as to what is right and what is wrong. And they articulate not just that consensus alone—good laws and customs express a higher law. Thomas Molnar asserts that "authority mediates between a higher law and the individual by articulating the higher law in terms of expected behavior, if possible, internalized, turned into a self–improving conviction."[9] Authority thus trains us in the habit of perceiving and obeying that higher law.

Furthermore, conservatives believe that much of human behavior is less the product of conscious intellection than it is the result of emulation. They think that men are by nature imitative. Molnar believes that "social life rests on a great deal of imitation—as is shown by the language we use, the fashions and fads we copy, the habits we assimilate—and *moral* imitation is one of its aspects."[10] Thus not only the teachings but also the teachers—those in authority, such as parents, teachers, and religious, social, and political leaders, or the people Kirk calls "the natural leaders in every order of society"[11]—help us to perceive and incorporate into our own behavior the truths by which men must live.

But teaching is not enough. Man fails to live up to the truths he possesses, conservatives believe, because by nature his reason is insufficient. Authority, writes Molnar, "supplies an indispensable persuasion as it possesses sanctions in cases where reason does not suffice."[12] For his own good and for the good of others, man must be enticed and persuaded and coerced to obey the truths of the moral order. Molnar acknowledges that "there are . . . strong personalities able to submit to self–authority. But the majority of men is not of this kind . . . ; they need authority to be exercised not inside but over them."[13]

One of the ways that authority helps us obey truth, according to conservatives, is to create within us good habits. "If men are courageous or virtuous, ordinarily this is because they are persons of good moral *habits*," argues Russell Kirk. Without the almost unconscious regulation of habit, man does not have the resolution to remain virtuous when a test comes; he becomes "either a coward or a brute in any personal or civic crisis."[14] Thomas Molnar agrees: "Actually, nothing better has been found in mankind's experience than the *training of habit*, which is also the formal character of education, manners, civilized attitudes, and even of higher virtues."[15] Authority can help us gain good habits. It holds us to virtuous action until it becomes habitual. "In this sense, authority is a permanent reminder, thus a reinforcer, of habits; since habits, however, spring from an initial conscious acceptance followed by an internalized automatization, it may be said that authority aims at the *ritualization of good habits*."[16] Authority can thus work to create habits out of the moral behavior that we have chosen, reinforcing and strengthening the good in our characters. Conservatives believe that authority works in this fashion because, as I will discuss soon, they believe that authority generally accords with our best understanding of what is right and good.

One of the habits we must develop is self–discipline. Conservative thinkers believe that discipline is essential to developing virtue. Discipline is essential to hold us to the struggle, exertion, self–denial, and endurance that are prerequisites to the taming of our evil tendencies and the forging of a virtuous character. Authority disciplines us and helps us to learn to discipline ourselves. But, says Richard Weaver, there exists in the world today a popular heresy about man's destiny. "The heresy is that man's destiny in the world is not to perfect himself but to lean back in sensual enjoyment . . . . Somewhere, moreover, the metaphysicians of publicity have absorbed the idea that the goal of life is happiness through comfort. It is a state of complacency supposed to ensue when the physical appetites have been well satisfied. Advertising fosters the concept, social democracy approves it, and the acceptance is so wide that it is virtually impossible today, except from the religious rostrum, to teach that life means discipline and sacrifice."[17]

Those physical appetites are never satisfied, conservatives believe, so the search for consumption is endless, destroying the capacity to endure toil, to obey truth, and to achieve virtue. Authority must discipline us so that we can subdue these appetites. This exercise of authority over man implies respect for him—respect for the potential inherent in his nature to overcome evil and cultivate good.

This respect implies that men can learn to discipline themselves and that the exercise of authority over them for the purpose of discipline may need only be temporary. For many this is true, but not for all; probably not for the majority, from the conservative perspective, and certainly not for the majority in all aspects of their lives at all times. Conservative thinkers believe that success in self–discipline in one area is most often accompanied by failure in others. "Man is always deficient in many areas so that authority is always rightfully exercised over him," asserts Molnar,[18] and Richard Weaver agrees: "The mass mind is incapable of seeing the virtue of selection and restraint."[19] Man must be restrained by authority in those areas in which he is not yet self–disciplined or is incapable of self–discipline. Otherwise, he will be unable to achieve virtue or attain the happiness that is dependent upon virtue. If his institutions are to serve him, they must restrain him at many points. "The possibilities that imagination, together with the penchant for moral evil presents to men, men fully exploit" unless restrained by authority, says Molnar.[20] Thus the need for restraint is rooted in man's nature. These restraints are not damaging, except in extreme cases in which they so severely restrict man as to leave him without the freedom to develop virtue. Short of that, however, they serve man by helping him to achieve his goal—virtue.[21]

One further way that conservatives think authority helps to shape man is to protect him. Authority must screen man from influences that would damage him. Weaver complains that in the mass media "all reserve is being sacrificed to titillation. The extremes of passion and suffering are served up to enliven the breakfast table or to lighten the boredom of an evening at home. . . . It is contended that such material is the raw stuff of life, and that it is the duty of organs of public information to leave no one deceived about the real nature of the world. The assertion that this is the real world begs the most important question of all. The real stuff of life is precisely what the civilized man desires to have refined, or presented in a humane framework."[22]

Refinement is necessary, conservatives believe, so that there can be understanding and not just thrills, reflection instead of just sensation. Authority must shield man from more temptation than he can handle. It must protect him from forces that would degrade him even when he desires to become virtuous. In the view of conservative thinkers, the reason that so many Americans have in recent years become active in organizations such as the Moral Majority is that they have been provoked—provoked by the conviction that society is jeopardizing souls and must be changed.[23]

Conservatives do not want authority to so protect man as to destroy the necessary struggle against evil that refines him. Yet despite any difficulty in deciding what restraint and protection are necessary in any particular case, Molnar assures us, there are "limits not to be transgressed."[24] Authority must be used to establish what Brent Bozell calls the "temporal conditions conducive to human virtue—that is, to build a Christian *civilization*."[25]

SOCIAL INTEGRATION

Conservative thinkers argue that in addition to needing authority to teach and shape him to be virtuous, man needs authority to help him fit successfully and harmoniously into society. Once again their perception of this need stems from their view of man's nature—he is a social being, with natural desires and needs to belong to a group, but his natural tendencies toward his own selfish interests often put him at odds with others. Molnar argues that "the selfish, self–centered, separatist nature which is one side of [man's] nature" must be tamed to the extent necessary to allow him to live peacefully with others. "Lacking the sure–footedness of animal instinct, [man] needs social enforcements enabling him to conform to his very nature as a social being." He is "so free of instincts that with almost every step he threatens the very community without which he would not exist and survive as a human being." Authority is necessary to mediate "between man's two basic needs: to be free and to be integrated with the group, and it mediates rationally because it is rational for man to live in the community of other men. If human groups are always precarious and precariously balanced between order and anarchy, it is because man is a place of conflict between his rational desire to be free and his equally rational desire to belong to the group."[26]

Conservatives believe that the authority exercised in the family, religious institutions, schools, and other like institutions helps train the individual in appropriate social behavior by inculcating habits of cooperation, courtesy, and deference, by teaching the value of self–sacrifice and service, and by providing an external reinforcement for the individual's ever–present but insufficient desire to belong. All this is for the individual's own good, Molnar tells us, for without the habit–forming training that can be obtained only in these relationships sustained by authority, the individual becomes "unstable, lonely, alienated, unreliable, confused—so atomized in his functions that he easily becomes an agent of destruction . . . [or] an easily housebroken member of unnatural and antisocial groups."[27]

AUTHORITY AND THE GOOD SOCIETY

So far the discussion of conservative views of authority has focused on the ways that authority helps the individual. The last topic—how authority helps the individual fit properly into society—brings us to a consideration of the role they believe authority has in creating the good society. Authority must shape men not only for their own individual good but also to ensure the existence of a good society for the benefit of all. Conservatives believe that authority is required to preserve order and prevent chaos and anarchy. If men are to enjoy the fruits of freedom, they must be protected in its exercise. They must live in an orderly society in which it is possible to predict at least to a degree what the outcome of their actions and the actions of others will be. They must be able to foresee what actions the rulers of the society will take, and they must be able to have some measure of confidence in the outcome of their plans. These things are not possible in the midst of chaos and disorder. The existence of society is a minimum requirement for a meaningful existence for the individual.

What causes disorder and how may it be prevented or overcome? According to conservatives, disorder, crime, riots, and chaos are not caused by an environmental deficiency, that is, by social or economic deprivation. Disorder is primarily the result of a lack of authority. Explanations that point to such social or economic causes "do not seem very plausible" to James Burnham "once we reflect that these conditions have existed in human society from its beginning, in orderly as in disorderly times and places. But even if [such explanations] are correct, they do not answer the *political* question. Politics deals with power, with rule. From a political standpoint, the cause of increasing disorder is the decay in the *authority* of the rulers, the sovereign. The cure is the restoration of authority."[28]

Conservative thinkers argue that a lack of authority also imperils freedom. When authority does not protect the freedoms that men wish to enjoy, they are left at the mercy of the strongest. An unlimited emphasis on freeing men from authority even for the purpose of following their consciences leads to the destruction of freedom. Tonsor proclaims that "the revolution made in the name of conscience and against authority did not always free men but, just as the reactionary conservatives had warned, it simply led to a war of all against all."[29] Conservatives believe this is true not only because the selfish tendencies of men must be restrained by authority to the extent necessary to protect the rights of others, but also because freedom depends upon a certain order that fosters the necessary conditions, including individual attitudes, for freedom to flourish. Russell Kirk argues that liberty arose "in consequence of an elaborate process. Its perpetuation depends upon retaining those habits of thought and action which guided the savage in his slow ascent to the state of civil social man."[30]

This order that is necessary for the existence and exercise of freedom is delicate. It must be protected and not taken for granted. Disorder is the more usual state of human association. As Kirk puts it, "quiet ages and safe lands are rare exceptions" and must be preserved by vigilant care.[31] Any culture is close to barbarism, no matter how settled and orderly it may seem, so that the preservation of order is a necessary function of authority if the society is to survive.

Conservative thinkers argue that the proper authority properly exercised not only helps bring about the existence of society, it helps create the good society. For one thing, it moves people toward a perception and an appreciation of the common good. Molnar believes authority "contains at least some concretization of the common (or partial) good, inasmuch as it is based on moral insight reinforced by social consensus in its widest sense."[32] As pointed out before, conservatives believe that authority teaches and persuades people to give up or moderate their individual interests in favor of the good of all. It also teaches what that good is and how it may be achieved. It thus contributes to a situation in which cooperative endeavors can flourish, in which mutual respect can exist.

Conservatives also believe that authority helps to maintain the standards without which good human relations would be impossible. This it does not only through the effect it has on those it punishes for antisocial behavior, but also through the effect it has on those who do not offend against the law but who witness both the offense and the punishment. Molnar believes that "the nature of sanctions is that it is indivisible: if those who deserve it are not appropriately penalized, then the so–far guiltless tend to fall, by a kind of social gravitational pull, to lower levels of discipline and civilization."[33] The punitive activity of authority teaches not only the guilty but also the rest of society, upholding the standards that make civilized life possible. With such punishment to sustain men's good intentions, they are less likely to give in to their evil tendencies.

Such punishment also helps to prevent antisocial acts in another way. Conservatives believe that it defuses the passions of retribution felt not only by those directly wronged by the original act but also by others who are outraged by the flouting of the standards of right and decency that they have internalized. It satisfies in an appropriate and controlled manner the natural human passions that might otherwise result in further violent antisocial behavior. George Will states this last point clearly: "There is also a cathartic function of expressive state action. The Nurenberg tribunals, however problematic they were jurisprudentially, performed the vital function of civilizing the vengeance that was going to be expressed, one way or another."[34]

ORTHODOXY

Another way that conservative thinkers believe authority preserves the existence of society and fosters a good society is through supporting an orthodoxy, what Tonsor calls the "minimum consensus which is necessary for the survival of any society."[35] As Willmoore Kendall contends, "any viable society has an orthodoxy—a set of fundamental beliefs, implicit in its ways of life, that it cannot and should not and, in any case, will not submit to the vicissitudes of the market place."[36] Conservative thinkers believe that this minimum moral consensus must be maintained or the society cannot survive. Since a society cannot protect its citizens unless it protects itself, it must sustain this consensus. To the extent that this is necessary, and only to that extent, the right of society to protect its existence must come before the rights of the individuals within it.[37]

Why do conservative thinkers consider this orthodoxy so vital? What does it do that they regard as essential? Without it they believe that the norms that are required to hold society together by restraining the evil in man's nature are threatened. Molnar asserts that "the partisans of permissiveness so completely trust the goodness of human nature that they believe that noninterference with the child's ways will automatically lead to good results. If we follow their logic, we find at the end a completely new society—or rather a 'dis–society'—at every generation or even at shorter intervals, since every child permissively brought up follows his own will, views, and norms, and they are by definition not transferred to the next. Thus, the consequence of permissiveness, if it were allowed free course, would be the extinction of society, in truth, anarchy."[38]

This quotation from Molnar is revealing in its negative reference to a new society, the goal of many a liberal or radical vision. The conservative attitude toward such a new society is negative not simply because it is new, but most fundamentally because it implies a wholesale rejection of the norms, standards, and customs of the past that conservative thinkers believe are necessary to mold both the individual and society for the good of all.[39]

Frederick Wilhelmsen sums up a number of other reasons why conservatives believe that a minimum orthodoxy is necessary: "Without this political orthodoxy . . . respect for the state withers; contracts lose their efficacy; the moral bond between citizens is loosened; the state opens itself to enemies from abroad; and the politeia sheds the sacral character without which it cannot long endure."[40] All of these have to do with the continued existence of society. By creating a minimum level of agreement on the most important questions that the members of a society face, the orthodoxy creates or sustains a moral bond between citizens that prevents the disruption of the social, economic, and political ties between them by disagreement over these questions. It also ties them to some common definitions of the nature of the world and of the nature of their relations with each other. And it ties them to some common purposes and tasks. Without this consensus, therefore, "society is dissolved into a war of all against all, into congeries of warring factions, pressure groups, and value systems," as Tonsor puts it.[41] The minimum consensus that authority must support also helps to hold society together by tying the citizens to the state. The state is not the only nor even the most important purveyor or supporter of this orthodoxy, nor do conservatives wish the state to be supported entirely without thought or question. But the State must be accorded some respect if it is to fulfill its functions.

What is this orthodoxy that conservative thinkers believe to be so essential? "What we point to, in a word," Wilhelmsen says, "is that matrix of convictions, usually enshrined in custom and folkways, often articulated formally and solemnly in charter and constitution, occasionally summed up in the creed of a church or the testament of a philosopher, that makes a society the thing that it is and that divides it from other societies."[42] This orthodoxy is not intended to suppress freedom. Indeed, conservative thinkers believe that it makes real freedom possible, for without this consensus people could not maintain the order necessary to support freedom. Willmoore Kendall states that "freedom of thought and freedom of expression there are and must be, but within limits set by the basic consensus; freedom of thought and freedom of expression there are and must be, but no anarchy of thought or anarchy of expression. . . . By no means are *all* questions open questions; some questions involve matters so basic to the consensus that the society would, in declaring them open, abolish itself, commit suicide, terminate its existence as the kind of society it has hitherto understood itself to be," and thus make it impossible to support and foster freedom.[43]

One of the questions that is not open for conservatives is the question of the merits of communism. They believe that some forms of political institutions make the development of a good society impossible. One of these is communism, what Meyer calls a "monstrous, atavistic attack on the survival of the very concepts of moral order and individual freedom."[44] Communism is not just an error that must be exposed or denounced, according to conservative thinkers. It is an evil that cannot be allowed to be part of the moral consensus, or even to coexist within the same culture. Communism is a threat to the very existence of our society, conservative thinkers believe, and we must be morally strong and loyal to our values and culture to be able to withstand this threat.

Even the appeal to academic freedom cannot be allowed to prevent the fighting of the battle against this threat. Richard Weaver believes that "Communist Party Members . . . are not free to teach the truth as they find it. They are bound by the dictates of the party line, which tells them *a priori* what views to hold, what ideas to propagate." This precludes the pursuit of truth that academic freedom exists to foster. "They are not exercising academic freedom, and they are not entitled to its prerogative." Weaver also questions the right of "fellow travelers" to academic freedom. He does not categorically deny their right, but he does question their qualifications to use it properly. When such a person defends the Soviet regime or "collaborates with it on the intellectual level, he must defend some things that our traditional morality has agreed not to condone—mass killings, planned aggression, systematic double dealing, and cynical disregard for pledges." He believes that we may have reached "the point at which the rhetoric of political and social survival becomes more persuasive than the rhetoric of academic freedom, just because in the present situation the second is a dependent of the first."[45]

Nonconservatives frequently complain that conservatives are trying to impose their values on society. Conservative thinkers respond that this is true in any society if the society wishes to survive. By "what it requires, encourages, proscribes, refuses to proscribe and prevents being proscribed," the government of any society establishes and supports certain values, according to George Will. "As liberalism has become a doctrine of 'liberation' it has spawned new 'rights', in the name of which government has been empowered to promote certain values by stipulating behavior. Defenders of competing values [e.g., conservatives] are castigated for trying to 'impose' their values."[46]

Conservatives believe that this enforcing of values not only does happen, it should happen. Society must protect itself by maintaining minimum standards of what can and what cannot be allowed to exist or take place within it. That this is a conservative conviction is perhaps made clearest when they consider communism and the attempts to fight it, such as the effort made by Joseph McCarthy. Even those conservative thinkers who disliked McCarthy and his methods believe that the battle he was waging had to be fought. "In some charismatic way that cannot be explained by his own often inept acts and ignorant words," explains James Burnham, "McCarthy became the symbol through which the basic strata of the citizens expressed their conviction— felt more than realized—that Communism and Communists cannot be part of our national community, that they are beyond the boundaries; that, in short, the line must be drawn somewhere. This was really the issue in the whole McCarthy business. . . . The issue was philosophical, metaphysical: what kind of community are we? . . . From the Liberal standpoint—secularist, egalitarian, relativist—the line is not drawn, Relativism must be absolute."[47]

From the conservative standpoint, the line must be drawn clearly: although society may not prescribe every appropriate belief, it must proscribe those that are inimical to its very existence.

If society is to exist it must have an orthodoxy. If it is to be a good society it must have a good orthodoxy. Ultimately, conservative thinkers support a public orthodoxy not so much for what it does as for what it is—an approximation or approach to truth. Wilhelmsen argues that the reason conservatives desire the acceptance of a public orthodoxy is not "on the grounds of its brute factuality," that is, on the grounds that it exists or is politically viable. The consequences of that approach are the "subordination of both religious and intellectual freedom to the state; reduction of transcendent truth to existential truth; the pressing of God into the service of man." The orthodoxy's claim to acceptance "cannot be mere political utility or historical sanction, but [its representation of] the very structure of things as they are in themselves" if the orthodoxy is to support a good society.[48] The ultimate purpose of this consensus is to teach the best understanding reached by the members of the society of the truths of the objective moral order, to represent their "common confrontation of the Absolute."[49] In Niemeyer's words, it must "elucidate the connection between the political system and the underlying transcendent truth."[50]

Conservative thinkers are not relativists. They do not desire just any existent or useful orthodoxy, but an orthodoxy that is as close to the truths of the objective moral order as men's understanding will allow. This poses a problem, however. No minimum consensus can fully represent the truths of the objective moral order. Men are incapable of completely understanding those truths. Any orthodoxy will fall short of the truth, yet some orthodoxy is necessary. Without it, society would collapse, making the pursuit of a closer approximation impossible. So conservative thinkers believe that it is good to support the prevailing orthodoxy.

But this presents a dilemma to "any man who is aware both of the demands of the transcendent and of society, any man whose soul is turned out towards the truth of things as they are . . . but also faces his responsibilities as a member within a society that incarnates a way of life involving a certain (at least apparent) commitment to the Absolute." If he does not find ultimate meaning within his society's orthodoxy, Wilhelmsen asserts, he must "face up to two alternatives: to seek meaning beyond that orthodoxy, and preach this new truth to the citizenry—thus corrupting the bonds that have hitherto kept his society in being; or to seek meaning beyond the public orthodoxy but keep the new truth to himself, thus living a lie. . . . Either choice is evil: to destroy an essentially decent society is wrong, even if that society reposes upon theoretically erroneous foundations; but to fail to speak the truth when truth demands that it be spoken is wrong, too."[51]

How to resolve this dilemma? On this point different approaches are taken by different conservative thinkers. The easiest way out, of course, is if there is little or no conflict between the orthodoxy and the truth. This can be the case if revelation supports the public orthodoxy. Then the personal inquiry into truth will not disturb the orthodoxy.[52] Conservatives tend to believe that this is true to a large extent of American society and of Western civilization in general. They believe that the values that sustain the best aspects of contemporary society derive from Christianity and that the chief reason that contemporary society is in trouble is that this foundation is neglected. Wilhelmsen argues that without these truths from Christianity, the central values of our civilization make no sense. "Unless Christ be a Divine Person, personal dignity is a sham; . . . unless we are all brothers under a common Father, the pretensions of a universal liberty for all men are ridiculous; unless we have been called into existence by a Providential Creator who fingers each one of us uniquely with life and being, then slavery is perfectly sensible: Aristotle showed how sensible it was in the *Politics*. Our entire legal and ethical world is sustained by a faith in the Christian God and in the consequences of his incarnation."[53]

Unfortunately, conservatives believe, all orthodoxies are partially false. None contains only truth or all truth. There is no guarantee that truth will win out on this earth. Yet conservative thinkers believe that there is more revealed and time–tested truth available to man than he is presently (or ever) willing to acknowledge or follow. The public task is to restore what can be restored and to preserve what is still intact. The private responsibility is to seek for as much truth as possible while disturbing the settled existence of society as little as necessary.[54]

SOCIAL STRUCTURE

Another end for which conservative thinkers regard authority as essential, beyond the need to sustain the moral consensus, is the structuring of society for the good of all. They believe that the inequality of human beings is a basic fact.[55] Society must be structured to reflect that fact if communal objectives are to be met by each person performing the type of task or tasks for which he is suited. Beyond that, there are a number of tasks necessary for the proper functioning of society that could be performed by a large number of people who are apparently equally qualified for them. People must in some way be divided into groups that will perform these tasks. To some extent this dividing will take place naturally, on the basis of people's interests. This is the desired outcome, from the conservative perspective, since it leaves individuals as free as possible to choose their own tasks. But this may not always work, due to such factors as the low social status of some important tasks or an imbalance between one generation's interests and the necessary tasks. In such cases, there must be some means of seeing that essential tasks are not neglected. Structuring society in some way leads most people in one stratum to feel that a certain category of tasks is appropriate or natural to them. Molnar argues that "authority is the means of ensuring that a seemingly homogeneous multitude divides into permanent strata and thus performs a certain number of ordered tasks among which there is a hierarchy of importance."[56] This is seen by conservatives as less restrictive of freedom than assigning each individual to a specific task, both because there is a great variety of options open within any category of tasks, and because any specific individual is not prevented from choosing to reach beyond that category of tasks, although the smooth operation of society depends upon the fact that most within any strata will be sufficiently persuaded by group norms and expectations and by tradition to find satisfaction within the appropriate category.

Structure is also required to discipline individual desires and hold people to their work within the communal activity when their selfish desires lead them to flee work.[57] "From all these illustrations," Molnar concludes "that authority presents in a reasoned manner the inequality that exists in every community; we realize, of course, that reason is compatible with the fact that in the community there are many orders grouping individuals, many sets of codes (code of honor, professional code), many rights and duties. Authority explains and justifies these differences."[58]

Authority serves the many social groups and institutions in society in much the same way it serves society as a whole. In addition, public authority supports the authority of these groups, so that, for instance, the authority of a father is supported by public authority manifested in laws and customs. Authority also maintains a balance between these groups and ensures that they do not disrupt the order of society and that they contribute somewhat to the common good by performing their proper functions. Conservative thinkers believe that the rise of powerful, narrow special interest groups is related to the decline of authority. When public authority becomes feeble, a power struggle takes place between groups like political parties, giant corporations, giant unions, the media, government bureaucracy, and pressure groups of various kinds. As Molnar points out, "in well–ordered societies all of [these groups] are institutions, . . . that is, single–function bodies." But when authority does not order society and hold each of these groups to its proper function, "each institution, for lack of a controlling authority, is determined to conquer as much space for itself as possible, soon at the expense of other institutions, of the governing authority, then of the citizens."[59]

SUMMARY

Conservative thinkers see authority as indispensable for both the individual and society. Authority cannot ensure that all of these good things will happen, but conservatives believe that without authority, they are very likely not to happen. As Molnar puts it, "all this does not mean that the use of authority automatically leads either to virtue or to the desirable social behavior; but it supplies an indispensable persuasion."[60]

Yet authority itself poses a danger to some of the ends that conservative thinkers hold most dear, such as the pursuit of virtue and the exercise of freedom. How conservatives think the need for authority is to be reconciled with these other ends is the subject of the next chapter.

NOTES

1. Tonsor, "The Conservative Search for Identity," in Meyer, ed., *What Is Conservatism?* (New York, 1964), p. 134. See also Will, *Pursuit of Virtue*, p. 83.

2. Meyer, *In Defense*, p. 6.

3. Ibid., p. 74. See also Will, *Pursuit of Virtue*, pp. 99–100.

4. Kirk, *Beyond*, p. 171. See also Will, *Pursuit of Virtue*, pp. 27, 99–100; Zoll, *Twentieth Century Political Philosophy*, p. 27; and Kendall, *Affirmation*, p. 109.

5. Meyer, "The Twisted Tree of Liberty," *National Review* (16 January 1962), p. 26.

6. Kirk, *Program*, p. 238.

7. See Will, *Statecraft*, p. 27; and Meyer, "Why Freedom?" *National Review* (25 September 1962), p. 224.

8. Will, "The Value of Punishment," *Newsweek* (24 May 1982), p. 92. See also Bozell, "Freedom or Virtue," *National Review* (11 September 1962), p. 185.

9. Molnar, *Authority*, p. 57.

10. Ibid., p. 29.

11. Kirk, *Program*, p. 238.

12. Molnar, *Authority*, p. 31. See also Bozell, "Freedom or Virtue," p. 184.

13. Molnar, *Authority*, p. 22. See also Will, *Pursuit of Virtue*, pp. 59–61; and Meyer, "Why Freedom?" p. 224.

14. Kirk, "Prescription," in Meyer, ed., *What Is Conservatism?* pp. 30, 31.

15. Molnar, *Authority*, p. 44.

16. Ibid.

17. Weaver, *Ideas Have Consequences*, pp. 91, 105.

18. Molnar, *Authority*, p. 93.

19. Weaver, *Ideas Have Consequences*, p. 33.

20. Molnar, *Authority*, p. 21.

21. This should become clearer when we discuss the types of institutions that conservatives believe should exercise authority and the types of authority they should exercise.

22. Weaver, *Ideas Have Consequences*, p. 29.

23. See Will, "Who Put Morality in Politics?" p. 108.

24. Molnar, *Authority*, p. 59.

25. Bozell, "Freedom or Virtue," p. 184.

26. Molnar, *Authority*, pp. 31, 79, and 90.

27. Ibid., p. 89.

28. Burnham, "Notes," p. 1286.

29. Tonsor, "Conservative Search," p. 142. See also Will, *Pursuit of Virtue*, p. 27; Weaver, *Ethics of Rhetoric*, p. 173; and Kirk, "Prescription," pp. 24, 29.

30. Kirk, *Conservative Mind*, p. 29. See also Will, *Pursuit of Virtue*, p. 32.

31. Kirk, *The Old House of Fear* (New York, 1961), pp. 189–90.

32. Molnar, *Authority*, p. 31.

33. Ibid., p. 46.

34. Will, "Value of Punishment," p. 92.

35. Tonsor, "Educating the Children of the 'Me' Generation," *Modern Age* 25 (Summer 1981), p. 258. See also Will, *Statecraft*, pp. 19–20.

36. Kendall, "Three on the Line," *National Review* (31 August 1957), p. 181.

37. See Kirk, *Program*, pp. 278–80.

38. Molnar, *Authority*, p. 33.

39. The conservative attitude to tradition and change will be discussed at greater length in chapter 7.

40. Wilhelmsen, *Christianity and Political Philosophy*, p. 36.

41. Tonsor, "Educating," p. 258.

42. Wilhelmsen, *Christianity and Political Philosophy*, p. 29.

43. Kendall, *Affirmation*, pp. 74–75. See also Will, *Pursuit of Virtue*, pp. 84–85, 113.

44. Meyer, *In Defense*, pp. 9–10. See also Vivas, *Relativism*, p. 2.

45. Weaver, *Academic Freedom* (Philadelphia, 1963), pp. 12–15.

46. Will, "Who Put?" p. 108.

47. Burnham, "Re-Legitimization," *National Review* (1 June 1957), p. 518. See also Will, *Pursuit of Virtue*, p. 105.

48. Wilhelmsen, *Christianity and Political Philosophy*, pp. 34–36.

49. Wilhelmsen, "My Doxy Is Orthodoxy," *National Review* (22 May 1962), p. 366.

50. Niemeyer, Review of Clinton Rossiter's *Conservatism in America,* in *Journal of Public Law* 4 (Fall 1955), p. 443.

51. Wilhelmsen, *Christianity and Political Philosophy,* pp. 36–37.

52. See ibid., pp. 58–59.

53. Ibid., p. 212.

54. See chapter 8, where the discussion of tradition will take up this problem again.

55. See chapters 6 and 7.

56. Molnar, *Authority,* p. 31. See also Kirk, *Conservative Mind,* p. 18; Burnham, *Suicide,* p. 107; Weaver, *Ideas Have Consequences,* p. 107; Kuehnelt–Leddihn, "Portland Declaration," p. 1190; Tonsor, "The New Natural Law and the Problem of Equality," *Modern Age* 24 (Summer 1980), p. 243; and Nisbet, *Twilight,* p. 238.

57. See Weaver, *Ideas Have Consequences,* pp. 78–79, 92.

58. Molnar, *Authority,* p. 24.

59. Ibid., p. 114.

60. Ibid., p. 31.

5

FREEDOM VS. AUTHORITY

Conservatives' beliefs about the nature of man and the objective moral order lead them to place great value on freedom, both for its own sake as an essential aspect of man's being and as necessary for other ends. One such end is human growth. According to Russell Kirk, conservatives seek "to preserve a society which allows men to attain manhood, rather than keeping them within bonds of perpetual childhood."[1] The goal of human growth is virtue. Conservatives believe that people become virtuous as they struggle to conquer their innate evil tendencies and attune their actions with the moral order. Achieving virtue requires freedom, for unless a man is free to choose good or evil, he cannot choose to be virtuous; there is no purifying struggle without freedom. If a man chooses evil, he will not achieve virtue, but neither can he become virtuous unless he is free to choose. A man may be coerced to act virtuously, but he is not then free to face and conquer his evil tendencies, and thus he is not virtuous. As Frank Meyer states, "virtue is the fruit of well–used freedom."[2]

Conservatives believe freedom is necessary to virtue in another way as well. Just as men may be coerced to act virtuously, they may be coerced to act evilly. Technically it is true that as long as a person's will is not controlled, he is free to act virtuously regardless of the force exerted upon him. But as John Chamberlain recognizes, that is "a truth that would hold only for a race of martyrs. For it takes a rare individual to follow the dictates of his own choice of virtue if the whole machinery of the state—the courts, the police, the army—happens to be against it."[3] People must be free from coercion that would prevent their virtuous action.

The conservative view of human weakness in yet another way dictates that freedom is essential to virtue. Those individuals who would coerce us to be virtuous are also prone to error and sin. Although conservative thinkers believe that in the properly ordered society the rulers are more virtuous than the majority of the citizens, they do not believe that the rulers are angels. "Even bishop–statesmen in history have been guilty of great monstrosities of behavior," Chamberlain reminds us.[4] It is likely, then, that the standards imposed by these rulers will not be unfailingly virtuous. Therefore, even "the church–run state is no guarantee of a virtuous society."[5] Even if men could be made virtuous by coercion, and conservatives believe they cannot, there is no guarantee that the standards to which they would be forced to conform by rulers themselves subject to ignorance and evil would be the standards that could lead them to virtue.

Another end for which conservatives believe freedom has instrumental value is variety. In the view of Russell Kirk, "variety and complexity . . . are the high gifts of a truly civilized society."[6] By nature people desire this diversity. In summarizing the beliefs of American conservatives, Erik von Kuehnelt–Leddihn states that they believe that "men share with the beasts a craving for sameness. . . . But it is exclusively human to have a thirst for diversity. . . . *The delight in the variations of creations distinguishes man from the beast as much as religion or reason.*"[7] This yearning for variety, for individuality, is so natural to man that uniformity "can be achieved only by brute force, by leveling, enforced assimilation, exile, genocide."[8] If men are to satisfy this innate yearning for variety and enjoy and develop their individuality, and if society is to reap the fruits of this variety, men must be left free to develop as they wish to the greatest extent compatible with the need for order in society.

Conservative thinkers also believe that freedom is instrumental to effective political and economic association. No one knows enough to successfully control society single handedly, nor does any group of men. But "there is a wonderful way of life, suited to humanity as it is—that is, made to order for all of us, no one of whom knows very much," states Leonard Reed. It is the "free market, private property, limited government way of life, . . . a method of social and economic cooperation that doesn't require a lot of knowledge on the part of any one person."[9] This system works, Reed argues, because "there is an order of Creation over and above [man's] mind. . . . This order works in diverse and wondrous ways through billions of minds and . . . [man] should not in any way abort these miracles." Even though man does not understand just how this system works and does not know enough to plan or mastermind it, and even "though, from his experience, he does not know what will happen, he gains a faith that miracles will happen if creative energies be free to flow."[10] The virtue of such a free system, according to John Chamberlain, "is that it allows energy to flow uncoerced into a thousand–and–one different forms, expanding goods, services, and jobs in myriad, unpredictable ways."[11] Economic or political control from the top by the state does not allow for the free flowing of human inventiveness and energy. These cannot be planned or coerced, and they would not be financed by bureaucrats.[12]

Conservative thinkers also believe that freedom is intrinsically valuable, beyond any instrumental usefulness it may have. Meyer asserts that man is "of such a nature that innate freedom is of the essence of his being."[13] "Freedom is inalienable and indefeasible as a right, not for any reasons of utility but because it is the true condition of man's created being. . . . It is because freedom is the truth of the order of things that the conservative, who is first of all one who respects the inborn constitution of creation, stands for freedom."[14] Conservative thinkers believe that freedom is a gift of the creator. Man is not controlled by fate, or by heredity or environment—it is only those who have lost belief in transcendent truth who believe that.[15] Notions of biological or environmental determinism that deny the freedom of the will are contrary to the core ideas of conservatism. Whatever influence environment or heredity may have on man—and some conservatives think that that influence is large—he is free to choose his own actions.

So far the focus has been on why conservatives value free-

dom—how their core beliefs lead them to stress freedom. Perhaps
even more important, more distinctive of American conservative
thought, is what the core leads them to believe about freedom.
As Gerhart Niemeyer correctly perceives, "conservatives have
differed from their opponents not on whether to have more or
less freedom but on how to conceive the truth about political
freedom."[16] Despite disagreements and differences of emphasis
among themselves, because of their core ideas conservatives do
share ideas about freedom that are essentially different from
those of their opponents.

When conservative thinkers focus on the content of freedom,
they stress as fundamental human rights some traditionally
American notions, such as freedom of speech, religion, and association, a position shared by their liberal counterparts. Where
they believe that they depart from nonconservatives, in the words
of Felix Morley, is in believing firmly that "these natural rights
are . . . gifts from the Creator" and are therefore grounded in
the objective order of reality—that is, they are based on absolute truths and cannot be defended without acknowledgement
of these truths.[17] Conservatives believe, for instance, that one
of the grievous flaws of liberalism is that while it has stood
for individual freedom, its utilitarian philosophy has denied
the validity of objective moral truths about man and about the
constitution of being.[18] Without these truths, freedom cannot be
defended against the will of the stronger, and there is nothing to
restrain and temper the desires of men that lead men to infringe
the freedom of others.

Another way that conservatives differ from their opponents
on the nature of freedom is in stressing a natural right that
they believe most contemporary nonconservatives downplay
or deny—the right to property. People must be left free to
use and enjoy their property to the greatest extent compatible
with the same right of others and with the need to fund the
legitimate functions of government. Conservatives believe that
the extent of that freedom should be much greater than allowed
by contemporary American government.

There are a number of reasons why this aspect of freedom is so
valued by conservatives. They view it as a natural right bestowed
on man by God. Because of this, "the property instinct is an in-

eradicable part of human nature, and . . . any successful attempt to abolish it can only result in suffering," argues Chamberlain.[19] William F. Buckley, Jr., points out another reason that conservatives value freedom: "It is part of the conservative intuition that economic freedom is the most precious freedom, for the reason that it alone gives to each of us, in our comings and goings in our society, sovereignty—and over that part of existence in which by far the most choices have in fact to be made, and in which it is possible to make choices, involving oneself, without damage to other people."[20] The sovereignty Buckley speaks of is dear to conservatives' hearts. They believe that many of the decisions that an individual makes daily presuppose his possession of and freedom to use property. If his possession and use of this property is as free as possible from interference or taxation, he can exercise this sovereignty to the greatest extent possible.

Furthermore, economic freedom is seen by conservatives as an essential support for other freedoms. As Buckley argues, "without economic freedom, political and other freedoms are likely to be taken from us."[21] By this conservatives mean that the effective expression of other freedoms is often dependent upon some measure of freedom in obtaining, having, and using property. The effective use of the freedom of speech, for example, may require funds for such things as renting a hall, advertising speeches, or printing and distributing literature. Even more important, the exercise of the freedom of speech is rendered doubtful and dangerous when a person's livelihood may be put in jeopardy by what is said. This danger may exist no matter who his employer is, but it becomes particularly acute, conservatives believe, when a society's primary employer is government. Even if a person is independently wealthy, the opportunities for having his freedom of speech curtailed multiply as fast as do the taxes and regulations to which he is subject. For these reasons conservatives such as Buckley warn: "Stifle the economic sovereignty of the individual by spending his dollars for him, and you stifle his freedom."[22] Furthermore, because the state has a monopoly on coercive power (by which conservative thinkers mean the power to take from a person his life or property or to incarcerate him), because it must be strong in some areas, and because the governors are subject to corruption by their power—the more so the more that power increases—"we must resist every single accretion of power by the state," including power that limits our right to property.[23]

Conservative thinkers also believe that the freedom to have and use property contributes significantly to virtue. Richard Weaver explains that "private property . . . provides an indispensable opportunity for training in virtue. Because virtue is a state of character concerned with choice, it flourishes only in the area of volition. . . . Here in the domain of private property, rational freedom may prove the man; here he makes his virtue an active principle."[24] The specific virtues that may be inculcated by the free use of property include thrift, providence, and industry. "Property shows itself a benevolent institution by encouraging certain virtues, notable among which is providence. . . . No society is healthy which tells its members to take no thought of the morrow because the state underwrites their future. A conviction that those who perform the prayer of labor may store up a compensation which cannot be appropriated by the improvident is the soundest incentive to virtuous industry."[25]

It is because of this stress on the right to property, at least in part, that conservatives oppose the welfare state. The rates of taxation necessary to support the welfare state seem to them to be little short of confiscation, and thus these taxes weaken and may eventually destroy the right to property. Such taxation also chips away at other freedoms by weakening the individual's sovereignty over his financial resources, thus reducing the effective exercise of other freedoms. Welfare measures may increase the security of individuals, an end that conservatives desire to a certain degree. But security is not freedom, nor is it as valuable as freedom. Conservative thinkers believe there are other, superior ways to provide security.[26]

Thus it can be seen that for conservatives freedom is largely negative rather than positive, as far as government involvement is concerned. It is freedom *from* interference both by government and by other people. It is not freedom *for* any particular thing, determined in advance: neither jobs, nor security, nor health, nor any other such end. Meyer argues that "the 'freedom for' is not freedom at all, but simply a set of ends conceived as the proper purpose of freedom. . . . Freedom does not lead inexorably and of itself to [specific] ends . . . , but only makes it possible for each individual person to choose between them."[27] It is the right to choose, not the end chosen, that for conservatives defines freedom.

FREEDOM VS. AUTHORITY

The tension between the need for authority and the desirability of freedom is acute in contemporary American conservative thought. The same human nature that makes authority necessary makes it dangerous to freedom. Furthermore, the authoritative truths on which man must base his life are known only imperfectly, so that it is dangerous to enforce them. On the other hand, freedom endangers the authority that is necessary for the existence of the state and the virtue of the individual. One solution to this conflict might be to give up one or the other of these values. For conservative thinkers this is not an option because both ideas derive from and are made necessary by the core of contemporary American conservative thought.

Another possibility is to so favor one over the other as to render the other impotent, or at least reduce its importance in conservative thinking. Some of the statements that conservative thinkers make, particularly traditionalist conservatives, seem to point in this direction.[28] Many seem to make freedom dependent upon authority to such a degree as to render it almost meaningless. Russell Kirk, for instance, believes that freedom is dependent upon the order created and maintained by authority. "Genuinely ordered freedom is the only sort of liberty worth having: freedom made possible by order within the soul and order within the state. Anarchic freedom, liberty defiant of authority and prescription, is merely the subhuman state of the wolf and the shark, or the punishment of Cain, with his hand against every man's." Civilized man lives by authority and by prescription, "that is, by ancient custom and usage, and the rights which usage and custom have established. Without just authority and respected prescription, the pillars of any tolerable civil social order, true freedom is not possible."[29]

These conservative thinkers believe that freedom cannot exist without authority and order, and therefore that freedom is not an independent value or idea. Donald Atwell Zoll argues that freedoms or rights stem from duties: " 'rights,' to the conservative, follow from the adequate discharge of duties and they do not exist *in vacu.*"[30] Therefore, it is not true "that freedom means that everybody may do as he wishes," insists Thomas Molnar. To believe that it means that "leads directly to the permissive situation we here deplore; for freedom to have a sense . . . it must be embodied in institutions under whose protection all can benefit by it."[31]

These statements make it appear that freedom is not as significant or valued in conservative thinking as is authority, that in the view of conservative thinkers it does not have as important a role in society or in the lives of individuals. As John Hallowell puts is, "freedom is not an end in itself, as the classical liberal was inclined to believe, but an essential means to the development of moral and spiritual perfection. And it loses its meaning and degenerates into license if it is not directed toward that end."[32] Freedom is a means to an end, rather than an end itself. The end for which it is a means is virtue. Therefore "liberty is not the power of doing what we like, but the right of being able to do what we ought," as Stephen Tonsor argues.[33] Some conservatives even go so far as to assert that the freedom that is essential as a means to attaining virtue is internal. L. Brent Bozell argues that the "morally significant choice is a *psychic* event." The good will that chooses virtue does not cease to be good if prevented from converting that psychic commitment into action. Therefore, *"the freedom that is necessary to virtue is presumably a freedom no man will ever be without."*[34] This freedom is untouched by government action, or by the action of any other group. Therefore, Bozell asserts, authority represents no danger to freedom, at least not to the really significant freedom—significant in terms of the end it exists to bring about.

Bozell goes even further to imply that on a more fundamental level, freedom is not essential to virtue at all. Virtue means conforming with divine patterns of order, he argues, which seems to imply that virtue does not require freedom and may be produced by coercion.[35] Few conservative thinkers seem willing to go this far in favor of authority over freedom. But to whatever extent conservative thinkers believe that freedom is important as a means of fostering virtue, they believe that too much freedom is inimical to that end. From this perspective, freedom cannot be regarded as an absolute; doing so would ignore the other necessities of the good society, like order and justice. For example, Willmoore Kendall believes that elevating freedom of speech or freedom of thought to the position of society's highest good undermines the public orthodoxy, threatening order. He prefers instead the freedom of speech that he believes was advocated by Plato and Socrates: to speak, to try to convince others of the truth of what you say, and to obey the public authority if you fail to convince them.[36]

However, there are also many statements made by conservative thinkers that emphasize freedom at the expense of authority. Many, especially libertarian conservatives, argue specifically that the end that freedom is meant to foster—virtue—is unattainable without freedom, so that authority cannot persuade and coerce individuals to become virtuous unless those individuals are free to choose whether to obey. Thus, the acceptance of moral authority must be voluntary, making the beneficial effects of authority with regard to virtue dependent upon freedom. Frank Meyer insists that "virtue is made inaccessible to the coerced citizen wherever and to the degree that the state compels his action. Being unfree to reject virtue, he is unfree to choose it."[37] Edmund Opitz makes the same point when he states, "People cannot be made good by law; they can only be made less free."[38] It is only the "internalized authority of the voice of conscience," as Tonsor puts it, that "possesses the moral and ethical energies" necessary to make an individual virtuous, and the conscience lies outside the authority of the state.[39] Therefore, although these conservative thinkers agree with the traditionalists that the achievement of virtue is ultimately the most important problem to be solved by man, they believe that it is not a political problem. Virtue cannot be enforced or brought about by political means and is not directly the concern of the state.[40]

Not only do Meyer and other libertarian conservatives argue that because freedom is essential to virtue it is not subordinate to authority, they also argue that for the same reason freedom not used for high ends is still freedom, not license.[41] To define freedom as recognition or acceptance of truth or duty is to make freedom meaningless—to turn it into something else. "Freedom means freedom: . . . not responsibility, but the choice between responsibility and irresponsibility; not duty, but the choice between accepting or rejecting duty; not virtue, but the choice between virtue and vice."[42] There is of course the danger that people will use their freedom unwisely. It is likely that many people in many situations and at many times will use their freedom in ways that are not beneficial to them. But, as William F. Buckley points out, "these are the perils of liberty, with which conservatives are prepared to live."[43] Meyer likewise recognizes yet is prepared to live with this danger. "If freedom is indeed the essence of man's being, that which distinguishes him from the beasts, he must be free to choose his worst as well as his best end. Unless he can choose his worst, he cannot *choose* his best."[44]

This statement by Meyer reminds us that conservative thinkers hold that freedom is part of the nature of man. As such it is valued independently of any usefulness or importance it may have in producing other ends, even virtue. Although freedom is part of man's nature, and the perfection of his nature implies the achievement of virtue and the creation of harmonious relations between men, libertarian conservatives do not believe that there is any pre–established harmony between freedom and virtue, or between freedom and order. As Meyer puts it, "freedom may be in accord with social order, or it may be in dis–accord."[45] If all men use their freedom for virtuous and unselfish ends, individual virtue and social order will result. But there is no guarantee that freedom will be exercised in this way, and the potential harmony between freedom and order or freedom and virtue does not provide a justification for the use of authority to force this harmony into existence. They do speak of ordered freedom, much like the traditionalist conservatives, but by this they mean something rather different: freedom based on the governmental order created by the Constitution, with its stress on the limitations of government, and its tension and balance between the state and federal levels and between the coordinate branches of the federal government, all of which protect freedom.[46]

Furthermore, the attempt to use authority to support order is potentially damaging to freedom. Enforcing an orthodoxy, for instance, no matter how necessary it may seem, threatens freedom of thought and speech. Libertarian conservatives are less confident than the traditionalists that an orthodoxy can produce benefits that may outweigh or at least justify the dangers to freedom. George Will, himself more a traditionalist than a libertarian conservative, expresses this concern with regard to the issue of school prayer. "Religious exercise should arise from a rich tradition, and reflect that richness. Prayer, properly understood, arises from the context of the praying person's particular faith." The lowest–common–denominator prayer that would come from holding prayer in school would be "a mere attitudinizing, a thin gruel of religious vocabulary" rather than authentic religious expression.[47]

In addition to threatening specific freedoms, the use of authority to support order is potentially inimical to freedom in general by adding to the size of the state's power. This contributes to what Stephen Tonsor sees as the major problem of modern society: "the growth of centralized authority," a trend that is "absolutely inimical to liberty."[48] Large central power is dangerous because of human nature. We cannot depend upon the men who exercise public authority to be sufficiently prudent and sufficiently virtuous themselves to use that power to make us virtuous, even if it were possible so to make us virtuous.[49]

For all these reasons, libertarian conservatives believe that freedom must take precedence over authority. All the institutions of society that involve authority must take as a primary goal the fostering of men's freedom. Frank Meyer argues that because "freedom is the essence of the being of man, and since all social institutions are subordinate to men, the virtue of political and social institutions should be judged by the degree to which they expand or contract the area of freedom. . . . Liberty is the political end of man's existence because liberty is the condition of his being. It is for this reason that conservatism, which in preserving the tradition preserves this truth, is only constant to itself when it is libertarian."[50]

BALANCING AUTHORITY AND FREEDOM

Despite the seriousness of the tension between freedom and authority within contemporary American conservative thought, conservative thinkers do no wish to reject either idea. Indeed they cannot do so and be true to the core ideas that give shape and coherence to all of contemporary American conservative thought. Therefore, positions that exclude one or the other of these ideas are rejected by conservative thinkers. They are not anarchists; that is, they do not believe that human society can exist without authority. Neither are they libertarians. Even the most libertarian conservatives see a much greater role for authority in society than is desired by a libertarian such as Murray Rothbard, and contrary to the libertarian position, they do not view authority as merely a necessary evil. Conservatives believe that freedom requires authority, and they therefore reject both anarchism and libertarianism.

But they are not authoritarians, holding that freedom is superfluous, inherently harmful, or merely to be allowed to exist at the pleasure of the state. They believe that authority defeats its own purpose of reforming individuals if the individual has no freedom. Conservative thinkers also do not believe that liberalism or socialism have the answer to the problem of authority and freedom. Both desire too much public authority in some areas, notably the economy, and liberalism exercises too little in others, especially the moral realm. Conservative thinkers desire both freedom and authority and believe that the two are inextricably intertwined.

How do conservative thinkers attempt to balance the need for authority and the need for freedom? To an extent, they do so by recognizing that the tension exists and will continue to exist. As Russell Kirk points out, part of our inheritance—an inheritance for which we ought to be grateful—is "the idea of a healthy tension between the claims of order and the claims of freedom."[51] George Will agrees that this tension is part of our heritage. He says that Americans have always been torn between two desires: for absence of restraint and for a sense of community, which implies restraint by authority.[52] The reason that conservatives see this tension as healthy is that it forces us to remember and to try to satisfy the claims of both ideas, neglecting neither, which is necessary if society and individuals are to achieve a meaningful existence.

They also believe that this tension is healthy because the two ideas seem at least partially reconcilable. Although freedom and authority pull in different directions, conservatives believe that if we keep the claims of both in mind, these claims can be balanced. Despite their disagreements, both libertarian and traditionalist conservatives have the same goals. All conservative thinkers believe that the ultimate purpose of human existence is the achievement of virtue. They all desire a peaceful order of society that will assist individuals in approaching this end. They all desire to secure as far as possible the freedom of the individual to develop according to his own lights and his own abilities—and this means especially freedom from interference by the state. Despite their divergences, all conservative thinkers agree that both freedom and authority are necessary for the attainment of these goals.

In order to make both freedom and authority possible, conservative thinkers recognize that it is necessary to modify or limit each for the sake of the other. Even the most libertarian conservatives believe that authority is necessary and acknowledges that freedom cannot be absolute, that it must be sufficiently limited to make the proper exercise of authority possible. Stephen Tonsor, for instance, agrees with the traditionalist conservatives that "lacking internal religious authority, society can exist only if an external secular authority is imposed."[53] They thus believe that freedom must be reconciled with authority.

Conservatives think that authority is necessary to protect each person's freedom from invasion by others. As we saw earlier, Meyer believes that the freedom of each individual must be limited to the extent necessary to achieve the closest approximation of unfettered freedom for all.[54] The traditionalist Russell Kirk agrees, arguing that "any coherent and beneficial freedom must have the check of social order: it must accord with a rule of law, regular in its operation, that recognizes and enforces prescriptive rights, protects minorities against majorities and majorities against minorities, and gives some meaning to the idea of human dignity."[55] Libertarian conservatives acknowledge the necessity of this type of authority and of other types as well. Meyer points out that moral authority is necessary. Indeed, he calls the "combination of freedom and moral authority" the most basic of "conservative assumptions."[56] By moral authority, Meyer means the authority of truth, the authority of teaching about the truths of the moral order. Without an assent to these truths by the members of society, the freedom of the individual cannot be protected, even by coercive authority. Thus Meyer argues that "the only possible vindication of the freedom of the individual person rests upon a belief in his overriding value as a person, a value based upon transcendent considerations."[57] The truths of the objective moral order are necessary not only to convince people to respect the freedom of others, but to give that freedom meaning. As Meyer asserts, "freedom is meaningless unless founded upon 'the laws of Nature and of Nature's God.'"[58] Kirk agrees that "freedom must have the sanction of moral order; it must accord with principles, religious in origin, that establish a hierarchy of values and set bounds to the ego."[59] Meyer reminds us that "freedom . . . is a means—as is the whole political structure—to the higher ends of the human person. Without reference to those ends, it is meaningless."[60]

Just as freedom must not be made subordinate to moral ends, in Meyer's view, those ends cannot be made subordinate to freedom.[61] Libertarian conservatives like Meyer and Tonsor are not in favor of using the coercive power of the state to force people to believe or follow these truths, to create an orthodoxy that will support the exercise of freedom. Nonetheless, they recognize that, as Tonsor asserts, "individual freedom is quite impossible without assent to some generally held set of beliefs."[62] They desire that other, noncoercive institutions support these truths that modify freedom, as does the traditionalist Robert Nisbet, who sees "individual freedom as an inextricable aspect of a kind of social pluralism, one rich in autonomous or semi–autonomous groups, communities, and institutions" that exercise various kinds and amounts of authority.[63] Freedom must be modified to mean the doing not just of whatever one wishes, but the acts that one's conscience demands, if freedom is to have its proper meaning in the eternal scheme of things.[64] As a result, Meyer tells us, the conservative "cannot accept the fundamental philosophical position . . . which is the historical foundation of pure libertarianism. He cannot posit freedom as an absolute end." Placing freedom as "the sole good and end of existence" is an "evasion of the dilemma of freedom and justice."[65]

On the other hand, traditionalist conservatives agree with their libertarian counterparts that authority must be limited for the sake of freedom. They clearly believe that authority must not be allowed to destroy freedom. Man needs social reinforcements to help him reach his goal of virtue and to enable him to live peacefully with his fellows, but those reinforcements must not be absolute, or so strong as to destroy freedom.[66] The need to restrain authority and the need to have authority come from the same source—the conservative view of human nature. As Thomas Molnar explains, the conservative view of "authority contains a guarantee that man is not totally subordinated to authority; the source of this guarantee is itself beyond authority, it is the divine stamp on man's soul."[67]

If authority is to shape and help man without removing his freedom, then ideally his compliance with authority should be largely voluntary. Conservative thinkers, even traditionalist conservatives, believe not only that this is possible but also that it is the normal state of affairs in a healthy society. Thomas Molnar, one of those most inclined to stress the importance and value of authority, believes of authority that "its essential nature is . . . that it is *accepted* voluntarily."[68] His position on this point is consistent with that of libertarian conservative Frank Meyer, who believes that "the conservative view of the human situation insists on the authority of truth, but by its very recognition of that authority it insists equally upon the sanctity of the individual person's freedom to accept or reject that authority."[69]

How can compliance with authority be voluntary and authority still be effective? For one thing, conservative thinkers put much faith in various kinds of noncoercive authority—noncoercive, in contrast to the coercive power of the state, in that they cannot incarcerate people or deprive them of life or property. As Kirk argues, "political authority, . . . though an important part of this complex of authority which rules our lives, is no more than a part."[70] Noncoercive authority is exercised by the family, by religious institutions, by the schools, by the local community, and by the other "autonomous and semi–autonomous groups . . . and institutions" which, Robert Nisbet asserts, make up the social pluralism in which freedom is embedded.[71] Libertarian conservatives agree that these institutions play an important role in helping individuals and protecting freedom, and thus they help answer the question posed by Tonsor: "How was freedom finally to be reconciled with authority? The answer was to come from America . . . federalism, the separation of church and state, an educational system not wholly dominated by the central government, and a free–enterprise, market economy."[72]

In addition to institutions that exercise noncoercive authority, there is what Meyer calls "the authority of truth and good," which includes "the ideas, the persuasions, the customs which go into forming every human person."[73] Russell Kirk agrees that we find authority "in a number of ways; but of these, the means for most men is what we call prescription or tradition." "Prescription . . . means those ways and institutions and rights prescribed by long—sometimes immemorial usage. Tradition . . . means received opinions, convictions religious and moral and political and aesthetic passed down from generation to generation, so that they are accepted by most men as a matter of course."[74] If these institutions and ideas exercise sufficient authority, the state will need to exercise only a minimum of coercive authority. Conservative thinkers clearly prefer the authority of these noncoercive sources. They are more concerned with restoring these than they are with increasing the power of government.

For one thing, these institutions and ideas can hold us to higher standards than the standards that we would dare entrust the state with the power to enforce. These higher standards are necessary for a healthy society, for without them, as George Will believes, "proper moral judgement is supplanted by a morally constricted legalism, the notion that whatever is legal—whatever there is a right to do—is morally unobjectionable. There are protected rights to do many things (such as sell pornography, incite hatred) that are wrong. . . . Comportment should be controlled by a morality of aspiration more demanding that a mere morality of duty."[75]

This noncoercive authority works because, as Kirk puts it, it is "accepted by most men as a matter of course."[76] Molnar also argues that this authority, if it is good authority, is obeyed to a large degree without the need for coercion because "its directives coincide with what rational men regard as rational, thus valid and natural to follow."[77] He also believes that authority is obeyed because "at all times it is rooted in its counterpart, the innate desire to respect authority."[78] Not only is it part of human nature to desire authority, people desire it because they want those things that can be achieved only or more readily or more assuredly through authority, such as community, order, and virtue. It is for such reasons that Molnar believes that authority is accepted voluntarily. "By 'voluntary' I do not mean that those who obey authority give the bearer of authority their explicit consent each time after a consultation; I mean, rather, that authority appeals to a number of motives in us, as varied as are the personal and social responses in general: loyalty, fear, prudence, regard for others, desire to imitate, corporate feelings, and so on. Thus while law coerces, authority addresses itself to a pre-existing consent of heart, mind, habit, and respect; while we *behave* before the law even if our intentions . . . contradict or oppose it, we *consent* to authority, (we are of one sentiment with it), we agree with its demands upon us. Ultimately we do so because respect for authority is as natural a response of our person as are love, contentment, pity, or pride of achievement."[79]

All this is not to say that conservative thinkers believe that to have coercive authority exercised by the state is not desirable or necessary. The state must support the civilizing effects of noncoercive institutions and ideas. It does so by stipulating certain minimum standards of behavior, punishing disobedience, and sustaining and preserving the existence of these other institutions. The state must even concern itself with virtue. George Will notes with approval that "the ancient and Christian theories of government hold that statecraft should be soulcraft; indeed, that government cannot avoid concerning itself with virtue."[80] But conservative thinkers hope that this can be accomplished with as little coercion as possible. They wish to limit authority for the sake of freedom. They also believe that nominally coercive authority often operates noncoercively. As George Will notes, "Law has an expressive function, expressing and thereby sustaining certain values."[81]

Furthermore, they believe that although the state is charged with aiding men to become virtuous, it is not charged with discovering and defining standards of virtue. Other institutions in society have that role, while the state is an instrument for defending the consensus achieved.[82] And even this role is limited. Authority is limited by its ends, or as Molnar puts its, "every type of authority carries within itself a limiting factor in conformity with its rationality; in the case of the family, love stands in the way of the parent's harsh authority, and in the case of the school, the respect for the potential scholar (or simply, educated man) prevents the teacher from becoming a despot. In the spiritual community the supernatural respect for a God–created soul is the inhibiting factor."[83] The law must accord with a higher law if it is to possess moral authority.

And the state's force can do little to civilize or even control man if other institutions abdicate their responsibilities or lose their power. The operation of the law presupposes an orderly setting in which most citizens obey and in which criminal acts are the exception rather than the rule, conservative thinkers believe.[84] When other institutions fail to restrain man's passions and to foster and give force to his desire to live peacefully with his fellows, the law cannot deal with the widespread lawlessness, injustice, and immorality that result, particularly in a democratic society where government must respond to some extent to the will of the majority, whether righteous or evil, public spirited or narrow and selfish. Ultimately, then, these other institutions must fulfill their functions. "The only redemption lies in restraint imposed by ideas" rather than by force, argues Richard Weaver. "I do not in truth see how societies are able to hold together without some measure of this ancient but now derided feeling [of piety] . . . The habit of veneration supplies the whole force of social and political cohesion."[85]

In addition to attempting to limit both authority and freedom for the sake of the other, conservative thinkers attempt in a number of ways to reconcile the two ideas or understand them in such a way that they are compatible, for they believe that each is essential for the existence of the other. A number of the statements examined so far reflect that belief. This belief does not, of course, automatically indicate how the two fit together, but it does lead conservative thinkers to conclude that despite their difficulties in resolving these ideas or even in agreeing on how to approach this resolution, such a resolution is both possible and necessary.

One approach to resolving the conflict is to view freedom and authority as pertaining to two different and separate realms. Frank Meyer in particular has tried to make this argument. He believes that it is possible to hold in tension the authority of truth and the freedom of men. The solution is to recognize

the absolute authority of truth in the intellectual and spiritual realm, while at the same time remaining aware of the contingency of institutions in the social realm and their consequent subordination to the transcendent value of the human person. . . . Understanding this, the West has always recognized . . . that the ultimate guardians of its essential truths could not be the possessors of material authority with their power to impose their own particular version of the truth and with their susceptibility to the corruptions of power. The guardians of intellectual and moral truth, to whom the West has always given its final deference . . . have been the learned, the priestly, the prophetic, skilled in the tradition—men devoted to the priority of persons over institutions, devoted not to power, but to truth and good.[86]

This means that authority more properly belongs in the moral realm, and that "in the *moral* realm freedom is only a means whereby men can pursue their proper end, which is virtue," while "in the political realm freedom is the primary end."[87] Therefore a good society requires two conditions: "the social and political order guarantees a state of affairs in which men can freely choose;" and the "intellectual and moral leaders, the 'creative minority', have the understanding and imagination to maintain the prestige of tradition and reason, and thus to sustain the intellectual and moral order throughout society."[88]

Both freedom and authority in contemporary American conservative thought are means to a higher end, rather than ends in themselves. That higher end is the good of the individual. Meyer expresses this clearly when he states that this combination of the ideas of freedom and authority comes from "the understanding—rooted in the Christian vision of the nature and destiny of man—of the primary value, under God, of the individual person. From his nature arises his duty to virtue and his inalienable right to freedom as a condition of the pursuit of virtue."[89] The traditionalist Thomas Molnar agrees when he states that "authority provides for its own limits; it includes the limits beyond which it is not to extend its exercise. Stated differently, authority is the guarantee that man is not totally subordinated to authority; the source of this guarantee is itself beyond authority; it is the divine stamp on man's soul."[90] The conflict between the two is resolvable on the basis of the pursuit of the higher end.

Resolvable is not the same thing as resolved, of course, and no final resolution appears yet in contemporary American conservative thought, at least not one that all or even the majority of conservative thinkers agree upon. It appears that most if not all conservative thinkers would agree that Meyer has taken the correct general approach to resolving the conflict, although many of the more traditionalist believe that he has not allowed sufficient scope for the use of authority to help make men virtuous.[91] All conservative thinkers would agree that the acceptance of moral authority must be voluntary if it is to result in genuine virtue.[92] But some add that state authority must sustain moral authority by restraining certain evils so that moral authority can exist to be assented to, and so that men do not become so degraded that they are unable to respond to the call to a higher way. All would agree with Meyer that compliance with state authority is not wholly voluntary and does not of itself create virtue. But some would argue that it does create in both the individual and society conditions favorable to virtue, without so restricting freedom as to make virtue impossible.

SUMMARY

For conservative thinkers, the problem of balancing freedom and authority remains. This problem has generated more disagreement among contemporary American conservative thinkers than any other. Yet this disagreement has taken place within limits set by conservatives' acceptance of the core ideas of contemporary American conservative thought. Indeed, the disagreement takes place precisely because of the nature of the core. Both freedom and authority are required by this core, but the exact nature of the balance between the two is not clear from the core, both because the core ideas and the positions that may be developed from them are sufficiently general to allow for differences of interpretation, and because the nature of the ideas of freedom and authority that stem from the core are inherently in tension.

NOTES

1. Kirk, *Program*, p. 19.
2. Meyer, *In Defense*, p. 66.
3. John Chamberlain, "The Morality of Free Enterprise," in Meyer, ed., *What Is Conservatism?*, p. 181.
4. Ibid.
5. Ibid.
6. Kirk, *Program*, p. 42.
7. Kuehnelt–Leddihn, "Portland Declaration," p. 1189.
8. Ibid.
9. Read, "Knowing That We Know Not," *The Freeman* 15 (October 1965), p. 11.
10. Read, in *The Freeman* 15 (September 1965), p. 64.
11. John Chamberlain, *The Roots of Capitalism* (Princeton, N.J., 1959), p. 165.
12. See ibid., pp. 10–11. See also chapter 6 for more on conservative thought on a free–market economy.
13. Meyer, *In Defense*, p. 23.
14. Meyer, "Champion of Freedom," *National Review* (7 May 1960), p. 305.
15. See Weaver, *Ideas Have Consequences*, p. 5.
16. Niemeyer, Review of Clinton Rossiter's *Conservatism in America*, p. 443.
17. Morley, *Freedom and Federalism* (Chicago, 1959), p. 27.
18. See Meyer, *In Defense*, pp. 1–2.
19. John Chamberlain, "Ignore Human Nature?" *The Freeman* 14 (February 1964), p. 59.
20. Buckley, *Up from Liberalism*, p. 179.
21. Ibid.
22. Ibid., p. 201. See also Weaver, *Ideas Have Consequences*, pp. 135–37.
23. Ibid., p. 183. Chapter 6 contains a more detailed discussion on conservative thought about government and the economy.
24. Weaver, *Ideas Have Consequences*, p. 137.
25. Ibid., p. 138.
26. See the discussion of community in chapter 7.
27. Meyer, *In Defense*, p. 60.
28. It should be remembered that these labels, libertarian conservative and traditionalist conservative, fit arguments and positions much better than they fit people.

29. Kirk, "Prescription," in Meyer, ed., *What Is Conservatism?* pp. 23, 24.

30. Zoll, *Twentieth Century Political Philosophy*, p. 127. See also Kendall, *Affirmation*, p. 109; and Kirk, *Beyond*, p. 166.

31. Molnar, *Authority*, pp. 107–8.

32. Hallowell, *Moral Foundation*, p. 87.

33. Tonsor, "Conservative Search," in Meyer, ed., *What Is Conservatism?* p. 141, quoting Lord Acton.

34. Bozell, "Freedom or Virtue," p. 182.

35. See ibid.

36. Kendall, "The People Versus Socrates Revisited," *Modern Age* 3 (Winter 1958–59), p. 101–3.

37. Meyer, "Why Freedom?" p. 223.

38. Opitz, "Painting Government into a Corner," *The Freeman* 14 (February 1964), p. 23.

39. Tonsor, "Conservative Search," p. 139.

40. See Meyer, *In Defense*, p. 136.

41. See, for example, Meyer, *In Defense*, pp. 55–56.

42. Ibid., p. 53.

43. Buckley, *Up from Liberalism*, p. 185.

44. Meyer, *In Defense*, p. 50.

45. Ibid., p. 59.

46. See chapter 6.

47. Will, "Opposing Prefab Prayer," *Newsweek* (7 June 1982), p. 84.

48. Tonsor, "Conservative Search," p. 144.

49. See chapter 6.

50. Meyer, "In Defense of John Stuart Mill," *National Review* (28 March 1956), p. 75.

51. Kirk, *Enemies*, p. 32.

52. Will, "Who Put?" p. 108.

53. Tonsor, "Conservative Search," p. 137.

54. See Meyer, *In Defense*, p. 74.

55. Kirk, *Beyond*, p. 170.

56. Meyer, *In Defense*, pp. 6, 7.

57. Meyer, "The Twisted Tree of Liberty," *National Review* (16 January 1962), p. 27.

58. Ibid., p. 28.

59. Kirk, *Beyond*, p. 170.

60. Meyer, "Twisted Tree," p. 27.

61. See Meyer, *In Defense*, p. 67.

62. Tonsor, "Conservative Search," p. 138.

63. Nisbet, *Twilight*, p. 48. See also chapter 7.

64. See Tonsor, "Conservative Search," p. 141.

65. Meyer, "Twisted Tree," p. 26; and *In Defense*, p. 67.

66. See Molnar, *Authority*, p. 135.

67. Ibid., p. 131.

68. Ibid., p. 13.

69. Meyer, "Caricature of Conservatism," *National Review* (17 June 1961), p. 385.

70. Kirk, "Prescription," p. 24.

71. Nisbet, *Twilight*, p. 48. For more on conservative views of these institutions, see chapter 7.

72. Tonsor, "Conservative Search," p. 147.

73. Meyer, "Why Freedom?" p. 274.

74. Kirk, "Prescription," p. 27. For more on conservative thought on tradition, see chapter 8.

75. Will, "Through Hoops for a Column," *Newsweek* (15 March 1982), p. 88.

76. Kirk, "Prescription," p. 27.

77. Molnar, *Authority*, p. 133.

78. Ibid., p. 32.

79. Ibid., pp. 13–14.

80. Will, "Who Put?" p. 108.

81. Will, "The Value of Punishment," *Newsweek* (24 May 1982), p. 92.

82. Even Bozell, the most authoritarian of traditionalists, makes this point; see Bozell, "Freedom or Virtue," p. 185.

83. Molnar, *Authority*, p. 39.

84. See Nisbet, *Twilight*, p. 150.

85. Weaver, *Ideas Have Consequences*, p. 36; and "Up from Liberalism," *Modern Age* 3 (Winter 1958–59), p. 27.

86. Meyer, *In Defense*, pp. 143–44.

87. Meyer, "Freedom, Tradition, Conservatism," in Meyer, ed., *What Is Conservatism?* p. 15.

88. Meyer, *In Defense*, p. 69.

89. Meyer, "Why Freedom?" p. 225.

90. Molnar, *Authority*, p. 131.

91. See for instance Bozell, "Freedom or Virtue," especially p. 184; and Kirk, "An Ideologue of Liberty," *Sewanee Review* 72 (April–June 1964), pp. 349–50.

92. With the possible exception of Bozell, who implies in "Freedom or Virtue" (p. 184) that virtue may be coerced, since it consists of compliance with divine order. But in the same article he also agrees that a full measure of virtue is unobtainable without freedom and assures the reader that he is not advocating theocracy.

6

GOVERNMENT AND
ECONOMY

The core of contemporary American conservative thought strongly influences conservatives' thinking about government. The core beliefs in an objective moral order and an unchanging human nature lead conservative thinkers to conclude that the chief problem of government is how to have a government that is strong enough to do that which conservatives believe government should do, but not so strong that it endangers freedom or other values that they hold dear. At several points the previous two chapters discussed or touched on this problem of government. This chapter will discuss the problem more directly, focusing on how the core beliefs influence both the conservative thinkers' perception of the problem and their approaches to solving it. While it is true that this problem is discussed by thinkers of many persuasions, for conservatives the problem is particularly acute. Because of their core beliefs, they think there is no easy or permanent solution. And the solutions they are willing to consider are only those compatible with their core beliefs.

Conservative thinkers believe, on the basis of their core beliefs, that there are legitimate functions for government to perform, functions that can best or only be performed by government. In other words, conservatives' distrust of the state stops far short of anarchism, as they sometimes have to remind themselves and others. Otherwise their concern that government may often over-reach itself and cannot do everything can turn from a reasonable concern into what George Will calls a "paralyzing anxiety" that government cannot do *anything* right. "It is one thing," he argues, "for people to conclude, after mature reflection, that government should not do this or that because inaction is preferable. But it is very different, and very dangerous, for people to conclude that government can no longer do the sorts of things it once did. Government undertook great projects and strenuous exertions . . . because they were necessary, and they will be again."[1]

There are several areas in which conservative thinkers believe government acts properly with strength. Many of these have to do with the roles of government mentioned in chapter 4 in the discussion of authority: preserving freedom from interference by individuals, groups, or nations; punishing crime and administering justice; preserving order; and sustaining a minimum moral consensus. Chapter 4 discusses how the conservatives' belief in the need for government authority in these areas stems primarily from their beliefs in an unchanging human nature and an objective moral order. In addition, they believe that government is properly entrusted with maintaining the conditions necessary for a stable economic order, in which individuals may pursue their own livelihoods and enterprises, and with the conduct of foreign affairs—but that both must be done in ways dictated by their core beliefs. Furthermore, they acknowledge that situations may arise that require government to exercise authority in other areas, such as the need for good roads that cross state boundaries. Although their view of human nature and traditional wisdom cautions against capriciously expanding government power, those same core beliefs also lead them to believe that no one can be certain what the future will bring and that no answer to the question of what power government should have is permanent. However prudent they may feel it is to limit government, they do not accept a rigid catalog of what government should do, excluding all else. They are not libertarians, per se.

There are proper ends to be sought through the means of government action, conservatives believe; but when people attempt to accomplish more through government, they imperil these proper ends. "If to the power naturally inherent in the state, to defend citizens from violence, domestic and foreign, and to administer justice, there is added a positive power over economic and social energy," Frank Meyer warns, "the temptation to tyranny becomes irresistible, and the political conditions of freedom wither."[2] As discussed in chapter 5, this belief is due to their view of human nature. "There is in power an impulsion to more power," Meyer argues. "The state will always tend to move beyond its natural bounds, and the men who hold its power will always attempt to gain more power."[3] This is the chief reason that conservatism represents what M. Stanton Evans calls the "limited government impulse."[4] They wish to limit government because they believe, as Meyer puts it, that "the power of the state rests in the hands of men as subject to the effects of original sin as those they govern."[5] Conservative thinkers are suspicious of concentrations of power, not only governmental but economic and social as well, because by nature people are tempted to use such power for their own selfish ends to the detriment of their fellows. Since the state must have a monopoly of physical force to maintain freedom and perform its other rightful functions, to give it any additional power is dangerous. Conservatives lack the liberal's faith in the power of democratic government to solve society's ills and the problems of individuals. They reject the Marxist belief that the state can be the instrument for creating the perfect society (and thus be the legitimate tool of class struggle), and that thereafter it will safely wither away.

Thus their positions on human nature and the objective moral order lead conservative thinkers to conclude both that there is need for government power and that such power is dangerous. Willmoore Kendall has this problem in mind when he says that "the best regime is that which is best for the nature of man."[6] This is taken in both the negative and positive senses. Clearly government must be of such a nature as to blunt or avoid the worst aspects of human nature. But it must also take into consideration the best possibilities inherent in human nature as well: to allow for freedom, to encourage civic and personal virtues, and to provide scope for the development of people's abilities. One of the chief mistakes of modern political philosophy, according to Kendall, is that it holds that "the purpose of society, government, and law is to minister [solely] to the self–interest of the members of society, rather than to the perfection of man's nature or to the attunement of human affairs to the will of God."[7]

To establish and maintain the right kind of government, according to conservatives, people must remember these proper purposes of government. Conservatives also believe it is essential to remember that government is only a means to these ends, and not an end itself—and with regard to the perfection of man's nature, it is not even the chief means. (Chapter 7 discusses the crucial role that nongovernmental institutions play in this process.) Meyer asserts that

social and political organization, however important as a condition of existence, is, like oxygen or water, a condition, not the end, of the life of the individual person. At the best, the proper social and political circumstances, like a rich and well–tilled seed–bed, can provide felicitous circumstances in which a man may work out his fortune or misfortune, his good or ill. At the worst, they may cramp the field of his existence to a compass scarcely recognizable as human, although even they cannot destroy the self–determination of his inner spiritual life.[8]

But at best or worst the political situation remains a means and not an end.

The general principle that conservative thinkers wish to see followed is clear, but achieving the proper balance between too little and too much government power is a problem that conservative thinkers acknowledge they cannot solve in any final way. While they offer a number of suggested means for approaching this balance, they do not believe that they have all the answers, or even that all the answers are attainable. Russell Kirk, for instance, argues that no "single fixed system of political concepts can bring justice and peace and liberty to all men at all times."[9]

James Burnham suggests that the dilemma of obtaining government that is both sufficiently strong and sufficiently weak draws "its force and historical relevance from the nature of man, from the fact that men are limited creatures moved by passion or interest more often than by reason. . . . If men were rational and good, or if their weakness and corruption were due only to social institutions that could be changed, then the dilemma would collapse."[10] The dilemma would also not exist for conservatives if they believed that men had no divine potential for achieving virtue, no inherent freedom; then there would be no reason to be concerned about the possibility that government might destroy that freedom and thwart the development of that potential.

Conservative thinkers propose a variety of ways to try to overcome this dilemma, to achieve the necessary balance in ways compatible with their core beliefs. For example, thing, rule by the right people is viewed as necessary to achieving this balance. Formal constitutional limits on the power of government and the scope of its activities are also seen by conservative thinkers as an important way to approach this balance. Another way to limit government is to strengthen less formal limits—traditional beliefs and practices that teach both governors and the governed to believe that government should be limited. Another way is to restrict the areas in which government operates, turning instead to other institutions or other means as much as possible. None of these means is seen as sufficient; all are viewed as necessary.

RIGHT RULERS

One way to balance the need for strong government and the need to keep government from being too strong, according to conservative thinkers, is to have the right people rule—people who will exercise governmental power wisely and with restraint. Although all people share human weakness, conservatives believe that some people are more successful than others at overcoming these natural tendencies toward evil and selfishness (whether through diligence, innate strength of character, or fortunate environmental circumstances). These people should rule. As Donald Atwell Zoll states, "governments ought to be restricted in their applications of power, principally by ethical self–restraint and constitutional inhibitions. . . . But the only guarantee of this circumspection, the conservative maintains, is the quality of governmental leadership—not the right system, as Babbitt said, but the 'right man.' "[11] To obtain such leaders, Kirk advocates that we "train the imagination," especially "its power of grasping in a single vision . . . the long course of history and of distinguishing what is essential therein from what is ephemeral," that is, of discerning what is in keeping with the objective moral order. Through this education "we return to the natural and informal aristocracy of Burke, the mingling of inherited position with rising talents, upon the principle of honor; I do not think we ever will discover another satisfactory method for calling to leadership the men who ought to lead us. A humane intellectual discipline aids greatly in their development,"[12] because understanding and appreciating an objective order that is more than human helps them achieve self–discipline and blunts the worst aspects of their unchanging human nature.

Conservatives do not regard this elite to whom they wish to entrust the power of government as a closed group. As Erik von Kuehnelt–Leddihn explains in summarizing the views of contemporary American conservatives, the search for people who have developed the character, wisdom, and self–discipline to rule for the common good "does not imply a closed, but an open society, without a caste system and with free movement from layer to layer. . . . Talent, achievement, dedication, personal discipline, character must be honored. . . . The formation of elites in a constant process of crystallization (and elimination) ought to be encouraged. There is no healthy society without leadership."[13]

Unfortunately, conservative thinkers acknowledge, there is no sure way of always selecting the correct people. And even though some people can more safely be trusted to exercise the power of government with wisdom and restraint than can others, they are still human and suffer from the same defects of human nature that bedevil their less refined or self–controlled brothers and sisters. Therefore, as Will Herberg states it, "no man, or group of men, no matter how good or wise they may be, possess the wisdom or virtue to be entrusted with unrestricted and irresponsible power over others."[14] Or as Harry Jaffa states, "there is no difference between man and man . . . that makes one *by nature* the ruler of another. This does not mean that there are not wide differences among men, or that it is not often to the advantage of some to be ruled by others."[15] But it does mean that none has the right to rule over another.

Conservative thinkers do not claim to have answered in any final way the question of how to obtain rule by the best without setting up a system that too narrowly restricts the chances for people of talent to rise within it. But they believe that workable answers can and must be found if government is to be both strong and good.[16] They wish to see the right people rule, yet they do not believe that this alone will finally solve the dilemma of government.

LIMITS AND ARRANGEMENTS OF POWER

Since conservatives do not believe that relying on the right rulers is sufficient to obtain the proper balance in government, they look for additional means to limit government power. One means is to employ a formal constitutional system to divide and control governmental power. Here they look toward the kind of limits and arrangements they see in the American constitutional system: the division of power between the branches of government on each level; federalism, or the division of power between various levels of government (federal, state, and local); limits on what types of functions government can perform; and the separation of power between government and other nongovernmental institutions. By limiting government power in these ways, conservative thinkers hope to limit the damage that can be done by rulers who yield to the defects of human nature.

The conservative insistence on the division of power within government, especially the federal government, is not remarkable—it is the stuff of American civics textbooks—although conservative thinkers believe that insufficient attention has been given to preserving such a division.[17] Neither is the notion of federalism unusual in American thinking, although the emphasis that conservative thinkers give federalism is unusual. They believe that local government must be restored to a place of prominence. State and municipal governments should take a more active role in making decisions and taking action on matters that properly pertain to their responsibilities to the citizens under their jurisdiction. Local governments should be wary of federal dollars and the federal control that accompanies them, recognizing that those dollars come from nowhere else than the pockets of the people in their own jurisdictions. Conservatives believe that doing these things will restore a more healthy and effective balance between levels of government by restricting the role of the federal government more to truly federal concerns. They believe it will produce more experimentation and a greater variety of solutions and approaches on the local level, rather than the stifling uniformity that arises from decisions made by distant bureaucrats who neither understand nor care much about the lives of the people they influence. It will also place more decision–making power in the hands of rulers who can more easily be held responsible to the people they rule.[18]

But it is the conservative emphasis on limiting the areas of government power and on the division of power between government of whatever level and other authoritative institutions that really sets conservative thinkers apart from others on these issues. Contemporary American conservative thinkers believe that the United States Constitution places serious limits on the use of government power. In general they are in favor of a strict interpretation of the Constitution's grant of power to the federal government, because, as Stephen Tonsor puts it, "the growth of centralized authority . . . is absolutely inimical to liberty."[19] As discussed in chapter 5, they think that one way to protect citizens against government power is to restrict the number and kinds of areas in which government is allowed to exercise power. Government must have power, but people can be relatively safe from that power only if it is restricted as much as possible to certain narrow and well–defined tasks.

That is part of the reason why, for instance, many responsible and charitable conservatives found themselves opposing civil rights legislation (although most of them have since come to feel that whatever good has been done by such legislation must be preserved).[20] They felt it was more important to preserve the constitutional limits on government power than to redress wrongs done to racial minorities by weakening those limits. They believe that their fears have been vindicated, that individual freedoms have been infringed by government action in these areas. George Will gives an example:

Liberal defenders of reverse discrimination say it is necessary during this "transitional" period of dealing with the consequences of slavery, racism, sexism, etc. But racial entitlements, once established, will be, like most such programs, immortal. The beneficiaries, including the administrators, of the racial and sexual spoils system will never say—on the basis of what criteria would they say?—that the consequences of racism, sexism, etc., have been corrected. . . . What began as a way of opening doors has become government action to determine, on the basis of race or sex, who can pass through doors. . . . Government has been drawn into the odious business of delineating the qualities—what percentage of Negro blood, what degree of Spanish–speaking skill—that constitute membership in a government–approved minority. . . .

This policy results in "inflicting injuries on persons who are guilty of no unlawful behavior and who have benefited from no unlawful behavior, and who are to be injured solely because of their sex or skin pigmentation."[21]

Conservative thinkers believe that some of the constitutional limits placed on government power have been misconstrued as grants of more power to government to restrict the rights of some citizens in favor of others. Burnham argues, for example, that the purpose of the first ten amendments to the Constitution has been obscured. "Instead of operating as limits on the power of government, they are on occasion accepted as authorizations or grants of additional government power over the daily affairs of citizens. The ironic result is that the enforcement of civil rights becomes an instrument not of liberty but of despotism"[22]—an instrument of despotism because it weakens constitutional restraints on the ruler's appetites for power and leaves citizens with less protection than before. And Will complains that "many new 'rights' " claimed by individuals "are not protections against [government's] power but claims against the freedoms of fellow citizens." He gives some examples:

Every December, they crawl out of the woodwork, Grinchy people who seem to live for the fun of trying to get Christmas trees, carols and creches banned from public places. These people advertise themselves as friends of freedom, naturally. Their aim is to get the First Amendment construed to say that carols sung, or trees and creches displayed, on public property constitute the unconstitutional "establishment" of religion. . . . These people want to use state power to purge the social milieu of certain things offensive, but not at all harmful, to them. . . . There are other examples of rights being asserted in aggressive, almost vicious, ways. The National Organization for Women, which speaks incessantly about freedom and "liberation"

and all that, is trying to assert a right to have a judge disqualified
from hearing a case pertaining to the ratification of the Equal Rights
Amendment: disqualified because . . . his church opposes ERA. What
NOW is seeking would violate the constitutional guarantee that "no
religious test shall ever be required as a qualification to any office
or public trust under the United States." It is, by now, a familiar
process: people asserting rights in order to extend the power of the
state into what once were spheres of freedom. And it is, by now, a
scandal beyond irony that thanks to the energetic litigation of "civil
liberties" fanatics, pornographers enjoy expansive First Amendment
protection while first–graders in a Nativity play are said to violate First
Amendment values.[23]

Implied in Burnham's statement is the belief that these limits
alone are not sufficient to check government power, for they can
be ignored. As Zoll's statement, quoted earlier, indicates, these
limits depend for their application on the correct rulers. Yet, on
the other hand, even good rulers need these checks to teach and
remind them, to prick their consciences.

Conservative thinkers believe that another way to limit government power is, whenever possible, to use government only
if other institutions have failed. Government must be strong in
the areas in which it must be used, but, due to the defects of
human nature, to give government power that it need not have
is dangerous and foolish. Government need not have power to
do things that can be done by other agencies and institutions.
So, whether by law or by custom, the power to do these things
should be withheld from government, except as a last resort. This
is what Meyer means when he says, "the power of the state rests
in the hands of men as subject to the effects of original sin as those
they govern. . . . If to the power naturally inherent in the state,
to defend citizens from violence, domestic and foreign, and to
administer justice, there is added a positive power over economic
and social energy, the temptation to tyranny becomes irresistible,
and the political conditions of freedom wither."

Furthermore, conservatives believe it is very often fruitless to
use government to try to solve social problems, for, as Meyer
states, "there is still a very small part of that which 'human hearts
endure' that the state can alleviate."[24] Or as Will puts it, "conservatism says many public problems can only be understood as

arising from citizens with inadequate habits of virtue, with virtue understood as self–control, respect for other's rights and concern for distant consequences."[25] Such causes are relatively resistant to state action, a better approach being moral persuasion. It is not only fruitless to use state power in this way, it is also dangerous, for, as Meyer argues, "so far as the increased power of the state to bring evil is concerned, that power is directly proportional to pretences the state makes to control men's lives for good."[26]

Conservatives argue among themselves about the practical application of this principle of limiting the areas of the use of government, as they do about the application of many of their ideas. But they agree that there must be limits, and they share a skepticism about the capacities of the state, based on their view of human nature. Even a president as sympathetic to their views as Ronald Reagan has received criticism from conservative thinkers for forgetting these limits and this skepticism. George Will, an outspoken supporter of Reagan in many areas, complains that Reagan and his advisers

had an unconservative faith in the ability of government to alter substantially, quickly and neatly the workings of a social mechanism as complicated as this $3 trillion economy. They abandoned conservative skepticism about the ability of one election and a passing mood to alter political habits developed over several generations. And they ignored the central tenet of conservative prudence, as taught by recent liberal practice: the unintended effects of any policy are apt to be larger and more lasting than the intended effects. They forgot what conservative analysis shows: almost everything, from the cost of kidney dialysis to the effects of urban renewal, has involved unpleasant surprises for government.[27]

Therefore, conservatives think that in most matters the state should be turned to last, only after the resources of other institutions have been exhausted or have proven inadequate, and perhaps not even then. Kuehnelt–Leddihn expresses this conservative approach as: "Whatever a person can do, he or she should do; the next step would be to turn to the family and then to the community. Only then should the State be asked for aid—and the central power of the State asked only as the very last resort."[28]

Conservatives acknowledge that many nongovernmental institutions have withered to various degrees and that government has stepped in to take over some of the functions these institutions previously performed; but they deny that these institutions are incapable of fulfilling those functions (see chapter 7). Evans argues that the federal government's intervention has been the cause and not the effect of the decline of these institutions. They have lost some of their effectiveness because the federal government has arrogated their authority, either because federal bureaucrats do not like the way these institutions are functioning, or because they do not like the lack of uniformity and of conformity to "enlightened" social scientific principles, or simply because they want more power. When the "federal government is drawn into various zones of activity," Evans argues, "the dominant motive cannot be that the problem isn't being solved. The more likely goad to action is the fact that it *is* being solved, and that in a few years' time there will be nothing left to intervene about."[29]

Not all conservative thinkers are as certain as Evans that nongovernmental institutions have usually fulfilled their functions adequately, nor are they all as confident about the future successes of these institutions. Nevertheless, they prefer to rely on these institutions, turning to government last if at all. Relying first on nongovernmental institutions sustains their authority; this makes them more effective checks to the power of government. And even if these institutions fail, conservatives believe that government intervention should often be rejected, even if that means that social problems go unsolved and human needs remain unfulfilled. For one thing, they are skeptical that government can solve the problems. And even if it could, using government in this way so increases its power as to threaten something their core beliefs lead them to value much more highly than the solution to any social problem—human freedom.[30]

Because of their approach in these and other matters, conservatives often seem, and are accused of being, unrealistic, contradictory, or vague. They express desires for certain outcomes, especially for a return to certain ways of life and thought, but seem to offer no practical means for accomplishing those ends. For instance, one critic writes of Russell Kirk that he "comes very close to asking for the dismantling of the industrial

economy. How this miracle is to be achieved without resort to the
governmental power Kirk abhors is not explained."[31] Those who
make this kind of criticism fail to understand that conservative
thinkers genuinely believe in the power of moral and intellectual
persuasion. They believe, to use the title of a book by Richard
Weaver, that *Ideas Have Consequences*. They believe that it is better
to persuade people than to force them—even for their own good.
As discussed in chapter 5, they believe that virtue must ultimately be freely chosen. And they see freedom as more valuable than
the good that might be achieved through paternalism.

Will presents one example of a conservative response to the
argument that government should force people to do what is
best for them. He discusses a case in which the Department of
Health, Education, and Welfare was considering intervening to
outlaw six–player basketball for girls because the girls who play
the six–player game are

marginally disadvantaged in the competition for athletic scholarships
from colleges, where the five–player game prevails. . . . One feminist
who wants HEW to intervene by declaring six–player basketball illegal
says, "I am sure there will be cries of federal intervention, but the girls
of Iowa will be the beneficiaries of such a decision. Ultimately they and
their parents will realize this." Study that last sentence. Not only does it
concede the obvious (that players and parents like the game they have),
it also is a perfect specimen of the bullying arrogance of ideologues.[32]

Where persuasion fails, conservative thinkers often prefer
failure to a "success" that would involve destroying, in whole
or in part, individual liberty and the conditions necessary for
the attainment of virtue. Failing to alleviate human suffering is
preferable, in their view, to destroying the liberty and virtue that
make people truly human—and that are inseparably connected to
human nature and the objective moral order that men ignore at
their own peril.

THE ECONOMY

One of the chief areas in which conservatives wish to restrict
the involvement of government is the economy. For one thing,

they believe that preventing excessive government involvement
in the economy is a primary means of limiting government's
power. Meyer declares that "the decisive virtue of a free economy . . . is the restriction of the power of the state," thus bringing
about "the preservation of the conditions of freedom by holding
from the state the control of a large segment of human life."[33]
The failings inherent in human nature lead conservative thinkers
to distrust even the best rulers and make them wish to keep
government from having the great power that would accrue
to it if it directed the economy. Even a mixed economy—one
that is nominally capitalistic but with a large amount of state
control, such as Great Britain's economy—is rejected. "It seems
odd indeed," to Stephen Tonsor, "that the contemporary Liberal
who finds the thought of an established religion so disgusting
because of its impact on personal liberty finds the thought of
state capitalism so comforting. Both are absolutely incompatible
with political liberty."[34]

They believe that private property allows those who disagree
with prevailing majorities, and especially with government, to
survive, even to protest and proselyte for their way of thinking.
Thus as Richard Weaver says, "the citadel of private property
[also makes] existence physically possible for the protestant."[35]
And Kirk asserts that conservatives are persuaded "that property
and freedom are inseparably connected, and that economic levelling is not economic progress. Separate property from private
possession, and liberty is erased."[36]

An economy as free from governmental interference as possible
(i.e., some form of a capitalist economy, for most conservatives)
not only protects freedom by limiting the state, it also bestows
freedom. William F. Buckley argues that economic freedom is the
most precious temporal freedom: "it alone gives to each one of
us . . . sovereignty—and over that part of existence in which by
far the most choices have in fact to be made, and in which it is
possible to make choices, involving oneself, without damage to
others."[37] Other economic forms are more inimical to freedom,
according to conservative thinkers, because they lead to statism.
There is great danger, Burnham warns, "if the welfare state (as
Americans and Englishmen prefer to call a centralized, bureau-
cratized statism) is carried through to its logical limit—that is,

to totalitarianism."[38] Conservative thinkers believe that Marxism and socialism deny natural rights, especially the natural right to property. The planning essential to state control of the economy coerces people "to work when the plan says they must," argues John Chamberlain, and exerts "compulsion on the consumer to take what the planner thinks is good for him."[39]

The conservatives' view of human nature plays a large role in their affection for free–market capitalism. Some go so far as to say that capitalism is the economic expression of human nature. For Leonard Read, "the free and unfettered market is but the unfrustrated economic manifestation of man's creative, emerging, spiritual dynamism."[40] Furthermore, conservative thinkers believe that capitalism best accords with a natural and largely wholesome human instinct—the desire for property. They believe other economic systems must try to suppress this instinct to various degrees. But "the property instinct is an ineradicable part of human nature," argues John Chamberlain, "and . . . any successful attempt to abolish it can only result in endless suffering."[41]

The property instinct and the property right corresponding to it also foster certain virtues, "notable among which is providence," explains Weaver; "no society is healthy which tells its members to take no thought of the morrow because the state underwrites their future. . . . A conviction that those who perform the prayer of labor may store up a compensation which cannot be appropriated by the improvident is the soundest incentive to virtuous industry."[42] Free choice is also necessary to the development of virtue—the bringing of man's character into harmony with the objective moral order. Therefore, according to conservative thinkers, a free economy contributes to virtue by fostering free choice. Meyer believes that by itself "a free economy can no more bring about virtue than a state–controlled economy. A free economy is, however, necessary in the modern world for the preservation of freedom, which is the condition of a virtuous society."[43] Furthermore, Weaver argues, "the citadel of private property . . . provides indispensable opportunity for training in virtue. Because virtue is a state of character concerned with choice, it flourishes only in the area of volition. . . . Here in the domain of private property, rational freedom may prove the man; here he makes his virtue an active principle."[44] Free choice is essential to man's nature. Therefore, "choice is fundamental to economics," says Chamberlain, "because it is fundamental to the moral nature of man. . . . Capitalism . . . is the economic expression of the morality which says a man must be free to choose between alternatives of good and evil if his life is to have Christian meaning."[45]

On the other hand, conservatives believe a state–controlled economy leads to corruption. Chamberlain states: "To be sure, economic freedom is no guarantee of virtue. . . . But when economic freedom is limited, virtue becomes more difficult. Whenever the state impinges on economics, corruption ensues" because the people in government who run the economy are tempted by the vast resources they administer and the power they have to use them for themselves. "The state being what it is, a mechanism of control that shares in the innate viciousness, or the original sin, of average mankind, it should follow axiomatically that the less power it has, to exert compulsion on human choices between good and evil, the less likelihood that it will be able to impose on people a total mistake. The surest way to limit state power is to keep it separate from the people's livelihoods."[46]

Furthermore, state interference in the economy aimed at aiding individuals does them more harm than good, most conservatives feel. The chief problem is that such attempts weaken men morally. As Kirk puts it, "Men are put into this world, [the conservative] realizes, to struggle, to suffer, to contend against the evil that is in their neighbors and in themselves, and to aspire toward the triumph of Love. They are put into this world to live like men, and to die like men. [The conservative] seeks to preserve a society which allows men to attain manhood, rather than keeping them within bonds of perpetual childhood."[47] Chamberlain also believes that the "real objection to Keynesianism is . . . that it debases men morally. Since the rachet–action of politics [by which programs, once begun, are never discontinued] makes a return to the voluntary society more and more unlikely, people become more and more cynical. With every increase in pressure group socialism, there is a corresponding increase in the psychology of 'what's in it for me' "[48] and less self–reliance and concern for others.

Conservative thinkers also believe that a free economy works best because it accords best with the nature of man in yet another way—it provides the best motivation to work. Man is by nature acquisitive, and "acquisition is the main motivation for hard work," says Kuehnelt–Leddihn. "Therefore an economy based on private enterprise and personal initiative will produce infinitely more than an economy based on state capitalism."[49]

A free economy accords best with man's limited reason. As Read puts it, a free economy "is a wonderful way of life, suited to humanity as it is—that is, made to order for all of us, no one of whom knows very much." He and other conservatives recommend "the free market, private property, limited government way of life" as a "method of social and economic cooperation that doesn't require a lot of knowledge on the part of any one person."[50] No one, they believe, knows enough to control from the top something as complex as a modern economy without stifling the free flowing of human inventiveness and energy and the responsiveness to individual tastes and wants that conservatives celebrate in a free economy.[51] So fear of the corruption of man and belief that men lack the ability to successfully direct a complex economy lead conservative thinkers to want to limit strictly limit government's influence over the economy.

Russell Kirk best sums up the conservative position toward a free economy when he says

Conservatism is not simply a defense of 'capitalism,' the abstraction of Marx. The true conservative does defend private enterprise stoutly; and one of the reasons why he cherishes it is that private enterprise is the only really practicable system, in the modern world, for satisfying our economic wants; but more even than this, he defends private enterprise as a means to an end. That end is a society just and free, in which every man has a right to what is his own, and to what he inherits from his father, and to the rewards of his own ability and industry; a society which cherishes variety and individuality, and rises superior to the dreary plain of socialism.[52]

Since conservatives view capitalism as a means rather than as an end, they are logically free to criticize the means without rejecting it or the end. And this they do on the basis of their core beliefs. Both traditionalist and libertarian conservatives criticize aspects of the modern capitalist economy that seem to them to threaten freedom, an essential part of human nature. And they are also concerned about the threats that capitalism in its modern forms poses to virtue, man's attempt to live in accordance with the objective moral order.

Their concern for the economic threats that capitalism poses to freedom is straightforward. They believe that one of the chief benefits of a free economy is that it helps to limit the size and power of government. When capitalism begins to involve the state as a partner, that value is in danger. John Chamberlain, a libertarian conservative and as staunch a defender of capitalism as can be found among the ranks of contemporary American conservative thinkers, complains that "it is not *laissez faire* when a businessman tries to use the state to get a special advantage for himself; indeed, it is its precise opposite. . . . To make [an economic] conspiracy effective there must be state cooperation in the creation and maintenance of a monopoly."[53]

The traditionalist Richard Weaver warns against the same dangers, which he sees as much more likely when the economy becomes dominated by large capitalist corporations. "The aggregation of vast properties under anonymous ownership is a constant invitation to further state direction of our lives and our fortunes. For, when properties are vast and integrated, on a scale now frequently seen, it requires but a slight step to transfer them to state control. Indeed, it is almost a commonplace that the trend toward monopoly is a trend toward state ownership. . . . Large business organizations, moreover, have seldom been backward about petitioning government for assistance."[54]

The concern of conservative thinkers for the threat to virtue posed by the faults of the modern capitalist economy is more complex than their concern for the threat to freedom. One problem that they see is that capitalism, with its focus on material values, can be destructive of the higher values derived from the objective moral order unless checked by other forces. As Weaver puts it, "the man of commerce is by the nature of things a relativist; his mind is constantly on the fluctuating values of the marketplace."[55] The economic philosophy of capitalism, Robert

Nisbet points out, "with its celebration of enlightened self–interest . . . and its general neglect of the moral and social," weakens older moral standards. Unless tempered by other values, such an economic philosophy influences all members of a society to focus on their own self–interest. That economic outlook also contributes to a moral philosophy that sees "nearly all social institutions as limits upon the individual's freedom and self–reliance," thus weakening support for these institutions that are so crucial for human virtue.[56] Even an enthusiastic exponent of capitalism like William F. Buckley believes that it must be tempered by a set of higher values—that materialism and self–interest are not enough. He argues, for instance, that Ayn Rand has been correctly excluded from the conservative community because "her philosophy is in fact another kind of materialism, . . . the materialism of the relentless self–server who lives for himself and for absolutely no one else." Thus she was excluded because of "her desiccated philosophy's conclusive incompatibility with the conservative's emphasis on transcendence, intellectual and moral."[57]

Furthermore, conservatives believe that the emphasis on self–interest and the "glorying in ruthless competition," as Kirk styles it,[58] that are part of the capitalistic outlook are destructive of community. Such an outlook denigrates co-operation, self–sacrifice, and compromise—values that make living together in genuine community possible. "The era of egotistical competition," argues Weaver, even makes "sabotage an approved instrumentality. The laborer feels justified in putting a stop to the whole productive process if his own appraisal of his service is not accepted; and this appraisal is not made with reference to what society exists for . . . but with reference to his own gratification."[59]

They also believe that because the self–interest fostered by capitalism is corrosive of traditional values, it can destroy the kind of ordered society held together by those traditional values—the kind of society required for the development of individual virtue. "Once supernatural and traditional sanctions [on behavior] are dissolved," Kirk argues, "economic self–interest is ridiculously inadequate to hold an economic system together, and even less adequate to preserve order. Prescription and prejudice are the defenses of justice and peace. Laugh them away, and in come those forces of delusion and unrest which Marxism exemplifies today; men refuse to live by economic reasonableness alone."[60]

Conservatives thus reject what they see as a simplistic choice between communism or Marxist socialism on one side and unfettered capitalism on the other. Kirk for instance accepts his critics' charge that he "would embrace neither capitalism nor communism." These critics "seem to be quite ignorant of the existence of Christian social principles, of private property which is not 'capitalistic' in the Marxist sense, or of traditions and political institutions far older than Keynes, or Marx, or even the modern industrial system."[61]

Another reason that conservative thinkers, especially traditionalist conservatives, have reservations about capitalism is that it can diminish the right to property, which they see as essential for both freedom and virtue. Richard Weaver has been most insistent on this point. He argues that conservatism is not a defense

of that kind of property brought into being by finance capitalism. . . . This amendment of the institution [of property] to suit the uses of commerce and technology has done more to threaten property than anything else yet conceived. For the abstract property of stocks and bonds, the legal ownership of enterprises never seen, actually destroy the connection between man and his substance without which metaphysical right becomes meaningless. Property in this sense becomes a fiction useful for exploitation and makes impossible the sanctification of work. . . . Respecters of private property are really obligated to oppose much that is done today in the name of private enterprise, for corporate organization and monopoly are the very means whereby property is casting aside its privacy.[62]

The solution, Weaver believes, is to restore property to its identity with the individual, for example in "the forms of independent farms, of local business, of homes owned by the occupants, where individual responsibility gives significance to prerogative over property. Such ownership provides a range of volition through which one can be a complete person, and it is the abridgement of this volition for which monopoly capitalism must be condemned along with communism."[63]

Not all conservatives, not even all traditionalist conservatives, agree with Weaver in all of his analysis or on the value of his proposed solution. But they do agree that capitalism can pose a threat to both virtue and freedom, and that reducing that threat requires humanizing economic activity by relating it to moral and intellectual ends. "The world's work, after all, must be done," acknowledges Kirk, "and once in an industrial society, we cannot get out of it without starving half the world's population. What we can do, however, is to humanize that industrial system, so far as lies in our power: to contend against its monotony, sacrificing Efficiency, if necessary, to variety of tasks and pride in work-manship; . . . to bring back to the industrial laborer the reality of community, and the taste for things beyond the pay–check."[64] And all conservatives agree that the way to tame the capitalist economy is not chiefly through the use of government. Instead the solution is the power of ideas and moral persuasion to change people's hearts and minds.

A few conservatives are more willing than their fellows to see government involved in the economy. Peter Viereck, a maverick conservative on many topics, asks, "When did we ever have laissez faire, and why is any merely material and economic system more sacred than the moral duty of compassion for want?"[65] George Will argues along similar lines, praising parts of the New Deal for bringing the large forces of the industrial revolution safely "within the scope of constitutional government" and protecting people from the impact of these forces. He even calls Franklin Roosevelt "a conserving politician" for his role in accomplishing this. And he argues that today we may need to involve government in the economy again in such things as the restriction of imports, a new Reconstruction Finance Cor-poration, and wage restraints—what he calls "Tory socialism." He acknowledges that this "is not conservatism as currently understood—an economic doctrine favoring free markets. But it might be a political doctrine for conserving the core of the industrial system, and the social fabric of many communities. A conservatism too pristine to accommodate those goals is pol-itically irrelevant, socially irresponsible, and not conservatism properly understood."[66]

But both Will and Viereck, and other conservatives who make similar arguments, agree with the majority of contemporary American conservative thinkers that the economy needs to be tamed or humanized to preserve freedom and to make virtue possible—to foster the values connected to their core beliefs. And they agree—which sets them apart from nonconservative critics of modern capitalism—that the use of government for this purpose is dangerous. As even Viereck acknowledges, a danger "does arise when the proposed reforms cross a line beyond which welfare laws are inflated into the welfare superstate." For him the line must be drawn when "the increase in security is less than the loss in liberty."[67] Most conservative thinkers want to draw the line much sooner, but what sets the conservatives apart from nonconservatives is that they draw it; and they do so on the basis of values that flow from their core ideas.

EQUALITY

A related issue is the conservative position on equality, particularly economic equality.[68] Contemporary American conservative thinkers are opposed to using government power to level, to create equality. Whatever value equality itself has, they believe that *enforcing* equality is unwise, unjust, and unsafe. For one thing, conservatives believe that human diversity is natural and that it would be destroyed by enforcing equality. One of the marks of American conservatism, according to Kirk, is "an affection for variety and complexity and individuality, even for singularity. . . . Variety and complexity . . . are the high gifts of truly civilized society. The uniformity and standardization of liberal and radical planners would be the death of vitality and freedom, a life–in–death, every man precisely like his neighbor."[69] Kuehnelt–Leddihn voices a more extreme conservative position when he says that "it is the low drive for sameness and the hatred of otherness that characterizes all forms of leftism, which *inevitably* are totalitarian. . . . The leftist vision enjoins uniformity: the nation with one leader, one party, one race, one language, one class, one type of school, one law, one custom, one level of income, and so forth. Since nature provides diversity, this deadening sameness can be achieved only by brute force, by leveling, enforced assimilation, exile, genocide."[70]

These last statements by Kirk and Kuehnelt–Leddihn also reveal that conservatives think that enforced equality poses a threat to freedom. Since diversity is natural, enforcing equality must mean destroying that diversity and with it a portion of human freedom. Conservative thinkers deny that freedom requires equality, that men cannot really be free if they are unequal. Meyer, for instance, argues that freedom does not require the "equalitarianism which would forbid to men the acquisition of unequal goods, influence or honor. . . . The only equality that can be legitimately derived from the premises of the freedom of the person is the equal right of all men to be free from coercion exercised against their life, liberty and property." Beyond that, "the capabilities of men . . . should determine their position, their influence, and the respect in which they are held."[71]

Conservative thinkers also believe that enforcing equality is not just. The right to property, as has been discussed, is very important to conservative thinkers. They believe that enforcing equality destroys that right. It also denies to each person the proper reward for his efforts and contribution. A society that rewards people justly would not "reduce all men to a single mode of existence," as Kirk puts it, but would be "marked by a variety of rewards."[72]

Furthermore, egalitarianism is not wise, according to conservatives. It is not good for anyone in society—if by good is meant those things that really count: freedom and virtue. "It frustrates the natural longing of talented persons to realize their potentials," says Kirk, by removing any reward for the struggle involved in doing so. And by frustrating their development, "it impedes any improvement of the moral, intellectual, and material condition, in terms of quality, of mankind. . . . It adversely affects the well-being, late or soon, of the mass of men" by depriving them of the leadership and the examples of excellence that they need.[73]

But decrying enforced equality is not the same as denying the value of equality or asserting that natural growth toward equality is harmful. Conservative thinkers recognize that, as Viereck puts it, freedom is threatened "by compulsory inequality, enforced by caste lines," as much as "by compulsory equality, enforced by guillotines."[74] And property, if it is to foster virtue, must be widely distributed, as indicated by Weaver's comments about property, cited earlier,[75] and by Tonsor's statement that "economic and social equality" are "a *sine qua non* for a stable democratic society. . . . Property, if it is a natural right, must be so broadly based as to fall to all men who make a genuine contribution to their society," rather than being an instrument of oppression in the hands of a few, as Weaver also points out. "Unless this [degree of equality] can be achieved through the instrumentality of a market economy and an advanced technology, it will be achieved by the hand of a demagogue or tyrant," with the destruction of liberty.[76] Conservatives see little middle ground. Some measure of equality will be achieved through moral persuasion and the charity and benevolence of one person toward another, or liberty will be destroyed.[77]

LIMITS ON DEMOCRACY

Limits on the power of government are particularly needed in a democracy, conservative thinkers believe. Any government is liable to degenerate into tyranny, but democracy is particularly prone. The problem, they believe, is that democracy is so easily taken to an extreme, so that the will of fifty percent plus one is elevated to be the supreme arbiter, jeopardizing freedom and truth. From their view of human nature they conclude that the will of the majority is as likely to be wrong as right, as likely to be evil as good. A higher standard is necessary to guide that will. It is one thing to use democracy "as a procedural method to get on with the business of government," according to Frederick Wilhelmsen, but quite another—and quite wrong—to accept it "as an unquestioned political and philosophical absolute."[78] Conservative thinkers believe that in a society in which democracy is the ruling principle in all spheres of life—what Wilhelmsen calls an ideological democracy—truth is at risk and no absolutes are accepted as untouchable.

However, if "a society sets up a public authority or watchdog charged with safeguarding duties and rights thought to be themselves untouchable absolutes, that society has declared that it is not an ideological democracy."[79] Therefore, according to Zoll, "the primary attack mounted by traditionalist conservatives [on the idea of democracy] has been ethical in nature: the accusation that popular democracy is possible, but not desirable, because it debauches moral values. The cardinal faults of popular democracy are seen as moral relativism, licentiousness, mediocrity, and egocentricity," all inimical to the truths of the objective moral order.[80]

Democracy is as dangerous to freedom as it is to truth, conservative thinkers believe. From their view of human nature they conclude that the unchecked rule of the majority threatens the freedom of anyone who disagrees. And they believe that democracy, whatever its adherents say, is not essential to political freedom. Conservatives believe that it can be one way to achieve political freedom, but it is not the only or necessarily the best way. Meyer, for instance, rejects the definition of political freedom as " 'the freedom to participate in the making of public policy.' This is emphatically *not* what is meant by political freedom. What is meant by political freedom is the limitation of the power of the state to the function of preserving a free order."[81] Confusing political freedom with participation, as conservatives believe advocates of democracy are prone to do, can threaten the proper limitation of the state, and thus freedom properly understood.

Zoll believes that one of the cardinal faults of democracy is that it produces mediocrity. In a good society, people are challenged or enticed to model their behavior and character on standards derived from the objective moral order. But democracy, as it affects the social and intellectual spheres, creates a spirit of social conformity that appeals to, assumes, or allows for primarily the lowest common denominator—the level expected of the common run of humanity. Conservatives believe that democracy is slow to recognize and reward native ability and industriousness. According to Richard Weaver, "every visitor to a democratic society has been struck by its jealous demand for conformity. Such a spirit is an outgrowth of competition and suspicion. The democrats well sense that, if they allow people to divide according to abilities and preferences, soon structure will impose itself upon the masses."[82] As pointed out in chapters 4 and 7, conservatives believe that in a good society, differences in one's abilities and the quality of one's contribution to society bring differences in rewards, which entails some structuring of society for the good of all. But democracy accepted as an organizing principle in all aspects of life (rather than as a political procedure) cannot allow for differences of reward, and thus it stifles talent and taste.

Nevertheless, whatever its faults, democracy is not rejected by contemporary American conservative thinkers. Whether by necessity or choice, they accept it as the prevailing norm in the United States and do not desire to abandon it—a position in keeping with their general attitude toward change.[83] Most believe that the American system of democratic government is best for this time and place—whatever its excesses and however much it may need reform. Kendall argues for instance that conservatives should have "no axe to grind for 'aristocracy,' no quarrel . . . with America's commitment to 'democracy.' . . . With Madison, and Hamilton, and with the subsequent American political tradition as a whole, [the conservative] shares the conviction that the United States must and should be governed by 'the deliberate sense of the community.' "[84]

Other conservatives are less celebratory than Kendall. The best that most have to say about democracy is reflected in Tonsor's argument that conservatives should not work for an artificial return to aristocracy but should work to determine "how to make liberty to proceed out of that democratic state of society in which God has placed us."[85] The problem for conservatives is not how to get rid of democracy but how to tame it, how to limit it in ways compatible with their core beliefs. They believe that some of the means available are the forms, arrangements, and limits on democracy established by the Constitution and by traditional governmental practice.

One of these means is the principle of representation. When Kendall and other conservative thinkers praise democracy and still others tolerate it, they do not mean by democracy a participatory democracy. By "deliberate sense of the community," quoted earlier, Kendall does not mean the momentary opinions of fifty percent plus one, but the best interests of the members of the community—what they would decide for themselves in their best moments—as determined through the deliberation of wise and good people whom they have chosen to represent them (the right rulers). In other words, conservatives believe that legislatures have "both representative and *deliberative* functions," as John Hallowell puts it. "The function of the legislative assembly is not only fairly to represent the people but to deliberate upon public policy and arrive at those decisions dictated by political prudence which will best promote the common good."[86] Legislators must consider not only what their constituents desire, but also what their understanding of the truths of the objective moral order requires.

Conservative thinkers clearly desire a *representative* democracy in which the representatives are relatively uninstructed by their constituents, being expected to represent not only those constituents but also the common good. They believe that the judgment of representatives is a better path to public policy than negotiations among interest groups. They believe that all too often representatives do not act on the best interests of their constituents and the common good, but respond instead to the demands of narrow, highly–organized interest groups. Conservative thinkers believe that democratic theory and practice as it has developed in America expects elected officials to balance the competing demands of such groups rather than attempt to do what they truly believe to be best. George Will, for instance, criticizes "the way we have institutionalized social pluralism. We have filled the government system with thousands of nooks and crannies from which factions can ambush democratically made decisions—all the while disguising ideological objectives in the arid language of 'due process.' "[87] And he characterizes the difference between the political parties and candidates in the 1984 presidential election in terms of their approach to representation. The Democratic party specializes in "the brokering function of interest–group liberalism. . . . What sort of mandate do you get when you build a majority by treating the electorate as a jumble of organized appetites? Reaganism is politics–as–evangelism, calling forth a majority with a hymn to general values. Mondaleism is politics–as–masonry, building a majority brick by brick. . . . Mondaleism suits the Democratic tradition, but perhaps not the national condition."[88]

The conservative view of democracy, as Kendall points out, emphasizes "specifically moral considerations; e.g., the kind of considerations involved in deciding who are the virtuous men."[89] Once again we see emphasis on finding the correct rulers. As Hallowell puts it, "Democracy places its faith in the ability of the average man to select men of sound judgement and good character to perform the functions of the legislator, but it does not demand that we regard every man as a competent legislator."[90] This need for moral considerations in the choosing of representatives is one more reason that conservative thinkers stress the need for more local initiative and local control in government. Local representatives are closer to the people they represent so that moral character can play a larger role in their selection.

As important as formal constitutional limits are in the conservative scheme of government, conservative thinkers regard them as insufficient. On the basis of their core beliefs, especially their view of human nature, conservative thinkers believe that formal limits cannot completely control the rulers' desire for power. As Burnham argues, "no written constitution could have been of itself an absolute guarantee against the centralization of power: men can always bend words to their passions. A nation that does not want liberty will not preserve it. But the Fathers did provide us with a framework marvelously apt for blocking the concentration of governmental power (sovereignty) in any single agency, *if* that is what we as a nation, or most of us, choose to use it for."[91]

Why should we wish to use this framework in this manner? Primarily, according to conservative thinkers, because of traditional beliefs and values. "The miracle of government, like other miracles, occurs in time," Burnham tells us. "In and through time, the paradox is resolved, reason merges with what is beyond or outside of reason. . . . If we translate into political and historical terms: the problem of government, insoluble by abstract reason alone, by ideology, becomes solved by social experience acting through time—that is, by *tradition*."[92] For conservatives, the problem of government has to do primarily with the nature of government power. Tradition, they believe, convinces us that political power must not be absolute, that it must be circumscribed if liberty is to exist. This is part of the tradition that conservative thinkers believe they are defending against the relativism of modern times. Tradition provides a standard for judging the acts of government, a standard to be ever more closely approximated through the day–to–day experience of governing.

According to conservative thinkers, some of these traditional ideas are embodied in the United States Constitution. Kirk quotes with approval Abraham Lincoln's statement that the founders "meant to set up a standard maxim for a free society which should be familiar to all, and revered by all, constantly looked to, constantly labored for, and even though never perfectly attained, constantly approximated, and thereby constantly spreading and deepening its influence and augmenting the happiness and value of life of all people of all colors everywhere." Kirk calls this a "prudent idea" and contrasts it with "the Jacobin dream of absolute right imposed immediately without respect for established interests and traditions."[93]

Conservative thinkers believe that without these traditional values and institutions to moderate and shape it, government, especially democratic government, is likely to degenerate into tyranny. Nisbet warns that this "pre–democratic strata of values and institutions which alone made political freedom possible" is crumbling.[94] Enlightened self–interest is not enough to create social harmony; the holding of values in common is required to temper the worst aspects of human nature, especially values that cause people to respect the liberty of their fellows and to feel a sense of public spiritedness.[95]

Furthermore, conservative thinkers believe that government must be in accord with the traditional ways of the people. "In every state the best possible—or least baneful—form of government," argues Kirk, "is one in accord with the tradition and prescriptive ways of its people. . . . The political institutions of a people grow out of their religion, their moral habits, their economy, even their literature; political institutions are but part of an intricate structure of civilization, the roots of which go infinitely deep. . . . Theory divorced from experience is infinitely dangerous, the plaything of the ideologue, the darling dagger of the energumen."[96] Conservative thinkers conclude from their view of human nature that a government that radically departs from the traditional ways of a people will not obtain their willing allegiance, and that if it demands their allegiance solely by force, it will damage the fragile norms and social bonds that hold the people together and hold in check the evil tendencies in individuals. They also believe that government must accord with traditional ways because tradition is one important source of knowledge about the objective moral order.[97]

But while government must accord with traditional beliefs and institutions, and requires them if it is to be just government, it is not government's role to define them. As discussed in the chapters 4 and 5, conservative thinkers believe that government may have some role in supporting these values and institutions, but their creation, regeneration, and definition is not a matter for politics. "The restoration of the ethical system and the religious sanction upon which any life worth living is founded," according to Kirk, "cannot be accomplished as a deliberate program of social reform. It must be its own end. . . . Society's regeneration cannot be an undertaking purely political."[98]

FOREIGN POLICY

Finally, a word about how conservatives' core beliefs influence contemporary American conservative thought on foreign policy is in order. There is one great theme that permeates this thinking and on which all conservatives agree. From their reading of the objective moral order, they conclude that the communist system of government should not be regarded as just another alternative or opposing form of government—it is evil. Because of the nature of that evil, it is morally necessary to combat it by whatever means necessary—including a military establishment, a draft, support for unsavory noncommunist governments against communist aggression, and a nuclear deterrence. It is impossible to understand the views of conservative thinkers on foreign policy issues without understanding the depth of their antipathy toward communism, especially Soviet communism. For instance, Gerhart Niemeyer warns of "the unprecedented character of evil in our time. . . . We are today facing evil that issues not so much from passions and misdirected loves as rather from . . . ideologies

established as public orthodoxies and practised by governing bodies and state institutions," ideologies in which "mur-
der is publicly legalized and justified"[99] and freedom is curtailed.

Accommodation with such evil is evil. We must try to establish peace, George Will acknowledges, but he contends that "the
rhetoric and policies of flexibility blunt the West's ideological
keenness and dilute its sense of purpose. . . . Such blunting
and diluting diminish the public's stamina for a foreign policy of permanent exertion. Thus détente tends to destroy its
prerequisite: it dissolves the clarity of purpose that alone can
prevent a desire for peace becoming an overwhelming impulse
toward accommodation. Détente is always possible; perhaps safe
détente never is."[100] "The most important dangers threatening
this country," he concludes, "are not denoted by the digits and
decimal points with which he [the president's budget director]
deals. The gravest dangers are the implacable and potentially
lethal challenge of the Soviet Union, and the rising tide of
terrorism for which it is largely responsible."[101] Therefore, as
Niemeyer argues, "the selective moral condemnation of Soviet
power has become a necessary and enduring component of
non–Communist governments,"[102] which fact influences all foreign policy decisions.

SUMMARY

As I hope this discussion has made clear, conservatives'
thinking about government and the economy is strongly influenced by their core beliefs in an objective moral order and
an unchanging human nature. Without understanding this, it
is difficult to understand conservative thinkers' views on the
nature of the chief problem of government and the types of
solutions they are willing to consider. The same is true of the
subjects to be considered in the next two chapters: the individual
and community (chapter 7) and change and tradition (chapter
8). Making sense out of contemporary American conservative
thought on these subjects requires seeing how it is shaped by
conservatives' core beliefs.

NOTES

1. Will, "Getting Big Things Done," *Newsweek* (30 March 1981), p. 90. See also Buckley, *Did You Ever See a Dream Walking?* pp. xxii–xxiii.

2. Meyer, "Freedom, Tradition, and Conservatism," in Meyer, ed., *What Is Conservatism?* p. 16. See also Kirk, "Prescription" in Meyer, ed., *What Is Conservatism?* p. 33.

3. Meyer, *In Defense*, p. 99.

4. Evans, *The Future of Conservatism* (New York, 1968), p. 11.

5. Meyer, "Freedom, Tradition, and Conservatism," p. 16. See also Zoll, *Twentieth Century Political Philosophy*, p. 129.

6. Kendall, *Affirmation*, p. 91. See also Morley, *Freedom and Federalism* (Chicago, 1959), p. xi; Voegelin, *New Science*, p. 63; and Burnham, *Congress and the American Tradition* (Chicago, 1959), pp. 11–12, 166–67.

7. Kendall, *Affirmation*, p. 99. See also Will, "Value of Punishment," p. 92.

8. Meyer, *In Defense*, p. 25.

9. Kirk, *Program*, p. 4.

10. Burnham, *Congress*, pp. 18–19.

11. Zoll, *Twentieth Century Political Philosophy*, p. 129. See also Kuehnelt–Leddihn, "Portland Declaration," p. 1192; and Kendall, *Affirmation*, p. 26.

12. Kirk, *Program*, pp. 72–73.

13. Kuehnelt–Leddihn, "Portland Declaration," p. 1190. See also Will, *Statecraft*, p. 16.

14. Herberg, "Presuppositions," p. 236.

15. Jaffa, "Another Look," p. 838, emphasis added.

16. See the discussion of the principle of hierarchy in chapter 7 for more on this subject.

17. See, for example, Tonsor, "Conservative Search," in Meyer, ed., *What Is Conservatism?* p. 147; Wilhelmsen, *Christianity and Political Philosophy*, p. 154; and Meyer, "Freedom, Tradition, and Conservatism," p. 17.

18. See, for example, Tonsor, "Conservative Search," pp. 145–46. See also Buckley, *Up from Liberalism*, pp. 183, 184; Evans, *Future*, pp. 11–12, 101; and Meyer, *In Defense*, pp. 97–99.

19. Tonsor, "Conservative Search," p. 147. See also Meyer, "Freedom, Tradition, and Conservatism," pp. 3–4; Kirk, *Program*, pp. 36, 150–51; Kendall, *Affirmation*, pp. 44–47; and Morley, *Freedom and Federalism*, pp. xi–xii.

20. While it is unlikely that all conservative thinkers opposed civil rights efforts for high–minded reasons (as conservatives, with their

emphasis on the inherent evil in men's nature, should be the first to admit), it is also clear that this position was not an easy one for conservatives aware of the suffering caused by racial discrimination. Indeed, a minority felt that the need to redress these wrongs was more important than the need to preserve the constitutional limits on government power and broke with the majority of conservative thinkers on this issue. For more on the apparently shifting attitude of conservative thinkers toward reform in prospect and in retrospect, see chapter 8.

21. Will, "Battling the Racial Spoils System," *Newsweek* (10 June 1985), p. 96.

22. Burnham, *Congress*, pp. 73–74. See also Nisbet, *Twilight*, p. 51; John Chamberlain, "Ignore Human Nature?" p. 59.

23. Will, *Pursuit of Virtue*, pp. 92–93.

24. Meyer, "Freedom, Tradition, and Conservatism," p. 16;

25. Will, "The Soul of Conservatism," *Newsweek* (11 November 1985), p. 92.

26. Meyer, *In Defense*, p. 26. See also Kirk, *Program*, p. 19.

27. Will, "What Stockman Really Said," *Newsweek* (23 November 1981), p. 130.

28. Kuehnelt–Leddihn, "Portland Declaration," p. 1190. See also Nisbet, *Twilight*, p. 50.

29. Evans, *Future*, pp. 237, 238. See also Thomas Molnar, *Authority and Its Enemies* (New Rochelle, N.Y., 1976), pp. 113–14; Burnham, *Congress*, p. 277; and Will, *Pursuit of Virtue*, p. 92.

30. See Buckley, *Up from Liberalism*, p. 186.

31. Young, *The Politics of Affluence: Ideology in the United States Since World War II* (San Francisco, 1968), p. 105.

32. Will, *Pursuit of Virtue*, pp. 89–90.

33. Meyer, *In Defense*, p. 150.

34. Tonsor, "Conservative Search," p. 149. See also Kirk, "Prescription," p. 25.

35. Weaver, *Ideas Have Consequences*, p. 137. See also William Chamberlin, "Conservatism in Evolution," p. 253; and Molnar, *Authority*, p. 51.

36. Kirk, *Conservative Mind*, p. 18. See also Buckley, *Up from Liberalism*, p. 210; and Meyer, "Why Freedom?" p. 225.

37. Buckley, *Up from Liberalism*, p. 179. See also John Chamberlain, *Roots*, p. 165.

38. Burnham, *Congress*, p. 277. See also Kuehnelt–Leddihn, "Portland Declaration," p. 1190; Buckley, *Up from Liberalism*, p. 179.

39. John Chamberlain, "The Morality of Free Enterprise," in Meyer, ed., *What Is Conservatism?* p. 186. See also John Chamberlain, *Roots*, pp.

181, 184–85; and Buckley, *Up from Liberalism*, p. 201.

40. Read, "On Freedom and Order," *The Freeman* 15 (January 1965), p. 33.

41. John Chamberlain, "Ignore Human Nature?" p. 59.

42. Weaver, *Ideas Have Consequences*, p. 138. See also Kuehnelt–Leddihn, "Portland Declaration," p. 1192; and John Chamberlain, *Roots*, p. 182.

43. Meyer, *In Defense*, p. 150.

44. Weaver, *Ideas Have Consequences*, p. 137. See also John Chamberlin, "Conservatism in Evolution," p. 253; Peter Viereck, *Conservatism Revisited*, pp. 13–14; and John Chamberlain, *Roots*, p. 208.

45. John Chamberlain, *Roots*, pp. 5, 10. See also Meyer, *In Defense*, p. 10.

46. John Chamberlain, "Morality," pp. 181, 182.

47. Kirk, *Program*, p. 19.

48. John Chamberlain, *Roots*, p. 208. See also Kuehnelt–Leddihn, "Portland Declaration," p. 1193.

49. Kuehnelt–Leddihn, "Portland Declaration," p. 1193. See also Zoll, *Twentieth Century Political Philosophy*, p. 127; and John Chamberlain, *Roots*, p. 182.

50. Read, "Knowing," p. 11. See also Opitz, "Let's Not Save the World," *The Freeman* 15 (January 1965), p. 10; and Kuehnelt–Leddihn, "Portland Declaration," p. 1193.

51. See Buckley, *Up from Liberalism*, p. 201; Read, "Knowing," p. 64; Opitz, "Let's Not," p. 10; and John Chamberlain, *Roots*, pp. 10, 165.

52. Kirk, *Program*, p. 40. See also Niemeyer, Review of Clinton Rossiter's *Conservatism in America*, p. 445.

53. John Chamberlain, "Morality," p. 187; see also p. 182.

54. Weaver, *Ideas Have Consequences*, p. 133. See also John Chamberlain, *Roots*, p. 189; and Meyer, *In Defense*, p. 154.

55. Weaver, *Ideas Have Consequences*, p. 32. See also Viereck, "But—I'm a Conservative!" p. 541; and John Chamberlain, "Morality," p. 181.

56. Nisbet, *Twilight*, p. 80. See also Molnar, *Authority*, p. 53; and Will, *Statecraft*, p. 19.

57. Buckley, *Dream*, p. xx–xxi.

58. Kirk, *Program*, p. 36.

59. Weaver, *Ideas Have Consequences*, p. 75.

60. Kirk, *Program*, p. 147. See also Viereck, "But—I'm a Conservative!" p. 541.

61. Kirk, *Program*, p. 11. See also Viereck, *Conservatism Revisited*, p. 16.

62. Weaver, *Ideas Have Consequences*, pp. 132–33.

63. Ibid. See also Molnar, *Authority*, p. 51.

64. Kirk, *Program*, p. 149. See also Molnar, *Authority*, p. 54.

65. Viereck, *Conservatism Revisited*, p. 16.

66. Will, "The Splendid Legacy of FDR," *Newsweek* (11 February 1982), p. 78, and "The Case for Automakers," p. 88.

67. Viereck, *Conservatism Revisited*, p. 16.

68. Other aspects of equality—social, racial, sexual—receive more treatment in chapter 7; but the basic conservative position is the same in these areas: opposition to government enforcement of equality.

69. Kirk, *Program*, p. 42. See also Zoll, *Twentieth Century Political Philosophy*, p. 127; and Kuehnelt–Leddihn, "Portland Declaration," p. 1189.

70. Kuehnelt–Leddihn, "Portland Declaration," p. 1189. See also Molnar, *Authority*, p. 51; and Tonsor, "Conservative Search," p. 143.

71. Meyer, *In Defense*, pp. 8–9. See also Zoll, *Twentieth Century Political Philosophy*, p. 127.

72. Kirk, "Prescription," p. 32. See also Kendall, *Affirmation*, p. 17.

73. Kirk, "Prescription," p. 34. See also Zoll, *Twentieth Century Political Philosophy*, p. 127.

74. Viereck, *Conservatism Revisited*, p. 19.

75. Weaver, *Ideas Have Consequences*, pp. 132–33.

76. Tonsor, "Conservative Search," pp. 148–49. See also Will, *The Pursuit of Happiness and Other Sobering Thoughts* (New York, 1978), pp. 7–9.

77. See chapter 7 for a further discussion of the less economic, more social aspects of equality.

78. Wilhelmsen, *Christianity and Political Philosophy*, p. 189. See also Nisbet, *Twilight*, p. 50; Herberg, "Presuppositions," p. 236; Weaver, "Up from Liberalism," p. 29; and Will, *Pursuit of Virtue*, p. 26.

79. Wilhelmsen, *Christianity and Political Philosophy*, p. 189. See also Burnham, *Congress*, p. 73.

80. Zoll, *Twentieth Century Political Philosophy*, p. 131. See also Molnar, *Authority*, p. 110; Burnham, *Congress*, p. 301; Wilhelmsen, *Christianity and Political Philosophy*, pp. 148–50; and Weaver, "Up from Liberalism," p. 29.

81. Meyer, "Why Freedom?" p. 225. See also Tonsor, "Conservative Search," p. 142; and Burnham, *Congress*, pp. 290ff.

82. Weaver, *Ideas Have Consequences*, p. 46. See also Tonsor, "Conservative Search," p. 142.

83. Chapter 8 discusses how the core beliefs influence the conservative attitude toward change.

84. Kendall, *Affirmation*, pp. ix–x. See also Hallowell, *Moral Foundations*, pp. 48ff.

85. Tonsor, "Conservative Search," p. 145.

86. Hallowell, *Moral Foundation*, p. 57. See also Molnar, *Authority*, p. 110; and Kendall, *Affirmation*, pp. 16–17.

87. Will, "Getting," p. 90. See also Molnar, *Authority*, p. 92; Kendall, *Affirmation*, pp. 26, 29; and Hallowell, *Moral Foundations*, p. 60.

88. Will, "A Broker for the Democrats," *Newsweek* (14 March 1983), p. 80.

89. Kendall, *Affirmation*, pp. 42–43.

90. Hallowell, *Moral Foundations*, p. 60.

91. Burnham, *Congress*, p. 38, emphasis added.

92. Burnham, *Congress*, p. 25. See also Jaffa, "Another Look," pp. 838–40; see chapter 8 for a discussion on what conservative thinkers mean by tradition.

93. Kirk, *Program*, p. 34. See also Buckley, *Dream*, pp. xvii; see also chapters 2, 3, 4, and especially 8 for more on the extent to which conservative thinkers value tradition over reason.

94. Nisbet, *Twilight*, p. 6.

95. See, for instance, Will, "The Madison Legacy," *Newsweek* (7 December 1981), p. 124; and Jaffa, "Another Look," pp. 838–40.

96. Kirk, "Prescription," pp. 33, 38, 39.

97. For more on tradition, see chapter 8.

98. Kirk, *Conservative Mind*, pp. 449, 452.

99. Niemeyer, "Foreign Policy and Morality" *Intercollegiate Review*, 15 (Spring 1980), p. 2. See also Will, "Nuclear Morality," *Newsweek* (21 December 1981), p. 84; Wilhelmsen, *Christianity and Political Philosophy*, pp. 103–5; and Meyer, "Freedom, Tradition, and Conservatism" p. 16.

100. Will, "Henry Kissinger's Craft," *Newsweek* (29 March 1982), p. 84. See also Evans, *Future*, p. 32; and Wilhelmsen, *Christianity and Political Philosophy*, pp. 106–8.

101. Will, "A Baptism of Fire," *Newsweek* (13 April 1981), p. 108. See also Will, "Reaping the Whirlwind," *Newsweek* (21 January 1980), p. 92.

102. Niemeyer, "Foreign Policy," p. 7. See also Buckley, *Dream*, p. xxiv.

7

COMMUNITY

Contemporary American conservative thought on the nature of
society and the relationship between individuals and society
is shaped by the conservatives' core beliefs in an objective
moral order and an unchanging human nature, and by the
tension between authority and freedom that stems from the
core. Conservative ideas in this area center on the notion of
community. Conservative thinkers see community and the institutions that constitute it as part of the solution to the tension
between freedom and authority discussed in chapters 4 and 5.
They also believe that the need for community arises out of
human nature. And they believe that community is necessary
for giving expression to the truths of the objective moral order.
This chapter discusses these aspects of conservative thinking on
community in the context of the core. It also provides illustrations
by discussing conservative thought on the part played by some of
the institutions that conservatives believe constitute community.

COMMUNITY AND HUMAN NATURE

When conservative thinkers refer to community, they sometimes mean the social unit consisting of people who share some

common interests and interact face–to–face with each other within a recognizable locality, such as a small town or neighborhood. More generally they use the term to refer to the complex of nongovernmental institutions and interactions that are natural (such as the family or local community) or that are constructed to meet natural human needs (such as religious and educational institutions and fraternal and philanthropic organizations). They are convinced that there are natural and necessary interactions between people in these institutions and that these interactions, while in an important sense voluntary, are not accidental.

Conservative thinkers believe that by nature people need community and are suited to it. People naturally desire the associations involved in community. As Thomas Molnar puts it, "aware that we are individuals—selfish, self–willed, 'separatist'—we also long for integration into the group. . . . It is rational for man to live in the community of other men. If human groups are always precarious and precariously balanced between order and anarchy, it is because man is a place of conflict between his rational desire to be free and his equally rational desire to belong to the group."[1] George F. Will agrees that people are generally "torn between two desires: for absence of restraint and for a sense of community."[2] Even libertarian conservative Frank S. Meyer agrees that community is a natural thing. He says that community means not only the "voluntary association of individuals in the myriad of relationships that are available for each person to choose or reject in a free society," but also the "necessary and inescapable associations that the conditions of existence prescribe for all men."[3] For conservatives "community is no mere aggregation of individuals under democratic despotism," as Russell Kirk puts it, but something essential and natural.[4]

Conservative thinkers conclude from their view of human nature that community is necessary for the proper development of human beings. Society "is natural to man," according to Willmoore Kendall; "its origin is to be sought in the nature of man, for whose perfection it is necessary."[5] Without the associations involved in community, people would be mere atoms, lacking the associations and integration that make them truly human. Molnar asserts that "man cannot function outside society." He needs membership in society, without which he would not be an individual, let alone a protected and integrated one. . . . I mean by integration and protection the fact that we learn society's language, mores, and traditions, without which we would be individuals physiologically, but not in the human sense, that is, infinitely rich in thought, modes of expression, and articulation, with a sense of identity and belonging, with rather clear reflective choices, preferences, refusals, and aspirations. Thus if nature shapes our immediately given body, society fashions our reflective life, our ethical being, our tastes, our personality.[6]

Of course, not every ordering of the institutions of community fulfills this human need for integration equally well. Part of the task of conservatives, according to Kirk, is "the recovery of a humane scale in the civil social order: a society made for the truly human person, not an impersonal collectivism forcing all men into a universal mold."[7] The best community is one that is shaped by men's understanding of the objective moral order and one in which the truths of the objective moral order are taught. One of the chief functions of the institutions of community is to teach, and what these institutions teach, at best, are the truths of the objective moral order. And the authority exerted by these institutions influences people to obey those truths.

INDIVIDUAL AND COMMUNITY

As much as conservative thinkers stress the need that people have for community, they do not believe that community or its institutions properly take precedence over the individual. What they seek in community is a balance between the needs of the individual and the needs of the community, which is part of the balance they seek between authority and freedom. They conclude from their core beliefs that both the individual and the institutions and groups to which he belongs are important. The quotation from Molnar about the human need for society, cited above, also mentions the other side of this balance: "Man cannot function outside society, and the latter does not exist without the individuals who compose it."[8]

The conservatives' concept of community is an attempt to express the proper relationship between people. Just as libertarian conservatives place more stress on freedom and less on authority than traditionalist conservatives do, so libertarian conservatives put more emphasis on the individual and are more wary of the influence of community than traditionalist conservatives. But traditionalist and libertarian conservatives agree that both the individual and community are important. Their desire is not to promote either at the expense of the other, but to find a balance that serves the individual best by recognizing and fulfilling both his need for freedom and his need for integration. They agree in rejecting both a collectivism in which they believe the individual counts for nothing and a radical individualism that tears apart the ties and interdependencies that make people real individuals.

Conservative thinkers acknowledge that community can pose a threat to individual freedom, but most do not feel that it is a very strong threat. In this area conservatives seem to take an approach rather different from their position on limited government and economic individualism. When discussing those topics, they are very concerned to limit power and authority, but when they turn their attention to community, they are much less concerned. A major part of the reason for this difference is that they see the authority exerted by community as a corrective for the necessary limits placed on the authority exerted in these other spheres. They believe that authority must be exercised; if its exercise in some areas is particularly dangerous, that is all the more reason that authority is needed in other areas. And since the authority exerted by community is largely noncoercive, it is safer. The more effective this safer authority is, the less authority need be exerted by coercive institutions like government.

So contemporary American conservatism stresses individualism versus the state but not versus community, family, or friends. In a eulogy for his friend and fellow conservative Frank Chodorov, William F. Buckley, Jr., explained that the individualism that Chodorov believed in—and that characterizes conservatism—is one "which called for aloofness from remote and synthetic and involuntary associations, but which flowered in the giving of oneself to one's family, and friends, and philosophical soul mates."[9]

Frank Meyer's position is a notable exception to the generally low level of concern among conservative thinkers over the threat that the authority of community poses to individual freedom. He becomes very heated when discussing this threat and takes many of his fellow conservatives to task for not treating it seriously. He is concerned that when they talk about community being organic, they mean that community is a real being that is more important than the individuals who compose it. He fears that "community (except as it is freely created by free individual persons), community conceived as a principle of social order prior and superior to the individual person, can justify any oppression of individual persons so long as it is carried out in the name of 'community' . . . or of its agent, the state. This is the principle of collectivism."[10]

There are a few conservative thinkers who take a position almost as extreme as Meyer describes.[11] But Meyer has over-stated the case for most conservative thinkers. When they talk about community being organic, what they mean is that it is not a machine that can be tinkered with or rearranged at will without serious consequences.[12] But they do not see community as superior to the individual. Their position is reflected in Kirk's emphasis on "the soft but effectual controls" exerted by community.[13] Most conservative thinkers believe that these controls pose no serious threat to individual freedom because they are noncoercive—yet very significant. Meyer himself argues that the noncoercive aspects of community are valuable. "To assert the freedom and independence of the individual implies no denial of the value of mutuality, of association and common action between persons [i.e., of community]. It only denies the value of coerced association."[14]

As one of the leading libertarian conservatives, Meyer consist-ently emphasizes the freedom of the individual, and thus he finds value in community only if it does not seem to threaten freedom—and most other conservative thinkers believe it does not. Meyer does not think the role to be played by the institu-tions of community is as significant as most other conservative thinkers do. Concerning "all sets of relationships between men," he argues that

those relationships may be of the kind best described as institutions, or as associations, or as communities. They may be in their essential form necessary to human existence, like the state and the family. They may fulfill a function which is necessary, but which can be fulfilled in many different ways, like the economic system or the educational system. Or they may be totally voluntary, like a professional association, or a charitable guild, or a chess club. But all of them are instrumentalities only. Depending on their structure, they can make movement toward virtue easier or more difficult—but that is all.[15]

Most other conservative thinkers agree in principle with Meyer, but for them that "all" is very important.

COMMUNITY, AUTHORITY, AND FREEDOM

Conservative thinkers believe that community plays a vital role in the solution to the freedom–authority dilemma. One of the best ways to protect freedom from the power of government, according to conservatives, is to divide power among many groups and institutions, so that power is not concentrated in any one of them. If "authority is diffused throughout the community by way of a plurality of institutions," argues Frederick Wilhelmsen, then no one institution can exert absolute authority over anyone.[16] The division of authority pits one institution against another, and one result of their competition is that each tends to protect the individual from the others. As a result, says Stephen Tonsor, "the freedom of the individual is most certain in that realm which [no institution] can successfully occupy and dominate."[17] There is some competition between all these institutions, but the main competition is between each of the institutions of community and government. These "mediating structures," as Will describes them, "(families, churches, neighborhoods, voluntary associations) . . . soften the exposure of the individual to the great megastructure, the state."[18]

It is especially true, conservatives believe, that the diffusion of authority is essential to check the power of the national state—so much so that Russell Kirk declares that "the true freedom of the person subsists in community. Associations such as family, local community, trade union, and religion protect the individual by standing between him and the state. When these are removed, the state acts directly upon the individual and exerts so much power that freedom is lost."[19] Robert Nisbet similarly emphasizes on these institutions when he declares that the heart of the problem of politics lies in "the relation of the state to other, nonpolitical institutions. These latter have been the essential walls of the political community, the indispensable means by which checks and limits have been placed upon the state's power and upon the tendency, always great in democracy, for that power to seek constantly to encompass all manner of ways of life."[20]

Conservative thinkers argue that these intermediary institutions also protect the freedom of the individual from encroachment by other people. Some of these institutions teach moral truth that, in Kirk's words, "has made men ashamed of their appetite for power," thus helping to restrain the natural human impulse to infringe on the rights of others for the sake of one's own interests.[21] Conservatives believe that the acceptance of such precepts is essential in a democracy. When the majority rules, it must exercise self–restraint or minorities will suffer. "Our system," says Felix Morley, "assumes that self–assertion will be for the good of all if balanced by self–discipline. To meet that proviso it relies heavily . . . on the services of organized religion" and other institutions.[22] The Founding Fathers understood this, Nisbet asserts. They expected institutional and shared values to control and restrain men's tendencies toward mischief and evil. When these institutions are weak or destroyed, there are fewer moral restraints on human tendencies to infringe the freedom of others.[23]

In addition to the self–restraint induced by moral teachings, the close personal relationships that people have within local communities and institutions help to restrain them. As Kirk puts it, "when no man feels settled into an order, then the individual has no dread of censure, but is restrained in his appetites only by the threat of force: the policeman supplants, so far as he is able, the old influence of emulation and the soft but effectual controls of good repute. Almost no one is afraid of 'public disapproval' in the abstract; what we fear is the loss of good repute within the little platoon we belong to in society, the reproaches of our parish, our club, our neighborhood, our partners, our guild or union."[24]

This discussion of the conservative belief that community must restrain men's appetites for the sake of freedom also illustrates the conservatives' belief that community has an essential role to play in exercising authority for the good of the individual. As chapter 4 points out, conservatives place great emphasis on authority. They believe that much of this authority should be exercised by institutions other than government. Indeed, many seem to believe that it is in the very nature of an institution to exercise authority—that exercising authority is part of its purpose. According to Molnar, "an institution . . . is not a mere aggregate of individual wills, efforts, and interests, entirely at the mercy of the whims of these individual members. An institution . . . has also an educative function, it is an embodiment (incorporation) of just such a function . . . a civilizational function."[25]

The institutions of community are noncoercive. They cannot make people act virtuously by force, nor can they take away the life, liberty, or property of a person who acts unvirtuously, as government can. But conservatives believe that these institutions can and must establish conditions that favor the growth of virtue and nurture that growth. The more they succeed, the less authority need be exerted by government, and thus the opportunities for the abuse of government power are restricted. But "the less control survives within private life and local community, the more control will be exerted by the centralized state, out of necessity."[26] Thus, Kirk says, "free community is the alternative to compulsive collectivism."[27]

HIERARCHY WITHIN COMMUNITY

The last general aspect of community that requires our attention—and perhaps the most controversial—is the principle of hierarchy. Conservative thinkers believe that the well-ordered society is indeed ordered, "that civilized society requires orders and classes," as Kirk puts it.[28] They disagree about the nature of the hierarchy that is needed—libertarian conservatives and traditionalist conservatives especially disagree with each other about what forms hierarchy should take. But they all agree that hierarchy is needed and that it is natural. Tonsor, a leading libertarian conservative, points out with approval that "one of the most obvious and widely observed behaviors in animal and human societies is what ethologists call the 'pecking order,' [or] 'hierarchy.' "[29] Traditional conservative James Burnham, agrees. He believes that we must restore "society as it really is—hierarchical and differentiating, not equalized or regimented."[30] Such hierarchy is unavoidable, Nisbet argues, arising as it does "from the very functional requirements of the social bond."[31]

Hierarchy—or order, to use Kirk's term—"is the harmonious arrangement of classes and functions which guards justice and gives willing consent to law and ensures that we all shall be safe together. . . . Order also signifies the honor or dignity of a rank in society; and it signifies some particular profession or class."[32] Kirk's statement indicates some of the benefits that conservatives believe are derived from hierarchy. When people accept their positions within such an order, accept the relationships with other people in other positions implied by such an order, and recognize that the order operates for the good of all within it, then they give "willing consent to law," the instrument of that order. They feel the dignity and usefulness of their position in that order. They are able to obtain justice and wish to see justice done to others. They feel safe with each other, and they feel a sense of fraternity. Kirk believes that "we are made for cooperation, not for strife; and order is not a corruption of the natural equality of man, but instead the realization of the providential design which made us one another's keepers."[33]

Nisbet argues that in society there must be "some form of stratification of function and role."[34] Without it, some necessary functions are not fulfilled. This is true not only of individuals, Molnar states, but also of institutions. "A reasonable society is structured according to the generalized principle of subsidiarity, which implies that in a society every group, from family to State, has distinct tasks it is best able to perform, and that these tasks are hierarchically organized."[35]

Another benefit of hierarchy, from the conservative perspective, is that giving distinction to people who have developed certain desirable character traits provides incentive for others to develop those traits and share in the distinction, at the same time helping people understand what is of real worth. As the traditionalist Richard Weaver argues, in a society in which the virtuous and knowledgeable have natural elevation, "it is possible for [a person] to live on the plane of spirit and intelligence because some points of reference are fixed."[36] Meyer agrees. A staunch libertarian conservative, he certainly does not want the conservative principle of hierarchy to be used to support rigid social structures; yet he points out that a necessary condition of the good society is that "the intellectual and moral leaders, the 'creative minority,' have the understanding and imagination to maintain the prestige of tradition and reason, and thus to sustain the intellectual and moral order throughout society. A failure of the responsible interpreters of the intellectual, moral, and spiritual order would make freedom a useless toy, depriving men of standards by which to guide their lives."[37]

The need for leadership is felt very keenly by conservative thinkers. The proper leaders can give force to the truths of the objective moral order by exemplifying the application of those truths. As discussed in chapter 6, finding the right leaders is part of the conservative solution to the problem of obtaining government that is both strong and safe—that meets the requirements of both authority and freedom. Conservative thinkers believe that a hierarchical order of society helps to create and sustain the proper leadership. As Weaver says, "a society in the true sense must have exclusive minorities of the wise and good who will bear responsibility and enjoy prestige. Otherwise either it will be leaderless, or its leadership will rest on forces of darkness."[38] Conservatives believe that there must be leaders—people demand them. A society that gives distinction to the best will have good leadership. One that does not will have leaders who obtain their positions through evil means.

The best leaders are those who are both wise and good—that is, those who know the truths of the objective moral order and who have sufficiently overcome the weakness of unchanging human nature sufficiently to base their lives on those truths. Donald Zoll believes that the concept of ethical realism—(Zoll's term for belief in the objective moral order)—requires as a corollary the "concept of legitimate leadership based upon ethical attainment."[39] These leaders, the wise and good, must receive prestige for two reasons: it makes others want to emulate them, and it provides an appropriate reward for them, without which either they would refuse to undertake the task of leadership or they would undertake it for some other, less noble reward—a reward that they would probably obtain at the expense of the people they lead. So, "for the good of all," as Weaver expresses it, "prerogative will attach to higher function, and this will mean hierarchy."[40]

This emphasis on the leadership and privileges of the wise and the good points out the precarious balance that conservatives are trying to achieve with regard to the principle of hierarchy. A proper hierarchy must be relatively open so that the good and wise can rise to leadership, but if it is to function properly as a hierarchy it must not be too open. Nisbet quotes Edmund Burke's statement that "everything ought to be open but not indifferently to every man."[41] It ought to be most open to the right people, those who demonstrate wisdom and virtue. Conservative thinkers acknowledge that the problem of determining who are the good and wise is a difficult one. Generally they rely upon other determinants that can be presumed to approximate these traits, such as education, class, wealth, and the opinion of peers. But what they really desire is a hierarchy based not on externals like race or ethnicity, or even class or wealth, but on virtue and knowledge.

With such emphasis on hierarchy, it is little wonder that conservative thinkers have disparaging things to say about equality, at least the enforced equality of condition and status. They support legal and moral equality, but, as Kirk says, they believe that "all other attempts at levelling lead to despair."[42] Richard Weaver summarizes very nicely the conservative argument against the egalitarianism that goes beyond moral and legal equality:

Equality is a disorganizing concept in so far as human relationships mean order. It is order without design; it attempts a meaningless and profitless regimentation of what has been ordered from time immemorial by the scheme of things. . . . If [democracy] promises equality of condition, it promises injustice, because one law for the ox and the lion is tyranny. . . . Nothing but a despotism could enforce anything so unrealistic, and this explains why modern governments dedicated to this program have become, under one guise or another, despotic . . . .

Nothing is more manifest than that as . . . social distance has diminished and all groups have moved nearer equality, suspicion and hostility have increased. In the present world there is little of trust and less of loyalty. People do not know what to expect of one another . . . .

The comity of peoples in groups large or small rests not upon this chimerical notion of equality but upon fraternity, a concept which long antedates it in history because it goes immeasurably deeper in human sentiment. The ancient feeling of brotherhood carries obligations of which equality knows nothing. . . . It places people in a network of sentiment, not of rights. . . . The basis of an organic social order is fraternity uniting parts that are distinct. . . . Fraternity directs attention to others, equality to self. . . .

However paradoxical it may seem, fraternity has existed in the most hierarchal organizations; it exists . . . in that archetype of hierarchy, the family. . . . The frame of duty which fraternity erects is itself the source of ideal conduct. Where men feel that society means station, the highest and the lowest see their endeavors contributing to a common end, and they are in harmony rather than in competition.[43]

There are several arguments presented here. Equality destroys the natural expectations that people have of each other in a well–ordered society. It creates envy and suspicion. It destroys the common emotions and obligations that people naturally feel when they know they are tied together in an understandable hierarchy and when they know their position and feel the rightness of their position in that hierarchy. It creates injustice, dictating like conditions for unlike individuals. And, of course, it destroys all the other goods that flow from hierarchy.

So conservatives wish to restore hierarchy within community—not just any hierarchy, but whatever aspects of good order and good ordering can be achieved without radical change. For as Kirk notes,

the conservative, knowing that radical backward–looking alteration is quite as perilous as radical forward–looking alteration, . . . will seek to utilize and improve the orders which already exist in our nation, not to impose an exotic pattern of abstract hierarchy. . . . I would sweep away none of [these orders], but would endeavor to repair them all. And I would employ for this purpose no ingenious novel devices, but simply the agencies for restoration which are accessible to us all—the church, the political caucus, the union, the club, the college, the newspaper, the publishing firm, the business establishment.[44]

Here as elsewhere conservative thinkers believe in the power of ideas to persuade people to respect the authority of virtue and knowledge and to restore prestige to a good and wise elite.

FAMILY

A look at some of the specific institutions that make up community should help to clarify conservative ideas about community and the relationship between individuals, government, and nongovernmental institutions. Chief among the institutions that together constitute genuine community is the family. It is within the family that conservatives believe human beings best receive the training and shaping that civilizes them. "The family is the number one and decisive civilizing agent of all human beings," asserts Molnar.[45] As discussed in chapter 4, conservative thinkers conclude from their core beliefs that people by nature need authority to be exercised over them to civilize them. The family plays a major role in this regard. In the family the truths of the objective moral order should be taught, and family members should support each other in living according to those truths. The family may delegate to other institutions some of this responsibility to civilize and educate, but as Erik von Kuehnelt–Leddihn points out in his summary of the positions of contemporary American conservative thinkers, conservatives believe that "the primary educator is the family."[46]

Molnar also expresses the conservative belief that, in addition to teaching, the family performs other important functions: "protection, the creation of an intimate and warm environment, the regulation of habits, the acquisition of a language and a frame of reference supplying and reinforcing the identity of the members."[47] These functions are essential to civilizing people and meeting the needs that stem from their human nature; as Molnar puts it, these functions arise out of "biological and psychological necessities, and also from an added element which we can only call *love*."[48] Conservative thinkers believe that it is the family that most properly exercises authority to fulfill these functions.

It is also within the family that the highest human impulses—such as honor, duty, cooperation, protection of the weak, and love—find their finest expression. Kuehnelt–Leddihn states that conservative thinkers believe that the family "offers fulfillment to the patriarchal and matriarchal drives," which they regard as natural human impulses.[49] In other words, the family is made necessary by human nature—it is required to meet human needs. The family is a natural and unavoidable unit, one of what Meyer calls "the necessary and inescapable associations that the conditions of existence prescribe for all men," made necessary by the nature of man.[50] And because conservative thinkers believe that the family is essential for meeting basic human needs that flow from human nature, they believe, as Kirk puts it, that "the degeneration of the family to mere common house–tenancy menaces the essence of recognizable human character."[51] They see as deplorable and dangerous the tendency to view marriage and family as relationships of convenience or mere life–style options. George Will warns about the sickness of a society in which people view these essential relationships so casually that the following symptoms appear:

[T]he casual contracting and dissolving of marriages in a society in which divorce is epidemic, and the casual conceiving and disposing of life in a society in which there are 1.4 million abortions a year. . . . A director of a shelter for runaway and "throwaway" youths says: "The whole '60s idea of 'do your own thing' has moved into the '70s and '80s with disposable relationships—if it doesn't work, if it's not perfect, I want something else." So, reports a social worker, at least once a week a parent drives up and drops off a child "with a suitcase and a quick goodbye."[52]

Conservatives believe that such casualness about an essential institution is destructive.

Conservative thinkers also believe that the family protects freedom. It mediates between the family members and government, sheltering family members from the direct influence of the government because to some extent the government acts on the family or on the person as a member of a family, and not on family members individually. Furthermore, beliefs and character are largely formed by the family and not by the State. This removes one area in which the State might influence the individual, and to that extent it limits the State's control over the individual. If the family, essentially a noncoercive institution, successfully exercises necessary authority over its members, there is less need for government—which inherently poses a greater threat to freedom—to do so.

Conservatives consequently believe that restoring the integrity and functions of the family is a high priority. How? Here as elsewhere the how of contemporary American conservative thought is difficult for nonconservatives to grasp.[53] In a liberal intellectual climate in which the tendency is to look to the power of democratic government to solve the ills of society and its members, the conservative approach seems pallid and ineffectual. Conservatives do not have a program to solve the ills of society in general or the problems that face the family in particular, if by program is meant a program of government action: no social scientists on the government payroll to study the problems, no commissions to propose government action, no legislation to bolster or restructure the family, no social workers sent in to counsel or to monitor the observance of government–established standards, no governmental carrots and sticks to produce the desired behavior—no money thrown at the problem. In the view of conservative thinkers, it is precisely government action that has largely caused the problem. The state has taken over the family's functions and parental authority,[54] leaving the family as "mere common house–tenancy."[55]

George Will provides one example of this conservative attitude when he discusses what he describes as a dilemma for government:

A child rejected by parents may need assistance more immediate and certain than a public agency's attempt to reform or compel the parents into acting more like parents. But the state's readiness to act *in loco parentis* can diminish parents' sense of urgent responsibility for acting as parents. There are many mentally handicapped children who should be with their families, but who are in institutions, or foster homes, because a too–solicitous society sometimes wrongfully offers parents the option of being less than parents to their handicapped child. Of course, some children must be institutionalized. And many extraordinary men and women provide splendid homes as foster parents of even seriously retarded children with serious physical handicaps. But regarding the retarded, society sometimes acts in ways that can work to weaken the natural threads of affection between parents and an infant.[56]

The solution to the problems facing the family, from the conservative perspective, is not government action but government inaction, for the most part—leave the family alone and stop expropriating its functions. Generally the only type of legislation that conservatives want in this area is inhibiting legislation—preventing government agencies from assuming the role of parent and provider, from undermining parental responsibility, and from taking from the family its functions of educating, civilizing, and shaping character. Other than that, the state must leave families alone.[57] If left alone, conservatives hope, the family will maintain its role and regain some of its lost functions. Furthermore, conservative thinkers hope that the power of ideas can be employed to persuade people of the importance and role of the family, and thus restore it to its rightful place, chief among the institutions of community.

Before leaving the topic of the conservative attitude toward the family, a few comments are in order to show how the conservative view of the role of the sexes is influenced by the core ideas. Conservative thinkers clearly believe that there are natural psychological differences between men and women and that both the biological and psychological differences *matter* in social, political, and economic ways. Conservative thinkers do not believe that either sex is superior to the other, but neither do they believe that the differences are inconsequential. That is, they believe that these differences should and do result in moral, social, political, and economic distinctions between men and women.

These distinctions are not as clear-cut and static as the biological and psychological differences from which they stem, but they are natural, conservative thinkers believe, and to destroy them is to destroy the natural order of things. Conservatives differ among themselves about the nature and importance of these distinctions, but they agree that distinctions exist and that to attempt to ignore or destroy them is to attempt to ignore or destroy human nature—sheer folly. Weaver expresses it this way: "I put forward here an instance which not only is typical of contempt for natural order but which is also of transcendent importance. This is the foolish and destructive notion of the 'equality' of the sexes. What but a profound blacking-out of our conception of nature and purpose could have borne this fantasy." He believes that the distinctions between men and women are so important and "of so basic a character that one might suppose the most frenetic modern would regard it as part of the *donnee* to be respected. What God hath made distinct, let not man confuse."[58]

Conservative thinkers believe that by nature both men and women are fit for certain types of activities, but their focus has mostly been on the proper roles for women because they believe those are the roles most neglected and most threatened. They believe that the general categories of roles most appropriate to the nature of women, as discovered by ages of experience and the accumulated wisdom of mankind, have their focus on love, affection, nurturing, and teaching—especially moral teaching. To pull women out of these roles is to threaten irreplaceable functions. For instance, conservative thinkers believe that it is a mistake to introduce women into the violent world of war. George Will writes that

the question is not just, or even primarily, whether women are physically 'tough' enough. The question, at bottom, is whether this society wants participation in war's brutality broadened to include women. . . . The almost instinctive and universal exemption of women from combat draws a line against the encroachment of violence upon havens of gentleness. It confers upon women a privilege of decency. It has been inseparably involved in the organic growth of societies committed to such things as the sanctity of the family, and civilian supremacy. Before a nation breaks the cake of custom, it should have a better reason than the presumption that the settled practice of civilization is, suddenly, anachronistic.[59]

As with the problems facing the family, conservatives do not believe that the answer to the confusion over roles is to legislate appropriate roles or coerce individuals to accept certain sexually defined goals. Kuehnelt–Leddihn, for instance, argues that conservatives believe that "the extraordinary careers and achievements of individual women—rulers, writers, artists, doctors, lawyers, business executives, civic organizers—indicate that, besides their nature–given roles, they should not be excluded from other careers, although certain activities are in contradiction to their nature and detrimental to their dignity—those of the coal miner, shock–trooper, or hangman, for instance."[60] To exclude people from certain careers on the basis of sex would limit their freedom, and that is not appropriate except in extreme cases, such as the example of women and military combat discussed by Will.[61]

The fact that conservative thinkers do not wish to use coercion to keep women in certain roles should not obscure their belief that some roles are more appropriate than others. As Kuehnelt–Leddihn puts it, conservatives believe that "the traditional role of women in our civilization is basically the result of experience and accumulated wisdom; its accent is on love, affection, life–giving, child–rearing, all immensely important, priceless, and irreplaceable activities."[62] Conservative thinkers believe society will be healthier when most men and women find fulfillment in their nature–given roles. The answer, they believe, is to persuade men and women to accept their natural roles and to make sure that the state does nothing to prevent them from fulfilling those roles.

RELIGIOUS INSTITUTIONS

Also very important within genuine community, conservatives believe, is the religious institution. "Conservatism ought not to confuse its cause with secularism," says Stephen Tonsor. "The doctrine of the separation of church and state does not and never has implied the theory of a wall of separation, and conservatism ought to do all in its power to strengthen and encourage religion."[63] We would expect such sentiments from a traditionalist conservative, but Tonsor is one of the more prominent libertarian conservatives. Strengthening and encouraging religious institutions is a high priority for all contemporary American conservative thinkers. They believe that any society, Western or non–Western, needs the support of religious institutions, but their primary concern is to strengthen the role of churches that teach Judeo–Christian principles, which they see as crucial to the vitality, even the survival, of Western civilization.

Conservatives think religion and the church exert an important influence—Tonsor and others believe the most important—that is needed "to check the aggressive, centralizing, and totalitarian tendencies of the modern state. Without a strong religion, which remains outside and independent of the power of the state, civil liberty is unthinkable."[64] One reason for this, presumably, is that religious institutions are able to command intense loyalties from large numbers of people, and they are thus able to compete with the state for people's loyalties better than many other institutions. This makes it impossible, or at least much harder, for the State to become sufficiently powerful to destroy liberty—especially when it is remembered how jealous of certain liberties religious institutions are.

Conservative thinkers believe that religion also protects freedom by the tenets it teaches. Peter Viereck argues that "the dikes of religious ethics" are the best protection against the "flood of pagan totalitarianism . . . [and] amoral statism," and further that religion acts as "a political and cultural stabilizer."[65] The church as an institution does not generally teach as part of its doctrine the value of a free form of government, yet it does teach values that support such government. As Kirk puts it, "though Christian doctrine insists upon no express frame of government and embraces no political party, nevertheless it is from the Church that we receive our fundamental postulates of order and justice and freedom, applying them to civil society. . . . Thus it is from religion that norms for social order grow; and when faith decays, those norms are flouted."[66] In other words, religion's teachings are not sufficient to ensure free government, but without them the norms that support free government lose their grip on people's minds and hearts.

An influence as valuable as the one exerted by religion deserves the support of government, at least indirectly. Even a libertarian conservative like Tonsor believes that

religious education, far from being divisive in a democratic society, can only strengthen and solidify the federalism of the state of which it is a part. Tax monies ought to be employed for the support of church schools; nonsectarian religious education should be a part of the educational program of the public schools; and faculties of theology should be associated with the state university systems. They will, by taking a large part of the educational structure out of the hands of the state, insure an area of liberty and nonconformity to the popular prejudices of Liberal secularism.[67]

"But just as certainly," Tonsor continues, "the coercive power of the state ought not to be employed to enforce religion's observation or intrude into the realm of private as distinct from public morality."[68] In other words, conservative thinkers see a difference between the State's giving indirect support to religious institutions in general and the State's giving direct support to one religious institution at the expense of others, thus, as Kirk puts it, supporting "the right of a clique of zealots to keep the consciences of all Christians."[69] One of the chief functions of strong religious institutions is the check they place on government. To help religious institutions stay strong by giving them the kind of support Tonsor describes does not threaten that function. But putting the power of government exclusively behind one church or denomination certainly does. The State must infringe neither the liberty of religious institutions nor the religious liberty of individuals.

Nor must the church try to extend its influence into the sphere of the state. As Russell Kirk reminds his fellow conservatives:

Christian faith surely must be concerned in some degree with political questions, and surely Christian belief has affected political forms from age to age, and will continue to affect political modes. But to assume that Christian dogmata, meant to order the soul, can be applied without qualification to the multitudinous prudential concerns of the civil social order—well, that way lies much confusion and violence. Christian faith may transform this world through working upon the minds and hearts of many human beings, with healthy consequences for the body politic. But the Christian Church is no instrument for administering secular justice, conducting secular diplomacy, or waging war.[70]

When religious fervor and commitment are applied to matters properly political, governing ceases to be the slow but steady process of adjusting the application of political principles to practical problems and changing circumstances. Instead, it becomes the rigid enforcement of political dogma for all people and all situations without variance, which conservative thinkers detest.

Conservative thinkers reject both the extreme of a complete wall of separation between church and state and the extreme of the control of one (state or religious institutions) over the other. Neither extreme balances properly between freedom and authority. Religious institutions and government must cooperate to some extent in exercising authority. Yet freedom is protected by the separation and competition between government and religious institutions. Government should provide some support to religious institutions, but it must not define religious doctrine or control those institutions. Religious institutions must support free government; yet religious control of the State would carry a high risk of tyranny. But despite the desirability of having each support the other, conservatives believe that the two will often be antagonists. George Will believes that "tension between religion and the state is perennial because it is inevitable: religion invokes claims to an authority superior to secular authorities."[71] They believe that this tension is healthy because it fosters freedom.

Ultimately, of course, conservative thinkers support religious institutions for reasons other than their contribution to the solution of the freedom–authority tension. For all the good that a thriving set of religious institutions can do for the community, the conservative concern for the health of these institutions is not merely pragmatic, nor do conservative thinkers believe that these institutions can be properly restored if they are regarded merely as instruments for maintaining the proper political balance. As Kirk puts it, the conservative

is concerned, first of all, with the necessity for regeneration of spirit and character—the perennial problem of the inner order of the soul, the restoration of the ethical system and the religious sanction upon which any life worth living is founded. This is conservatism at its highest; but it cannot be accomplished as a deliberate program of social reform, "political Christianity." . . . Recovery of moral understanding cannot be merely a means to social restoration: it must be its own end, though it will produce social consequences. In the words of T. S. Eliot, "If you will not have God (and He is a jealous God) you should pay your respects to Hitler or Stalin."[72]

EDUCATIONAL INSTITUTIONS

Another set of institutions that conservatives believe to be part of genuine community are educational institutions. From their core ideas conservative thinkers conclude that educational institutions have a vital role to play in society, teaching the truths of the objective moral order and helping to overcome the evils and improve the strengths of man's unchanging human nature. Therefore, educational institutions must play their part in exercising authority. "In every society," asserts Stephen Tonsor, "education has served, in the first instance, to inculcate and transmit those values necessary to the continuity of ordered life in the society. . . . The current effort in America to provide a value free education is not only doomed to failure but is socially destructive."[73] It is socially destructive, conservative thinkers believe, because people, by nature, cannot live together successfully unless they are taught and persuaded to believe certain values—values based on society's perceptions of the objective moral order. Thus, "the school has an obligation to communicate and enforce those moral rules without which a society cannot function. The currently asserted notion that values are simply private prejudices is nonsense. Values are the language of social coherence."[74] The conservative view of education is at odds with what conservative thinkers see as the relativism of contemporary society. As Tonsor puts it, "Perhaps the greatest enemy of . . . education is the growing irrationalism of our society; an irrationalism which is reflected in our educational system. In part this irrationalism is the consequence of the relativization of all values and attitudes. Increasingly large segments of our society, intellectuals among them, have come to believe that every mode of thought, . . . every life style, . . . every attitude no matter how idiosyncratic, is equally valuable and legitimate so long as it is held with passionate conviction and sincerity."[75] Such a relativistic attitude, of course, is anathema to conservatives, who hold the core belief that there is an objective moral order to which people must attune their lives for their own good and for the good of others.

The primary function of educational institutions, then, is not helping children express themselves, but exercising authority to refine their character by creating within them unbreakable ethical habits and to foster intellectual and moral discipline. "The primary need of man is to perfect his spiritual being and prepare for immortality," argues Richard Weaver. Once this is recognized, "then education of the mind and the passions will take precedence over all else. The growth of materialism, however, has made this a consideration remote and even incomprehensible to the majority. . . . The prevailing conception is that education must be such as will enable one to acquire enough wealth to live on the plane of the bourgeoisie. That kind of education does not develop the aristocratic virtues. It neither encourages reflection nor inspires a reverence for the good."[76]

The fact that conservatives want education to be concerned with the inculcation of values does not mean that they wish to see government, especially the national government, involved in determining which values are to be taught. They believe such action would be inimical to freedom. Determining what values are to be taught is a local community responsibility, from their perspective. By taking out of the hands of the national government an important aspect of the exercising of authority, educational institutions help to divide authority and protect freedom. "Because values are an essential aspect of education the school must always be related in a fundamental way to community and must reflect the aspirations and ideals of both the particular and the larger community," argues Tonsor. "The participation of the community in the management of the school and the formulation and direction of its educational program is not simply an old–fashioned idea; alongside the franchise and the jury system, it is the basis of our democratic society."[77] Schools are thus an integral part of genuine community.

This is not to say that conservative thinkers wish to see the schools operating as a kind of quasi–religious institution whose chief purpose is to drill students in the proper understanding of the objective moral order. As we have seen, conservative thinkers believe that families have the primary responsibility in this area; the role of educational institutions is one of support. Values that are taught in schools "need not be taught as a cut and dried system, a kind of catechism of the American way," says Tonsor. "They may be directly and almost unconsciously appropriated from the living experience of the past which continues to speak to us from literature and history. . . . There is another and very practical way in which the civic virtues are taught in school. That is in the maintenance of decorum in the school and in athletics."[78] But note the *almost* in Tonsor's statement. The teaching of values is not the teacher's chief concern; it occurs best as a by–product of a good education. But neither should teachers ignore their responsibility in this regard. Conservatives believe that the teaching of values must remain a conscious goal of education, a goal that is tied to the community's perception of the objective moral order.

SUMMARY

For conservatives, human life is at its best when lived within the influences of genuine community. Each institution cares for its members and helps them in certain aspects of their lives, without infringing the proper sphere of other institutions. Each does its share to help its members overcome the defects of their human nature and attune their lives to the objective moral order.

NOTES

1. Molnar, *Authority*, pp. 63, 79.

2. Will, "Who Put?" p. 108.

3. Meyer, *In Defense*, p. 140.

4. Kirk, *Beyond*, p. 99.

5. Kendall, *Affirmation*, p. 91.

6. Molnar, *Authority*, pp. 10–11; see also Hallowell, *Moral Foundation*, pp. 84–85.

7. Kirk, "Humane Political Economy," *Modern Age* 3 (Summer 1959), p. 226.

8. Molnar, *Authority*, p. 10.

9. Buckley, *Jeweler's Eye*, p. 311.

10. Meyer, *In Defense*, p. 130; see also John Chamberlain, *Roots*, p. 178.

11. One example is Molnar, *Authority*.

12. For example, see Nisbet, "Conservatism and Sociology," *American Journal of Sociology* 58 (1952), p. 169; Kirk, *Conservative Mind*, pp. 17 and 29; Hallowell, *Moral Foundation*, p. 85; and Molnar, *Authority*, p. 25.

13. Kirk, *Program*, p. 227.

14. Meyer, *In Defense*, p. 146.

15. Ibid., pp. 164–65.

16. Wilhelmsen, *Christianity and Political Philosophy*, p. 172.

17. Tonsor, "Conservative Search," in Meyer, ed., *What Is Conservatism?*, p. 150.

18. Will, *Pursuit of Virtue*, p. 92.

19. Kirk, *Beyond*, p. 99. See also Molnar, *Authority*, pp. 90–91; Nisbet, *Twilight*, pp. 6 and 48; Tonsor, "Conservative Search," p. 142; and Wilhelmsen, *Christianity and Political Philosophy*, p. 163.

20. Nisbet, *Twilight*, p. 74.

21. Kirk, *Program*, p. 263.

22. Morley, *Freedom and Federalism*, p. 12.

23. See Nisbet, *Twilight*, pp. 75–77.

24. Kirk, *Program*, p. 227.

25. Molnar, *Authority*, p. 108.

26. Kirk, *Program*, p. 229.

27. Kirk, *Conservative Mind*, p. 450.

28. Ibid., p. 18.

29. Tonsor, "The New Natural Law and the Problem of Equality," *Modern Age* 24 (Summer 1980), p. 243.

30. Burnham, *Suicide*, p. 107. See also Weaver, *Ideas Have Consequences*, p. 35; Weaver, *Southern Tradition*, pp. 392–94; and Kuehnelt–Leddihn, "Portland Declaration," p. 1190.

31. Nisbet, *Twilight*, p. 238.

32. Kirk, *Program*, p. 227.

33. Kirk, *Program*, p. 240.

34. Nisbet, *Twilight*, p. 238.

35. Molnar, *Authority*, p. 24. See also Weaver, *Southern Tradition*, p. 49; Wilhelmsen, *Christianity and Political Philosophy*, p. 163; and Zoll, *The Twentieth Century Mind* (Baton Rouge, 1967), pp. 126–27.

36. Weaver, *Ideas Have Consequences*, p. 36.

37. Meyer, *In Defense*, p. 69.

38. Weaver, *Southern Tradition*, p. 36. See also Kirk, *Conservative Mind*, p. 18; and Kuehnelt–Leddihn, "Portland Declaration," p. 1190.

39. Zoll, *Twentieth Century Mind*, pp. 124–25.

40. Weaver, *Ideas Have Consequences*, p. 36.

41. Nisbet, *Twilight*, p. 239.

42. Kirk, *Conservative Mind*, p. 18.

43. Weaver, *Ideas Have Consequences*, pp. 41–45.

44. Kirk, *Program*, pp. 247–48.

45. Molnar, *Authority*, p. 33.

46. Kuehnelt–Leddihn, "Portland Declaration," p. 1193.

47. Molnar, *Authority*, p. 9.

48. Ibid.

49. Kuehnelt–Leddihn, "Portland Declaration," p. 1190.

50. Meyer, *In Defense*, p. 140.

51. Kirk, *Conservative Mind*, p. 450.

52. Will, *Pursuit of Virtue*, pp. 113, 114.

53. See also the discussion of this point in chapter 5.

54. See, for example, Molnar, *Authority*, pp. 32–33; and Will, *Pursuit of Virtue*, p. 92.

55. Kirk, *Conservative Mind*, p. 450.

56. Will, *Pursuit of Virtue*, p. 114.

57. See, for example, Kuehnelt–Leddihn, "Portland Declaration," p. 1190; and Will, *Pursuit of Virtue*, pp. 92 and 113–14.

58. Weaver, *Ideas Have Consequences*, p. 177.

59. Will, "Armies Should Win Wars," *Newsweek* (18 February 1981), p. 120.

60. Kuehnelt–Leddihn, "Portland Declaration," p. 1190.

61. Even here there is some disagreement among conservative thinkers. All conservatives agree that women should not be conscripted into combat. But not all agree that women should be prevented from voluntarily becoming part of combat units.

62. Kuehnelt–Leddihn, "Portland Declaration," p. 1189.

63. Tonsor, "Conservative Search," p. 149. See also Kirk, *Conservative Mind*, p. 43.

64. Ibid., p. 150.

65. Viereck, *Conservatism Revisited*, p. 26.

66. Kirk, "Promises and Perils of 'Christian Politics,' " *Intercollegiate Review* 18 (Fall/Winter 1982), p. 21.

67. Tonsor, "Conservative Search," pp. 149–50.

68. Ibid., p. 150.

69. Kirk, "Promises," p. 22.

70. Ibid., p. 14.

71. Will, *Pursuit of Virtue*, p. 92.

72. Kirk, *Conservative Mind*, p. 449.

73. Tonsor, "Educating," p. 258–59.

74. Ibid., p. 259. See also Molnar, *Authority*, p. 33.

75. Ibid., p. 262. See also Will, *Pursuit of Virtue*, p. 25; and Weaver, *Ideas Have Consequences* p. 8.

76. Weaver, *Ideas Have Consequences*, p. 49. See also Will, *Pursuit of Virtue*, p. 25; Viereck, *Conservatism Revisited*, p. 10; and Kuehnelt–Leddihn, "Portland Declaration," p. 1193.

77. Tonsor, "Educating," p. 259. See also Weaver, *Ethics of Rhetoric*, p. 45ff.

78. Ibid., pp. 259, 260.

8

CHANGE AND TRADITION

Respect for tradition and the wisdom of the past is a distinguishing characteristic of contemporary American conservative thought. Tradition is so significant in conservative thinking that some people, including some conservative thinkers, see respect for tradition as the chief mark of conservatism. James Burnham, for instance, believes that "the attitude toward tradition probably furnishes the most accurate shibboleth for distinguishing conservatives from liberals. We may put the question this way: does the fact that a particular institution or mode of social conduct has been established for some while create a presumption in favor of continuing it? To this question a conservative will answer with a definite Yes; and a liberal with No, or 'very little.' "[1]

To the extent that conservatives share a common view of tradition because of the influence of the core ideas they share, Burnham's statement is true. And to the same extent those who define conservatism as a rejection of change or a defense of the status quo are on the right track. But such a definition of contemporary American conservative thought is insufficient. The conservative attitude toward change and tradition is more complex. It is only understandable when we see how it flows from the two core ideas of an objective moral order and an unchanging human nature.

TRADITION AND THE CORE IDEAS

Conservative thinkers see tradition as one of the best sources of knowledge of the truths of the objective moral order. Given their view of human nature, they believe that tradition is generally a better source of this crucial knowledge than reason. Reason alone is insufficient to find these absolute truths and to translate them into institutions and ways of living. People are unable to create in the abstract a social order or even to order their individual lives, without the aid of tradition and custom. Awareness of these limits inherent in human nature should lead, conservative thinkers believe, to humility and to respect for the insights and experiences of past generations, accepting them as part of the total reality. Conservatives believe that tradition reinforces this wariness about man's ability to understand and the need for man to be guided by inherited wisdom. "Awareness of the past is an antidote to both egotism and shallow optimism," argues Richard Weaver. "It restrains optimism because it teaches us to be cautious about man's perfectibility and to put a sober estimate on schemes to renovate the species."[2] Therefore tradition and the status quo must be granted a presumption of approximating the objective moral order because by nature man is unlikely to discover the truths of the objective moral order on his own.

Conservative thinkers therefore seek to conserve tradition and the status quo, but not primarily or necessarily just because it exists or is old or venerable. What they really wish to conserve is what is eternally true, the truths of the objective moral order. Yet because man's ability to perceive these truths is limited, conservatives believe that we should hold a presumption in favor of the traditional (or the orthodox—see chapter 4) as an approximation of the true, as proven over time by experience, by wise men, and by divine revelation. The antiquity of a value, belief, institution, or custom is a probable sign of its goodness, for if it has endured in the traditions of a society it is probably because the members of that society have found it good. As Russell Kirk puts it, conservatives believe that "by trial and error, by revelation, by the insights of men of genius, mankind has acquired, slowly and painfully, over thousands of years, a knowledge of human nature and of the civil social order which no one individual possibly can supplant by private rationality." "It is folly to ignore this inherited wisdom in favor of our own arrogant little notions of right and wrong, of profit and loss, of justice and injustice."[3] Traditional wisdom and the order it has established are more likely to approximate the moral order than are the efforts of any one individual or generation. It is wise and pious, Weaver argues, to accept the people of past generations, "their words and deeds, as part of the total reality, not to be ignored. . . . Are those who died heroes' and martyrs' deaths really dead? It is not an idle question. In a way, they live on as forces, helping to shape our dream of the world."[4]

The conservative regard for tradition is based on "the conviction that there is an order more than human," asserts Russell Kirk.[5] Tradition teaches about this order, expressing "a spreading mystery too great for our knowledge to compass," as Richard Weaver claims.[6] Or as Frederick Wilhelmsen puts it, "A sense of the sacred lies over all things, and man . . . [should be] content simply to 'let being be.' If modern man is the Demiurge who reworks creation in his own image, traditional man—even as he survives into our day—is the man who celebrates the things that are."[7] To understand what conservative thinkers mean by these kinds of statements is crucial to understanding their view of tradition. In their view, the objective moral order is unchanging. Living in accordance with this order is what brings individual happiness and social order. By nature, all people desire such happiness and are capable of attaining some measure of it, but only to the extent that they live in harmony with the truths of the moral order. By experience they learn something of what can make them truly happy, and this they cherish and attempt to preserve. The longer something has endured and the more that it has been regarded as good, the more likely it is to actually be good. Therefore, whatever is—what endures and is regarded as good, or what Wilhelmsen calls "being"—must be presumed to have some value. Conservative thinkers acknowledge that evil persists, too. Prostitution has endured, and given their view of human nature, they believe that it will continue. But despite human weakness in repeatedly succumbing to this temptation, prostitution has not been regarded as good by most people—it is always outlawed and condemned.

Conservative thinkers realize that truth transcends tradition. It transcends the wisdom of any age or of any institution, no matter how ancient or venerable. But conservatives believe that truth is no enemy to tradition. Tradition can reveal some of the truth, but never the whole, yet man must live by what tradition does reveal. The conservative view of man precludes the clear and unambiguous perception of truth. Absolute, universal truths exist, they believe, but we see them as through a glass darkly. That is not the same as not seeing them at all, however. With the aid of tradition—the accumulated wisdom gained through revelation, experience, and the insights of genius—we can come to see much of what is on the other side of that glass. What is perceived can and must be used to shape society and one's own life. But one may never be confident of having a complete and clear vision of those truths, and conservative thinkers are suspicious of anyone who claims to see the content of the objective moral order without limitation or qualification.

Conservatives warn that the limitations of tradition should not lead us to try to understand the world solely in terms of reason. "Theory divorced from experience is infinitely dangerous," Kirk warns. "No James Mill, however learned, can rightfully make laws for India."[8] "Every society has its roots in a particular historical tradition," John Hallowell reminds us. "It was one of the weaknesses of liberalism that it tended to ignore these roots and to exalt abstract reason to the neglect of custom and tradition."[9]

For all its value, tradition is not regarded by conservative thinkers as the only guide, nor as always beneficent. Respect for tradition does not exclude the need for the use of reason. In its rightful role, tradition serves as a guide to the operation of reason, not as a means to suppress reason. There must, as Wilhelmsen suggests, be a presumption "in favor of age in our evaluation of the decency of a political order" and of other institutions and of beliefs, "but this presumption must be tested."[10] Conservatives believe that the proper tool for that evaluation is reason, used in the light of experience. After all, conservatives believe that the consensus of modern American society has strayed far from the genuine tradition of Western civilization, so that tradition alone is inadequate to combat the liberal, collectivist consensus. Thus reason has an essential role to play. As Gerhart Niemeyer reminds us, the conservative position on reason "has been an argument not against reason but against intellectual *hubris* and a call to heed the fence posts of reality."[11]

But we must never forget, conservatives warn, that reason alone is insufficient as a means to discover truth. We must remember "the finite bounds of the purview of any one man or any one generation," as Frank Meyer puts it, and "employ reason in the context of continuing tradition."[12] Men must employ their reason to attempt to restore an understanding of truth and an expression of it in institutions and customs when it appears that the tradition of their nation has gone astray; but it is to the authentic tradition of the West, what conservative thinkers often refer to as the Great Tradition, and not to their own speculations that they must look for the source of that understanding and to get guidance on how they might structure their institutions to support and give expression to that understanding. Tradition is superior to reason as a guide to the truths of the objective moral order. It is the Great Tradition that is the chief standard against which the tradition of any particular nation or age can be judged by reason.

Because of these beliefs, conservative thinkers argue that conservatism is not an ideology, with predetermined answers for all problems in all circumstances, without reference to precedents and to limiting and shaping historical conditions. William Buckley argues that "conservatives are sufficiently anti–ideological to resist totally closed systems which do not provide for deep and continuing mysteries."[13] Conservatives write and act not on what Kirk calls "bodiless abstraction," but "on the foundation of convention, custom, and historic experience."[14] This means not that conservatives do not embrace principles, but that they draw those principles from tradition rather than from abstraction.

Furthermore, conservative thinkers do not believe that there is necessarily one best form for the institutions and customs that attempt to express the truths of the objective moral order. "It is only the rationalist mentality," asserts Wilhelmsen, "enamored of books and degrees, ignorant of history and innocent of the mystery of life," that insists on judging societies on the basis of:

an abstract company of essences inhabiting a ghostly republic of ideals foreign to the rhythm of being and becoming. A venerable society, born in necessity, nurtured in courage and annealed in conflict, is the creation of experience. It throws around itself a mythic cape woven of symbols—poetic, social, religious—representing its marriage with reality and its compromise with the absolute. These symbols cannot be penetrated by reason. They touch the springs of being and there sounds about them the drama of salvation and damnation.

Before a society toughened by the impact of nature and hallowed by the passage of time, the wise halt in contemplation and wonder. Only the rationalist presumes to judge the goodness of an ancient community by an unreal and abstract standard of what society and government ought to be.[15]

Conservatives attempt to preserve the tradition and roots they find, treating the existing and enduring institutions with a respect sometimes bordering on awe. As Gerhart Niemeyer notes, "in essence, conservative theorizing has consisted in attempts to restate the understandings on which a given country actually was based."[16]

Another reason the conservative thinkers prefer tradition to reason is that, according to the conservative view of human nature, reason is insufficient to hold men to obedience to the truth. As Kirk points out, men are "kept obedient to a moral law chiefly by the force of habit and custom."[17] Customs and institutions can help restrain man's bad intentions, helping him to overcome his evil tendencies and achieve self–mastery. It is for this reason that Richard Weaver believes that

forms and conventions are the ladder of ascent. In the way that our cognition passes from a report of particular details to a knowledge of universals, so our sentiments pass from a welter of feelings to an illumined concept of what one ought to feel. This is known as refinement. Man is in the world to suffer his passion; but wisdom comes to his relief with an offer of conventions, which shape and elevate that passion. . . . Thus we invariably find in the man of true culture a deep respect for forms. He approaches even those he does not understand with awareness that a deep thought lies in an old observance. Such respect distinguishes him from the barbarian, on the one hand, and the degenerate, on the other.[18]

Conservatives believe that tradition provides a definition of morality in behavior and in social organization. It gives to a people, says Eliseo Vivas, "the forms through which their more or less clear conceptions of excellence are expressed."[19] Tradition provides forms and definitions that can guide good intentions to fruitful results.

Among the most important elements of tradition are the beliefs and prejudices that are accepted without question. Conservatives believe that these spare us the effort and pain of having to experiment in all things ourselves and the danger of having to make moral decisions solely on a case by case basis. To the extent that tradition expresses the truths of the objective moral order, and to the extent that these truths become part of us—become "internalized, turned into a self–improving conviction" as Thomas Molnar puts it[20]—tradition becomes sound prejudice, and, according to Niemeyer, conservatives praise "the prejudices that are the embodiment of the experiences of generations."[21] The guidance of sound prejudice helps us overcome the temptation of passion and the misguidance of ignorance and inexperience.

With the restraints of custom and tradition abandoned or weakened in the modern world, conservative thinkers see violence, hatred, and moral disintegration. With veneration for tradition gone, only force can prevent disorder, both in the soul and in society. That is what Wilhelmsen is referring to when, as we have seen, he describes the modern world as "abstract perfection running riot, uniting with a subterranean passion, divorced from the constraints of tradition."[22]

Another of the functions of tradition is to teach men a common world view. As we have seen already in the discussion of authority, conservative thinkers believe that a common world view is necessary for common endeavor. A shared tradition links people together, acting as an essential social cement, "the more so as we proceed from a small well–linked group like the family, to larger and heterogeneous groups like the community of believers in a church or the citizens of a nation," as Thomas Molnar argues. Traditional "rites and symbols make up for the unity that is lacking in the group where individuals do not know each other. And these rites and symbols are the more effective as their origin reaches further back, because then the participants feel linked to each other not only horizontally, but also to the long line of ancestors in the past and descendants in the future."[23] This shared view of the world also helps men make sense of their lives and experiences. As Weaver tells us, conservatives believe that tradition presents a "way of looking at the world through an aggregation of symbols, so that empirical facts take on significance."[24]

The conservative belief in an unchanging human nature influences their attitude toward change in yet another way. Conservative thinkers tend to support the status quo not because they see the status quo as an end in itself, but because they see the preservation of the status quo as a means of ensuring the stability required by the nature of man. They believe that human beings in general are not able to cope intellectually or psychologically with rapid or continual change. If man is to have some measure of control over his life and some measure of meaning in that life, he must have stability and continuity. Man is a creature of habit, he takes comfort in the familiar and the accustomed. That does not mean that conservative thinkers believe that man is entirely static. By nature he also has a yearning for the excitement of innovation. Some of those excitements are merely passing phenomena, ephemeral changes; man requires stability to prevent those changes from destroying the framework of his life. Other innovations are more significant and enduring and must be incorporated into that framework; this too requires stability. Preserving the status quo helps to provide this stability.

Conservative thinkers also oppose change because it threatens other things that they believe are required by unchanging human nature and the objective moral order. Conservatives believe that nearly everything discussed in the last chapters that they regard as good—authority, freedom, orthodoxy, community, hierarchy—require stability, the absence of radical change, and the support of tradition and custom.

THE MEANING OF TRADITION

Since conservatives in general favor tradition over change, what do they mean by tradition? They are referring to the understanding gained through experience by people in the past and transmitted to later generations, or as Burnham puts it, tradition is "social experience acting through time."[25] Kirk amplifies this definition, stating that "tradition . . . means received opinions, convictions religious and moral and political and aesthetic passed down from generation to generation, so that they are accepted by most men as a matter of course."[26] These received opinions include not only conscious convictions but also a people's myths. The best of these myths contain the understanding, however partial, that past generations gained of absolute truths that are beyond rational understanding. Thus Kirk says that "great myths are not merely susceptible of rational interpretation: they *are* truth, transcendent truth."[27]

When conservative thinkers speak of reverence for the past and for the wisdom of the past, they are not speaking of any particular period or group as having attained a complete understanding of the truth, nor do they wish to return to any particular time or place. "In truth," says Kirk, "great political ideas transcend particular institutions and periods. The reflecting conservative adheres not to some idealized historical era, but to what Dr. Leo Strauss calls 'the Great Tradition.' "[28] As Meyer puts it, "the conservative is committed to conserve not simply whatever happens to be the established conditions, but the real consensus of his civilization as that consensus reflects truth drawn from the very constitution of being."[29]

Willmoore Kendall identifies this Great Tradition as composed of Greek classical philosophy, the teachings of the Old and New Testaments, and Christian theology.[30] Russell Kirk agrees, singling out Aristotle, Cicero, the Fathers of the Church, the Schoolmen, and the great English divines for particular mention, while in another place he speaks more broadly of "Christian faith (with its Judaic roots); the Roman and medieval heritage of ordered liberty; and the continuity of great 'Western' literature."[31] Of course conservative thinkers disagree on the precise content of the Great Tradition, just as they disagree on the content of the objective moral order. But whatever figures or groups conservative thinkers point to as contributors to the Great Tradition or bearers of it, what they are trying to identify are not the peculiar features of a single nation's inheritance, but what Frank Meyer calls "the authentic tradition of the West."[32] "Our normative inheritance in the United States is of European and Asiatic origin," argues Kirk. "Normality does not recognize frontiers. . . . It is a legacy of belief, not of blood."[33] What conservatives are striving to preserve are the values found good by what they regard as all civilized peoples. Thus Viereck claims that "common sense is the oracle of conservatism—the common and universal sense of mankind, the value common to every civilized society and creed."[34]

However, conservatives believe, as Kirk puts it, that the truths contained in this Great Tradition "cannot be divorced from the historical experience of a people."[35] Man is unable to create completely new institutions and values, even when trying to embody the truths conveyed by tradition in new forms. To be successful in making improvements, man must build on the foundations left him by his predecessors, respecting the wisdom that went into the creating of those foundations and the historical experience that they represent. "Every society has its roots in a particular historical tradition," John Hallowell reminds us. "It was one of the weaknesses of liberalism that it tended to ignore these roots and to exalt abstract reason to the neglect of custom and tradition."[36] Conservative thinkers believe that those foundations must be brought into closer harmony with the moral order, but they also believe that the historical experience of a nation or people must not be ignored. We can never know for sure how close a particular tradition is to the true order of things. For this reason, as Niemeyer reminds us, conservative thinking has usually consisted of "attempts to restate the understandings on which a given country actually was based. . . . It might elucidate the connection between the political system and the underlying transcendental truth, or recall the prejudices that are the embodiment of the experiences of generations, or the emotional patterns of political allegiance, or the principles of political and legal tradition to which the people have been attuned."[37] There is some disagreement among conservative thinkers about how much respect is due any particular tradition, regardless of its content. Yet all recognize that just as no particular tradition exactly matches all truth, so no tradition is empty of truth. This acknowledgment, when coupled with their belief that men cannot endure rapid change, even from falsehood to truth, dictates respect for particular traditions.

It is in this context that we can understand the attitude of conservative thinkers to the American tradition. Conservative thinkers believe that the American tradition of beliefs and institutions expresses much of this Great Tradition, even that it has contributed to it through such things as the Declaration of Independence, the Constitution, and the debates at the time of the adoption of the Constitution. But they do not think that American values, beliefs, and institutions comprise the whole of the Great Tradition, or that everything in the American tradition rightfully belongs in that Great Tradition.

For all these reasons, conservative thinkers accept as a general principle the need to avoid change and to foster the acceptance of tradition. As Russell Kirk argues, a guiding conservative principle must be: "never disturb, except under the greatest necessity, a thing that is at rest."[38]

CHANGE

Yet there are also compelling reasons for contemporary American conservative thinkers to favor change. Since conservative thinkers do not regard tradition as sufficient or infallible, they recognize that certain circumstances can make change desirable. Despite their defense of the status quo in general as a defense against chaos, many conservatives are profoundly alienated from the present status quo. As Eliseo Vivas puts it, "one of the essential marks of decency today is to be ashamed of being a man of the twentieth century."[39] Kirk's dictum that we must "never disturb, except under the greatest necessity, a thing that is at rest" is coupled with the recognition that "that dread necessity, however, is upon us; the conservatism of enjoyment must be exchanged for the conservatism of labor."[40] They feel this necessity chiefly because of their view of the modern world.

Frederick Wilhelmsen sums up the conservative view of the modern world in this fashion: "Abstract perfection running riot, uniting with a subterranean passion, divorced from the constraints of tradition and fed by a resentment born of boredom; this is the modern world."[41] That is, they see the worst in man—abstract reason and untamed passion—fostered in the modern world, while the best means of knowing the objective moral order and of convincing men to live according to this order are ignored. Thus their hostility to modernity stems from their core ideas. The conservative movement involves a spirit of resistance to the modern world, or at least to certain prominent trends of it, even if it appears that this resistance is doomed to failure. Frank Meyer argues that the conservative is one "who will set his face against [the wave of the present] if he finds it bad—even if this means he will be dashed to pieces on the rocks."[42]

Conservative thinkers reject much of the twentieth century because they believe that the twentieth century rejects the truths of the objective moral order. The forms and conventions that the modern world rejects are necessary, conservatives think, to express absolute truths and encourage men to obey them. The rejection of these truths has led to moral confusion. Frederick Wilhelmsen believes that the fact "that a million children can be aborted in New York in one year with hardly a ripple of protest and that the Watergate bugging case, a moral triviality, can produce a storm of protest around the nation indicates that our moral priorities are somehow perverse."[43]

Under these circumstances, conservative thinkers acknowledge that change is necessary, that the present state of affairs requires change in order to better express and support truth. Frank Meyer expresses the conservative position in this manner:

What the conservative is committed to conserve is not simply whatever happens to be the established conditions of a few years or a few decades, but the consensus of his civilization, of his country, as that consensus over the centuries has reflected truth derived from the very constitution of being. We are today historically in a situation created by . . . slow and insidious revolution at home and . . . violent open revolution abroad. To conserve the true and the good under these circumstances is to restore an understanding (and a social structure reflecting that understanding) which has been all but buried; it is not to preserve the transient customs and prescriptions of the present.[44]

As Meyer points out, "either the whole historical and social situation in which [conservatives] find themselves, including the development of collectivism, statism, and intellectual anarchy, is Providential, . . . or there is a higher sanction than prescription and tradition; there are standards of truth and good; . . . in which case reason, operating against the background of tradition, is the faculty upon which they must depend."[45] In other words, the existence of an objective moral order means that any particular tradition may be criticized, indeed that it must be. That is, although conservative thinkers believe that there is no one best form of representing and expressing the truths of the objective moral order and that great respect is due existing traditions, they believe that they can and must attempt to differentiate between good and bad forms and seek to reconcile existing traditions with the best available understanding of the truth, drawn not just from the consensus of their own contemporary society but from both the past of their society and the larger Western civilization.

They believe that it is necessary for conservatives to strive to carefully and gradually bring present institutions and beliefs into closer harmony with the best understanding they have of the truths of the moral order. They acknowledge the need for reasoned evaluation of a particular tradition and the need for change when traditional beliefs, customs, and institutions degenerate from the patterns dictated by the Great Tradition and the objective moral order. Consequently, conservative thinkers believe that one of their first tasks must be frank criticism of present society, of the status quo. This means, says Weaver, that the "conservative is sometimes found fighting quite briskly for change."[46]

Speaking of modern problems, Kirk says: "I hope that conservatives will encounter these troubles in the light of the wisdom of their ancestors; yet precedent alone will not suffice to rescue American society from its present distresses. The modern conservative must improvise and create, as well as obey prejudice and prescription."[47] Kendall recommends to his fellow conservatives the example of Burke, who wanted not only to preserve his heritage but to preserve *and* improve it "in the interest of an expanding justice and an ever–greater well–being for the country as a whole."[48]

One kind of change that from the conservative perspective may become necessary at any time is the altering of the expression of permanent principles to make them understandable and effective in changed circumstances. William F. Buckley, Jr., for instance, argues that ancient truths need modern formulations, not because they have ceased to be true—an impossibility, given the conservative belief in an objective moral order—nor because they do not fit present society, "but because the idiom of life is always changing, and we need to say things in such a way as to get inside the vibrations of modern life."[49]

It may also be necessary at times to change the forms, conventions, and institutions that give force to these unchanging truths. This is particularly true when these beliefs and institutions have gone astray, as conservative thinkers believe has happened in the modern world. Thus Meyer asserts that we must establish "in new circumstances forms of thought and institutional arrangements which will express the truth of the great tradition of the West."[50] Change may be necessary not only to better express unchanging truths, but to more closely approximate those truths as experience brings greater insight about them. Weaver reminds us that conservatives must distinguish "between respect for tradition because it is tradition and respect for it because it expresses a spreading mystery too great for our knowledge to compass." The first is idolatry; the second is reverence and is creative, allowing for change and development.[51]

Conservative thinkers reject much of the twentieth century not only because the twentieth century rejects the truths of the objective moral order, but also because it encourages an untamed human nature. Richard Weaver, for instance, believes that throughout the modern world "there are dangerous signs that culture, as such, is marked for attack because its formal requirements stand in the way of the expression of the natural man."[52] Conservatives belive that men must be taught and persuaded to obey eternal truths, but the forms, conventions, and beliefs that could do that are being rejected in the modern world. Instead, modern society has accepted false views of human nature and of life, what Weaver calls "a sickly metaphysical dream. . . . Somewhere, moreover, the metaphysicians of publicity have absorbed the idea that the goal of life is happiness through comfort. It is a state of complacency supposed to ensue when the physical appetites have been well satisfied. Advertising fosters the concept, social democracy approves it, and the acceptance is so wide that it is virtually impossible today, except from the religious rostrum, to teach that life means discipline and sacrifice."[53]

A good example of the conservatives' view that human nature is misunderstood in modern society can be seen in their criticism of modern science. They see science as a particular culprit in the corruption of modernity. As a tool in man's quest to both understand and control himself and the world, science has an appropriate and respected place. But conservatives believe that science is regarded by many people, including many of its practitioners, as a messiah, a false messiah from the conservative perspective. Science is believed to offer the potential to reveal unambiguous truth about man and the world, banish mystery, and solve all man's problems. Conservatives regard these as false claims. They believe that there are aspects of human suffering that can never be solved because they are part of the human condition. Man can never know all truth, certainly not through his own efforts, unaided by God. Science thus feeds man's hubris and leads him to have unfulfillable expectations of ease and comfort, unfitting him for the struggle necessary for him to attain his moral purpose, the achievement of virtue. Therefore, conservatives regard science as being impious toward God and toward nature, and they consider scientists poor guides to the way we ought to live our lives and organize our societies.[54]

Conservative thinkers believe that by nature people need stability. As we have seen, they believe that human beings in general are not able to cope intellectually or psychologically with rapid or continual change. Necessary change must not destroy that stability but must be of such a nature and be introduced in such a way that people can cope with it without damage to the framework of their lives.

And necessary change must take into account the need for a

strong presumption in favor of established beliefs and institutions, conservatives believe, and must come only after "very sober consideration of ultimate consequences."[55] Even institutions, customs, and beliefs that are clearly defective might be better left alone unless careful consideration shows that significant gains will outweigh any unforeseen and detrimental consequences.[56] There must be urgent and express reasons for any change. Whatever change is undertaken after such sober reflection should be guided by permanent principles drawn from the Great Tradition. Changes that are necessary must be reconciled with the best in the old order. As Kirk puts it, conservatives "seek, reasonably and prudently, to reconcile the best in the wisdom of our ancestors with the change which is essential to a vigorous civil social existence."[57] Therefore, change must be slow so that it does not disrupt what is still good in the old order of things.

Furthermore, Kirk asserts that conservatives must recognize that "change and reform are not identical, and that innovation is a devouring conflagration more often than it is a torch of progress. Society must alter, for slow change is the means of its conservation, like the human body's perpetual renewal; but Providence is the proper instrument for change, and the test of a statesman is his cognizance of the real tendency of Providential social forces," so that he may support and shape those forces to accomplish appropriate change in the appropriate manner and at the appropriate time.[58]

Therefore, if change is to be truly beneficial to individuals and societies, "evolution is to be preferred to revolution," as Viereck argues, "because it is less disruptive to the moral and psychological framework."[59] For these reasons conservative thinkers do not believe they are inconsistent when as a general policy they resist proposed changes, yet accommodate and even come to defend a change once it has been accomplished. They do not claim that every reform is evil, merely that much reform is, especially if attempted wholesale and pell–mell. But if, once a reform has been accomplished, its fruits are found to be good, they believe there is nothing inconsistent in accepting it; they can do so without giving up principled opposition to change in general and more specifically to rapid and fundamental change. However, conservatives do not believe that principled opposition to change should become categorical, blind opposition. Nor do they believe that their arguments against change in general require them to accept whatever happens to exist merely because it exists. George Will derides the argument of "some liberals . . . [that] liberalism promotes change, conservatism respects tradition and precedent, so when liberals are in power they should institute whatever changes please them, and when conservatives are in power they should treat liberal precedents as hallowed traditions. Conservatives are not delighted with this division of political labor."[60]

SUMMARY

Conservative thinkers believe that in a healthy society both preservation and change are necessary, but the changes they desire are primarily aimed at restoring what should have been preserved but has not been. In the words of Russell Kirk:

Coleridge says that there are two great elements in any society, its Permanence and its Progression. The Permanence of a state, roughly speaking, is its conservative interest; its Progression, what nowadays we call its liberal interest. There are ages in which intelligent people would do well to ally themselves with the Progression of their nation, to contend against stagnation; for a society without the means of renewal is not long for this world. But our time is not such an age. Our modern peril, rather, is that the traditions of civility will be swallowed up in the rush of appetite and will; with us the expectation of change is greater than the expectation of continuity, and generation scarcely links with generation. In the twentieth century, it is our Permanence, not our Progression, which needs the assistance of thinking men and women.[61]

Conservative thinkers consequently place more emphasis on tradition than on change, which is probably why some people define conservatism as resistance to change. But seeing how conservatives' attitudes to change and tradition flow from their core beliefs gives a clearer understanding of conservatives' beliefs.

NOTES

1. Burnham, *Congress*, p. 30. See also Kirk, *Conservative Mind*, p. 17; and Kendall, *Conservative*, p. 99.

2. Weaver, *Ideas Have Consequences*, p. 177.

3. Kirk, "Prescription," p. 28, and *Enemies*, p. 29.

4. Weaver, *Ideas Have Consequences*, p. 176–77.

5. Kirk, *Program*, p. 41.

6. Weaver, "Up From Liberalism," p. 28.

7. Wilhelmsen, "The Conservative Vision," p. 297. See also Zoll, *Twentieth Century Political Philosophy*, p. 128; and Kirk, *Conservative Mind*, p. 18.

8. Kirk, "Prescription," p. 39.

9. Hallowell, *Moral Foundation*, pp. 85–86. See also Kirk, "Prescription," p. 39; and Buckley, *Did You Ever Seen a Dream Walking?* pp. xxxv–xxxvii.

10. Wilhelmsen, *Christianity and Political Philosophy*, p. 19. See also Kirk, *Program*, p. 305; and Meyer, *What Is Conservatism?* p. 16.

11. Niemeyer, Review of Clinton Rossiter's *Conservatism in America*, (Fall 1955), p. 443.

12. Meyer, *What Is Conservatism?* p. 11. See also Kirk, *Program*, p. 110.

13. Buckley, *Dream*, p. 5.

14. Kirk, Letter to the Editor, *National Review* 33 (13 November 1981), p. 1334. See also Wilhelmsen, *Christianity and Political Philosophy*, p. 20; and Will, *Pursuit of Virtue*, pp. 45, 83.

15. Wilhelmsen, "The Conservative Vision," p. 298.

16. Niemeyer, Review of Clinton Rossiter's *Conservatism in America*, p. 443. See also Viereck, "The Rootless 'Roots': Defects in the New Conservatism," *Antioch Review* 15 (June 1955), p. 219.

17. Kirk, *Conservative Mind*, p. 27.

18. Weaver, *Ideas Have Consequences*, pp. 22–23, 26. See also Kirk, *Conservative Mind*, pp. 18 and 51; and Molnar, *Authority*, p. 33.

19. Vivas, *Moral Life*, p. 26.

20. Molnar, *Authority*, p. 57.

21. Niemeyer, Review of Clinton Rossiter's *Conservatism in America*, p. 443.

22. Wilhelmsen, "Conservative Vision," p. 299. See also Burnham, "Notes," p. 1286; Kirk, *Conservative Mind*, p. 51; Kirk, *Program*, p. 31; Molnar, *Authority*, p. 33; and Weaver, *Ideas Have Consequences*, p. 2.

23. Molnar, *Authority*, p. 44. See also Weaver, *Ideas Have Consequences*, p. 21.

24. Weaver, *Ideas Have Consequences*, p. 19.

25. Burnham, *Congress*, p. 25. See also Kirk, *Program*, p. 302.

26. Kirk, "Prescription," p. 27. See also Wilhelmsen, *Christianity and Political Philosophy*, p. 29.

27. Kirk, *Program*, p. 15.

28. Kirk, "Conservatism Is Not an Ideology," *National Review* 12 (30 January 1962), pp. 59, 74.

29. Meyer, "Freedom, Tradition, Conservatism," p. 10. See also Viereck, *Conservatism Revisited*, p. 5; Kirk, "Conservatism Is Not an Ideology," pp. 59, 74; and Kendall, *Affirmation*, chapter 5.

30. See Kendall, *Affirmation*, pp. 93–94.

31. See Kirk, *Program*, p. 26, *Enemies*, p. 30.

32. Meyer, "The Separation of Powers," *National Review* 12 (30 January 1962), p. 59. See also Will, *Pursuit of Virtue*, p. 32.

33. Kirk, *Enemies*, pp. 29–30.

34. Viereck, "But—I'm a Conservative!" p. 539.

35. Kirk, "Prescription," p. 39.

36. Hallowell, *Moral Foundation*, pp. 85–86.

37. Niemeyer, Review of Clinton Rossiter's *Conservatism in America*, p. 443. See also Kendall, *Affirmation*, p. ix; and Kirk, "Norms, Conventions, and the South," *Modern Age* 2 (Fall 1958), p. 343.

38. Kirk, *Program*, p. 8.

39. Vivas, *Moral Life*, p. x. See also Buckley, *Dream*, pp. xxxv–xxxvii; and Kirk, *Program*, p. 24.

40. Kirk, *Program*, p. 8.

41. Wilhelmsen, "Conservative Vision," p. 299.

42. Meyer, *In Defense*, p. 52.

43. Wilhelmsen, *Christianity and Political Philosophy*, p. 190. See also Weaver, *Ideas Have Consequences*, p. 105.

44. Meyer, "Freedom, Tradition, Conservatism," p. 10. See also Wilhelmsen, *Christianity and Political Philosophy*, p. 201.

45. Meyer, *In Defense*, p. 41. See also Viereck, "But—I'm a Conservative!" p. 539; Kirk, *Conservative Mind*, p. 48; and Kendall, *Affirmation*, p. x.

46. Weaver, *Ethics of Rhetoric*, p. 113. See also Hallowell, *Moral Foundation*, p. 25; and Kirk, *Program*, p. 9.

47. Kirk, *Program*, p. 16.

48. Kendall and George W. Carey, "Towards a Definition of 'Conservatism,' " *Journal of Politics* 26 (May 1964), p. 414. See also Viereck, "But—I'm a Conservative!" p. 539.

49. Buckley, *Dream*, p. xxxix.

50. Meyer, "Freedom, Tradition, Conservatism," p. 13. See also Kirk, *Conservative Mind*, p. 17; and Weaver, *Ideas Have Consequences*, p. 52.

51. Weaver, "Up From Liberalism," p. 28.

52. Weaver, *Ideas Have Consequences*, p. 25.

53. Weaver, *Ideas Have Consequences*, p. 105.

54. See, for example, Weaver, *Ideas Have Consequences*, pp. 25, 55–58; Vivas, *Moral Life*, pp. ix–x, 133, 175; Voegelin, *New Science of Politics*, chapter 4; and Will, *Statecraft*, pp. 118–20.

55. Kirk, "Prescription," p. 31.

56. See, for example, Wilhelmsen, *Christianity and Political Philosophy*, p. 20.

57. Kirk, *Program*, p. 6. See also William Chamberlin, "Conservatism in Evolution," p. 254.

58. Kirk, *Conservative Mind*, p. 18. See also Will, *Pursuit of Virtue*, p. 78.

59. Viereck, "The Rootless 'Roots'," *Antioch Review* 15 (June 1955), p. 220. See also Kirk, *Program*, p. 30.

60. Will, "Battling the Racial Spoils System," p. 96.

61. Kirk, "Norms," p. 343.

BIBLIOGRAPHY

Aaron, Daniel. "Conservatism, Old and New." *American Quarterly* 6 (Summer 1954): 99–110.

Adorno, Theodore W., Else Frankel–Brunswick, Daniel J. Levinson, and R. Nevitt Sanford. *The Authoritarian Personality*. New York: Harper and Row, 1950. Abridged ed. New York: Norton, 1983.

Auerbach, M. Morton. *The Conservative Illusion*. New York: Columbia University Press, 1959.

Bell, Daniel. "The Dispossessed." In *The Radical Right*. Edited by Daniel Bell, 1–45. Garden City, N.Y.: Doubleday and Co., 1963.

——. "Interpretations of American Politics." In *The Radical Right*. Edited by Daniel Bell, 47–73. Garden City, N.Y.: Doubleday and Co., 1963.

——, ed. *The Radical Right*. Garden City, N.Y.: Doubleday and Co., 1963.

Berns, Walter. "The Need for Public Authority." *Modern Age* 24 (Winter 1980):16–20.

Bozell, L. Brent. "Freedom or Virtue." *National Review* (11 September 1962): 181–87, 206.

Brown, Stuart Gerry. "Democracy, the New Conservatism, and the Liberal Tradition in America." *Ethics* 56 (October 1955): 1–9.

Buckley, William F., Jr. *The Jeweler's Eye: A Book of Irresistible Political Reflections*. Revised ed. New York: G. P. Putnam's Sons, 1958.

——. *Right Reason*. Garden City, N.Y.: Little, Brown and Co., 1985.

——. *Up from Liberalism*. New York: McDowell, Obolensky, 1959.

Revised ed., New York: Stein and Day, 1984.

———, ed. *Did You Ever See a Dream Walking? American Conservative Thought in the Twentieth Century.* Indianapolis: Bobbs-Merrill Co., 1970. Revised, with Charles R. Kesler, ed. *Keeping the Tablets: Modern American Conservative Thought.* New York: Harper and Row, 1988.

Burnham, James. *Congress and the American Tradition.* Chicago: Henry Regnery Co., 1959.

———. "Notes on Authority, Morality, Power." *National Review* (1 December 1970): 1283–89.

———. "Re–Legitimization." *National Review* (1 June 1957): 518.

———. *The Suicide of the West: An Essay on the Meaning and Destiny of Liberalism.* New Rochelle, N.Y.: Arlington House, 1964. Reprinted Washington, D.C.: Regnery Gateway, 1985.

Carson, Clarence B. "Cutting Loose from Reality." *The Freeman* 15 (January 1965):45–58.

Chamberlain, John. "Ignore Human Nature?" *The Freeman* 14 (February 1964): 58–61.

———. "John Randolph of Roanoke." *The Freeman* 15 (July 1965): 58–61.

———. "The Morality of Free Enterprise." In *What Is Conservatism?* Edited by Frank S. Meyer, 181–87. New York: Holt, Rinehart and Winston, 1964.

———. *The Roots of Capitalism.* Princeton, N.J.: D. Van Nostrand Co., 1959. Reprint. Indianapolis: Liberty Fund, 1976.

Chamberlin, William Henry. "Conservatism in Evolution." *Modern Age* 7 (Summer 1963): 249–54.

Chapman, Philip C. "The New Conservatism: Cultural Criticism versus Political Philosophy." *Political Science Quarterly* 75 (March 1957): 17–34.

Chase, Richard. "Neo–Conservatism and American Literature." *Commentary* (March 1957): 254–65.

Christie, Richard, and Marie Jahoda, eds. *Studies in the Scope and Method of "The Authoritarian Personality."* Glencoe, Ill.: Free Press, 1954.

Coser, Lewis A., and Irving Howe, eds. *The New Conservatives: A Critique from the Left.* New York: New American Library, 1976.

Crick, Bernard. "The Strange Quest for an American Conservatism." *Review of Politics* 17 (July 1955): 359–76.

Doenecke, Justus D. "Conservatism: The Impassioned Sentiment." *American Quarterly* 28 (Winter 1976): 601–9.

East, John P. *The American Conservative Movement: The Philosophical Founders.* Chicago: Regnery Gateway, 1986.

————. "Eric Voegelin and American Conservative Thought." *Modern Age* 22 (Spring 1978): 114–32.

Etzioni, Amitai. "The Neoconservatives." *Partisan Review* 44 (1977): 431–7.

Evans, M. Stanton. "A Conservative Case for Freedom." In *What Is Conservatism?* Edited by Frank S. Meyer, 67–77. New York: Holt, Rinehart and Winston, 1964.

————. *The Future of Conservatism.* New York: Holt, Rinehart and Winston, 1968.

————. "Techniques and Circumstances." *National Review* (30 January 1962): 58.

Freund, Lugwig. "The New American Conservatism and European Conservatism." *Ethics* (October 1955): 10–17.

Fryer, Russell G. *Recent Conservative Political Thought: American Perspectives.* Washington, D.C.: University Press of America, 1979.

Gottfried, Paul and Thomas Fleming. *The Conservative Movement.* Boston: G. K. Hall, 1988.

Guttmann, Allen. *The Conservative Tradition in America.* New York: Oxford University Press, 1967.

Haiman, Franklyn S. "A New Look at the New Conservatism." *Bulletin of the American Association of University Professors* 41 (Autumn 1955): 444–53.

Hall, Chadwick. "America's Conservative Revolution." *Antioch Review* 15 (June 1955): 204–16.

Hallowell, John H. *Main Currents in Modern Political Thought.* New York: Henry Holt, 1950. Reprinted Washington, D.C.: University Press of America, 1985.

————. "Modern Liberalism: An Invitation to Suicide." *South Atlantic Quarterly* 46 (October 1947): 453–66.

————. *The Moral Foundation of Democracy.* Chicago: University of Chicago Press, 1954. Reprinted Chicago, 1973.

————. "Obstacles to the Recovery of a Christian Perspective on Human Nature." *Modern Age* 27 (Winter 1983): 2–14.

Harbour, William R. *Foundations of Conservative Thought.* Notre Dame, Indiana: University of Notre Dame Press, 1982.

Hartz, Louis. *The Liberal Tradition in America.* New York: Hartcourt, Brace, and World, 1955.

Herberg, Will. "Conservatives, Liberals, and the Natural Law, II." *National Review* (19 June 1962): 438, 458.

————. "The Presuppositions of Democracy." *Commonweal* 62 (3 June 1955): 234–36.

Himmelfarb, Gertrude. "The Prophets of the New Conservatism." *Commentary* (January 1959): 78–86.

Hofstadter, Richard. *The Paranoid Style in American Politics and Other Essays.* New York: Alfred A. Knopf, 1965. Reprinted Chicago: University of Chicago Press, 1979.

———. "Pseudo–Conservatism Revisited." In *The Radical Right.* Edited by Daniel Bell, 97–103. Garden City, N.Y.: Doubleday and Co., 1963.

———. "The Pseudo–Conservative Revolt." In *The Radical Right.* Edited by Daniel Bell, 75–95. Garden City, N.Y.: Doubleday and Co., 1963.

Huntington, Samuel P. "Conservatism as an Ideology." *American Political Science Review* 52 (June 1957): 454–73.

Jaffa, Harry V. "Another Look at the Declaration." *National Review* (11 July 1980): 836–40.

———. "On the Education of the Guardians of Freedom." *Modern Age* 30 (Spring 1986): 111–17.

Kendall, Willmoore. *The Conservative Affirmation.* Chicago: Henry Regnery Co., 1963. Reprinted Washington: Regnery Gateway, D.C., 1985.

———. "The People Versus Socrates Revisited." *Modern Age* 3 (Winter 1958–59): 98–111.

———. "Three on the Line." *National Review* (31 August 1957): 181.

Kendall, Willmoore, and George W. Carey. "Towards a Definition of 'Conservatism.' " *Journal of Politics* 26 (May 1964): 406–22.

Kerlinger, Fred N. *Liberalism and Conservatism: The Nature and Structure of Social Attitudes.* Hillsdale, N.J.: L. Erlbaum Assocs., 1984.

Ketcham, Ralph L. "The Revival of Tradition and Conservatism in America." *Bulletin of the American Association of University Professors* 41 (Autumn 1955): 425–43.

Kirk, Russell. *Beyond the Dreams of Avarice: Essays of a Social Critic.* Chicago: Henry Regnery Co., 1956.

———. "Conservatism Is Not an Ideology." *National Review* (30 January 1962): 59, 74.

———. *The Conservative Mind: From Burke to Eliot.* 4th ed. rev. New York: Avon Books, 1968. 7th ed. rev., Chicago: Regnery Gateway, 1986.

———. "Edmund Burke and the Future of American Politics." *Modern Age* 31 (Spring 1987): 107–14.

———. *Enemies of the Permanent Things.* New Rochelle, N.Y.: Arlington House, 1969. Reprinted La Salle, Ill.: Sugden, Sherwood and Co., 1984.

———. "Humane Political Economy." *Modern Age* 3 (Summer

1959): 226.

———. "An Ideologue of Liberty." *Sewanee Review* 72 (April–June 1964): 349–50.

———. Letter to the Editor. *National Review* (13 November 1981): 1334, 1336.

———. "Norms, Conventions, and the South." *Modern Age* 2 (Fall 1958): 338–45.

———. *The Old House of Fear.* New York: Fleet Publishing, 1961.

———. "Prescription, Authority, and Ordered Freedom." In *What Is Conservatism?* Edited by Frank S. Meyer, 23–40. New York: Holt, Rinehart and Winston, 1964.

———. *A Program for Conservatives.* rev. ed., Chicago: Henry Regnery Co., 1962.

———. "Promises and Perils of 'Christian Politics.' " *Intercollegiate Review* 18 (Fall/Winter 1982): 13–23.

———. "Prospects for a Conservative Bent in the Human Sciences." *Social Research* 35 (Winter 1968): 580–85.

———. "The Tension of Order and Freedom in the University." *Modern Age* 27 (Spring 1983): 114–19.

———. *The Wise Men Know What Wicked Things Are Writen on the Sky.* Washington: Regnery Gateway, D.C., 1987.

———. ed. *The Portable Conservative Reader.* New York: Penguin, 1982.

Kronick, Bernard L. "Conservatism: A Definition." *Southwestern Social Science Quarterly* 27 (September 1947): 171–79.

Kuehnelt-Leddihn, Erik von. "The Portland Declaration." *National Review* (16 October 1981): 1188–90, 1192–96.

Lewis, Gordon K. "The Metaphysics of Conservatism." *Western Political Quarterly* 6 (December 1953): 728–41.

Lief, Leonard, ed. *The New Conservatives.* Indianapolis: Bobbs-Merrill, 1967.

Lipset, Seymour Martin. "The Sources of the 'Radical Right.' " In *The Radical Right.* Edited by Daniel Bell, 307–71. Garden City, N.Y.: Doubleday and Co., 1963.

———. "Three Decades of the 'Radical Right': Coughlinites, McCarthyites, and Birchers." In *The Radical Right.* Edited by Daniel Bell, 373–446. Garden City, N.Y.: Doubleday and Co., 1963.

Lora, Ronald. *Conservative Minds in America.* Chicago: Rand McNally, 1971. Reprint Westport, Conn.: Greenwood Press, 1979.

McClosky, Herbert. "Conservatism and Personality." *American Political Science Review* 52 (March 1958): 27–45.

MacDonald, H. Malcolm. "The Revival of Conservative Thought." *Journal of Politics* 19 (February 1957):66–80.

Mark, Max. *Modern Ideologies*. New York: St. Martin's Press, 1973.

Meyer, Frank S. "Caricature of Conservatism." *National Review* (17 June 1961): 385.

———. "Champion of Freedom." *National Review* (7 May 1960): 304–5.

———. "Conservatism." In *Left, Right, and Center: Essays on Liberalism and Conservatism in the United States*. Edited by Robert A. Goldwin. Chicago: Rand McNally, 1965.

———. *The Conservative Mainstream*. New Rochelle, N.Y.: Arlington House, 1969.

———. "Freedom, Tradition, and Conservatism." In *What Is Conservatism?* Edited by Frank S. Meyer, 7–20. New York: Holt, Rinehart and Winston, 1964.

———. *In Defense of Freedom: A Conservative Credo*. Chicago: Henry Regnery Co., 1962.

———. "In Defense of John Stuart Mill." *National Review* (28 March 1956): 23–24.

———. "The Separation of Powers." *National Review* (30 January 1962): 59.

———. "The Twisted Tree of Liberty." *National Review* (16 January 1962): 25–26.

———. "Why Freedom?" *National Review* (25 September 1962): 223–25.

———, ed. *What Is Conservatism?* New York: Holt, Rinehart and Winston, 1964.

Mills, C. Wright. "The Conservative Mood." *Dissent* (Winter 1954): 22–31.

Molnar, Thomas. *Authority and Its Enemies*. New Rochelle, N.Y.: Arlington House, 1976.

———. "Crisis." *Modern Age* 31 (Summer/Fall 1987): 215–21.

———. *The Pagan Temptation*. Grand Rapids, Mich.: Eerdmans, 1987.

Morley, Felix. *Freedom and Federalism*. Chicago: Henry Regnery Co., 1959. Reprinted Indianapolis, Ind.: Liberty Fund, 1981.

Murphy, Dwight D. *Modern Social and Political Philosophies: Burkean Conservatism and Classical Liberalism*. Washington, D.C.: University Press of America, 1982.

Nash, George H. *The Conservative Intellectual Movement in America Since 1945*. New York: Basic Books, 1976.

Newman, William J. *The Futilitarian Society*. New York: George Braziller, 1961.

Niemeyer, Gerhart. *Aftersight and Foresight: Selected Essays*. Lanham, Md: University Press of America, 1988.

———. "A Christian Sheen on a Secular World." *Modern Age* 31 (Summer/Fall 1987): 355–61.

———. "Conservatism and the New Political Theory." *Modern Age* 23 (Spring 1979): 115–22.

———. "Foreign Policy and Morality". *Intercollegiate Review* 15 (Spring 1980): 2–9.

———. Review of Clinton Rossiter's *Conservatism in America*. In *Journal of Public Law* 4 (Fall 1955): 441–47.

Nisbet, Robert A. *Conservatism: Dream and Reality*. Minneapolis: University of Minnesota Press, 1986.

———. "Conservatism and Sociology." *American Journal of Sociology* 58 (1952): 167–75.

———. *The Present Age: Progress and Anarchy in Modern America*. New York: Harper and Row, 1988.

———. *The Twilight of Authority*. New York: Oxford University Press, 1975.

Oakeshott, Michael. "On Being Conservative." In *Rationalism in Politics and Other Essays*. London: Methuen, 1962.

Opitz, Edmund A. "Let's Not Save the World." *The Freeman* 15 (January 1965): 3–11.

———. "Painting Government into a Corner." *The Freeman* 14 (February 1964): 14–27.

O'Sullivan, Noel. *Conservatism*. New York: St. Martin's Press, 1976.

Preece, Rod. "The Anglo–Saxon Conservative Tradition." *Canadian Journal of Political Science* 13 (March 1980): 3–32.

Read, Leonard E. "A Blessing of Extremism." *The Freeman* 14 (February 1964): 42–56.

———. In *The Freeman* 15 (September 1965): 64.

———. "Knowing That We Know Not." *The Freeman* 15 (October 1965): 11–14.

———. "On Freedom and Order." *The Freeman* 15 (January 1965): 29–38.

Riesman, David. "The Intellectuals and the Discontented Classes: Some Further Reflections." In *The Radical Right*. Edited by Daniel Bell, 137–59. Garden City, N.Y.: Doubleday and Co., 1963.

———. and Nathan Glazer. "The Intellectuals and the Discontented Classes." In *The Radical Right*. Edited by Daniel Bell, 105–35. Garden City, N.Y.: Doubleday and Co., 1963.

Rossiter, Clinton. *Conservatism in America: The Thankless Persuasion*. New York: Alfred A. Knopf, 1955.

Schlesinger, Arthur, Jr. *The Politics of Hope*. London: Eyre and Spottiswoode, 1964.

Spitz, David. "Freedom, Virtue, and the New Scholasticism." *Commentary* 28 (October 1959): 313–21.

Tonsor, Stephen J. "The Conservative Search for Identity." In *What Is*

Conservatism? Edited by Frank S. Meyer, 133–51. New York: Holt, Rinehart and Winston, 1964.

———. "Educating the Children of the 'Me' Generation." *Modern Age* 25 (Summer 1981): 255–63.

———. "The Father of Totalitarian Democracy: Jean–Jaques Rousseau." *Modern Age* 31 (Summer/Fall 1987): 243–51.

———. "The New Natural Law and the Problem of Equality." *Modern Age* 24 (Summer 1980): 238–47.

Viereck, Peter R. E. "But—I'm a Conservative!" *Atlantic Monthly* (April 1940): 538–43.

———. *Conservatism: From John Adams to Churchill.* Princeton, N.J.: Van Nostrand, 1956.

———. *Conservatism Revisited: The Revolt Against Revolt.* New York: Charles Scribner's Sons, 1949.

———. "The Philosophical 'New Conservatism.' " In *The Radical Right.* Edited by Daniel Bell, 185–207. Garden City, N.Y.: Doubleday and Co., 1963.

———. "The Revolt against the Elite." In *The Radical Right.* Edited by Daniel Bell, 161–83. Garden City, N.Y.: Doubleday and Co., 1963.

———. "The Rootless 'Roots': Defects in the New Conservatism." *Antioch Review* 15 (June 1955): 217–29.

Vivas, Eliseo. *The Moral Life and the Ethical Life.* Chicago: University of Chicago Press, 1950. Reprinted Washington, D.C.: University Press of America, 1984.

———. *Relativism: Its Paradoxes and Pitfalls.* Philadelphia: Intercollegiate Society of Individualists, 1962.

Voegelin, Eric. *From Enlightenment to Revolution.* Durham: Duke University Press, N.C., 1975.

———. *The New Science of Politics.* Chicago: University of Chicago Press, 1952. Reprinted 1987.

———. "On Classical Studies." *Modern Age* 17 (1973): 2–8.

———. *Order and History.* Vol. 1, *Israel and Revelation.* Baton Rouge: Louisiana State University Press, 1956.

———. *Order and History.* Vol. 2, *The World of the Polis.* Baton Rouge: Louisiana State University Press, 1957.

Weaver, Richard M. *Academic Freedom.* Philadelphia: Intercollegiate Society of Individualists, 1963.

———. *The Ethics of Rhetoric.* Chicago: University of Chicago Press, 1953. Reprinted Davis, Ca.: Hermagoras Press, 1985.

———. *Ideas Have Consequences.* Chicago: University of Chicago Press, 1948. Reprinted 1984.

————. *Relativism and the Crisis of Our Times*. Philadelphia: Intercollegiate Society of Individualists, 1961.

————. *The Southern Tradition at Bay: A History of Postbellum Thought*. Edited by George Core and M. E. Bradford. New Rochelle, N.Y.: Arlington House, 1968.

————. "Up from Liberalism." *Modern Age* 3 (Winter 1958–59): 21–32.

Weisman, Steven R. "What Is a Conservative?" *New York Times Magazine* (31 August 1980): 13.

Wilhelmsen, Frederick. *Christianity and Political Philosophy*. Athens, Ga.: University of Georgia Press, 1978.

————. "The Conservative Vision." *Commonweal* 62 (24 June 1955): 295–99.

————. "My Doxy Is Orthodoxy." *National Review* (22 May 1962): 365–66.

Will, George F. "Armies Should Win Wars." *Newsweek* (18 February 1981): 120.

————. "A Baptism of Fire." *Newsweek* (13 April 1981): 108.

————. "Battling the Racial Spoils System." *Newsweek* (10 June 1985): 96.

————. "A Broker for the Democrats." *Newsweek* (14 March 1983): 80.

————. "The Case for Automakers." *Newsweek* (7 March 1981): 88.

————. "Getting Big Things Done." *Newsweek* (30 March 1981): 90.

————. "Henry Kissinger's Craft." *Newsweek* (29 March 1982): 84.

————. "The Madison Legacy." *Newsweek* (7 December 1981): 124.

————. "Nuclear Morality." *Newsweek* (21 December 1981): 84.

————. "Onward and Upward." *Newsweek* (8 June 1981): 108.

————. "Opposing Prefab Prayer." *Newsweek* (7 June 1982): 84.

————. *The Pursuit of Happiness and Other Sobering Thoughts*. New York: Harper and Row, 1978.

————. *The Pursuit of Virtue and Other Tory Notions*. New York: Simon and Shuster, 1982.

————. "Reaping the Whirlwind." *Newsweek* (21 January 1980): 92.

————. "The Soul of Conservatism." *Newsweek* (11 November 1985): 92.

————. "The Splendid Legacy of FDR." *Newsweek* (11 February 1982): 78.

————. *Statecraft as Soulcraft: What Government Does*. New York: Simon and Shuster, 1983.

————. "Through Hoops for a Column." *Newsweek* (15 March 1982): 88.

————. "The Value of Punishment." *Newsweek* (24 May 1982): 92.

————. "What Stockman Really Said." *Newsweek* (23 November 1981): 130.

————. "Who Put Morality in Politics?" *Newsweek* (15 September 1980): 10.

Young, James P. *The Politics of Affluence: Ideology in the United States Since World War II*. San Francisco: Chandler Publishing Co., 1968.

Zoll, Donald Atwell. "The Philosophical Foundations of the American Political Right." *Modern Age* 15 (Spring 1971): 114–29.

———. *The Twentieth Century Mind*. Baton Rouge: Louisiana State University Press, 1967.

———. *Twentieth Century Political Philosophy* Englewood Cliffs, N.J.: Prentice Hall, 1974.

INDEX

Absolutes, 37–39, 41, 44–45, 48
Academic freedom, 68–69
Anarchism, 88
Anticommunist conservatives, 12
Authority, 55–74, 77–96, 142–44;
    and core ideas, 55; and
    freedom, tension between,
    83–97; and the individual,
    57–63; necessary for freedom,
    64–65; noncoercive, 91–93,
    140–41, 144; and society, 62–74;
    and virtue, 91–94; voluntary
    compliance with, 91–93

Berns, Walter, 11
Bozell, L. Brent, 11
Buckley, William F., Jr., 12
Burnham, James, 12

Capitalism, 115–16, 118–22
Chamberlain, John, 11
Chamberlin, William Henry, 11
Chambers, Whittaker, 12
Change: must be slow, 178;
    reasons to favor, 173–79; re-
    quired by the objective moral

order, 173–75; resistance to,
    inadequate as a definition, 4–5,
    15 n.4, 163; threatens stability
    required by human nature,
    170; and tradition, 43,
    163–79
Chodorov, Frank, 140
Civil rights, 108–9, 132 n.20
Common good, 65
Communism, 68–70, 120, 130–31
Community, 137–60; and
    authority, 91–93, 94; and free-
    dom, 90; part of the solution to
    the freedom-authority dilem-
    ma, 142–44
Consensus, 46, 66–72. See also
    Tradition
Conservative thought, unity and
    diversity, 3, 9–10
Constitution of being, 37, 40, 43
Constitution of the United States,
    129
Constitutional limits on
    government, 107–13;
    misinterpretation of, 109–10

Core ideas of contemporary American conservative thought, 8, 10; influence on rest of conservative thought, 8–9, 13–14; and tension between freedom and authority, 55, 96–97

Definitions, previous, 3–7
Democracy, 124–30; restrained by community, 143
Dignity of man, 27–32, 89
Distinction between conservative thinkers and nonconservatives, 8, 10
Diversity in conservative thinking, 3, 9–10
Divine order, 38–41
Division of powers, 107–8
Doenecke, Justus D., 17 n.9
Duties and rights, 84

East, John P., 24
Economic freedom, 80–82
Economy and government, 113–22
Educational institutions, 157–60
Elites, 106, 145–49
Emotion, 26, 30, 31
Equality, 72–73, 122–24, 147–48
Evans, M. Stanton, 11
Evil inherent in human nature, 21–28

Family, an essential institution, 149–52
Federalism, 107–8
Foreign policy, position on, influenced by core beliefs, 130–31
Free market economy, 79
Freedom, 77–87; and authority, tension between, 83–97; and core ideas, 55, 77, 87; and

equality, 123; political, 125; preserved by free economy, 113–15; and private property, 114–15; protected by community, 143–44; and social organization, 78–79; supported by religious institutions, 155; threatened by democracy, 125; threat to, from community, 140–42; and variety, 78; and virtue, 77–78, 84-85, 86

God, author of the objective moral order, 38–39, 40; source of freedom, 79
Good in human nature, 27–32
Government: balancing too little and too much, 101, 104–5; and economy, 113–22; last resort for solving social problems, 110–12; legitimate functions, 101–2, 103–4; means to an end, 104; negative functions, 103; positive functions, 103; relationship to other authoritative institutions, 108–13
Great Tradition, 171–73

Habits, 60
Hallowell, John, 11
Happiness and objective moral order, 47–48, 165
Harbour, William R., 19 n.18
Hayek, Friedrich A., 11
Herberg, Will, 11
Hierarchy, 144–49
History of contemporary American conservative movement, 7, 10–13
Human nature: and capitalism, 115; and community, 137–39;

creates need for authority, 55,
57; and democracy, 124; misunderstood in modern world,
176–77; and objective moral order, 40, 41–42, 47, 49–51; makes
power dangerous, 78, 81, 87,
105–6, 110; view of conservative thinkers, 21–31
Human reason and capitalism,
117

Imperfectibility of man, 23–24
Individual, balance between and
community, 139–40
Individual improvement, 31
Individual rights, 39, 58, 80; and
duties, 84; misconstrued,
109–10
Individuality, 78
Institutions, social, 90, 91–93, 94,
142–43
Interest groups, 73

Jaffa, Harry V., 11

Kendall, Willmoore, 11
Kirk, Russell, 12
Knowledge of objective reality,
40–44
Kuehnelt-Leddihn, Erik von, 28

Law, 59, 65–66, 93, 94
Leaders, natural, 60, 95, 146–47
Leadership, 146–47
Legitimate functions of government, and core ideas, 101,
102, 103–4
Liberal relativism, opposition to
by conservative thinkers, 37–38,
44–48. See also Relativism
Libertarian conservatives, 10–11,
56

Libertarianism, 88
Limits on government, 103
Local government, 107–8

McCarthy, Joseph, 69–70
Marxism, 115
Mediocrity, produced by democ-
racy, 125–26
Meyer, Frank S., 11
Modern society, conservative
hostility to, 173–78
Molnar, Thomas, 11
Moral foundations of democracy,
127–28
Moral order, view of conservative
thinkers, 37–51
Morley, Felix, 11
Myths, value of, 171

Nash, George H., 7, 18 n.16
National Review, 12
Natural law, 40–42, 47–48, 59
Natural rights, 39, 58, 80–81
Niemeyer, Gerhart, 12
Nisbet, Robert, 12
Nongovernmental institutions,
108–13

Oakeshott, Michael, 16 n.9
Objective moral order: and community, 139; and freedom, 80,
90; and government, 46–47, 48;
and human nature, 40, 41–42,
47, 49–51, 166; must be recognized by leaders, 146–47; and
tradition, 164–65; view of
conservative thinkers, 37–51
Objective reality, 37–39, 41, 44–45,
166
Opitz, Edmund, 11
Order, social, 144–49

Original sin, 22–23
Orthodoxy, 66–72, 85–87
O'Sullivan, Noel, 15 n.4

Paternalism and virtue, 113
Permissiveness, 46, 67
Persuasion, moral and intellectual, power of, 113, 143, 152, 154
Power and human nature, 78, 81, 87, 103, 106, 116
Prefectibility of man, 23–24
Prejudice, sound, 169
Property, 80–82, 120–21; appropriate to human nature, 115–17; and equality, 123, 124; fosters virtue, 82, 115–16; and government, 114–22; protects freedom, 114–15
Psychological explanations, inadequate as definition, 5–6

Read, Leonard, 11
Reality, objective, 37–39, 41
Reason, 25–27, 29–31; and authority, 60; insufficient as guide to objective moral order, 164; as source of knowledge of reality, 41–44, 164–66; and tradition, 42–44, 164–67, 168, 174–76
Relativism: effects on government, 46–47; opposition to by conservative thinkers, 37–38, 44–48, 70, 158; and permissiveness, 46; threat to freedom, 46
Religious institutions, 154–57
Representation, limit on democracy, 126–27
Revelation, divine, 40–41, 43, 71
Reverse discrimination, 108–9
Rothbard, Murray, 88

Rulers, right ones essential for right government, 105–7, 126–27, 128, 146–47

Science, conservative view of, 177
Security, 82
Self-discipline, 60–61
Self-interest, 27, 57, 63, 119–20, 129
Sexes, roles of, 152–54
Skepticism about capacities of government, 111–12
Social integration, 63. See also Hierarchy
Social structure and authority, 72–73
Socialism, 88, 115
Sociological explanations, inadequate as definition, 5–7
Stability required by nature of man, 170
Statism, 46
Status quo, defense of, inadequate as definition, 4–5

Tonsor, Stephen J., 11, 13
Tradition, 42–43, 163–79; an approximation of the objective moral order, 164–65; and reason, 42–44, 164–67, 168, 174–76; respect for based on belief in objective moral order, 165; source of knowledge of objective moral order, 164; tames democracy, 128–30
Traditionalist conservatives, 11–12, 56
Truth, 37–39, 41, 44–45; and orthodoxy, 70–72; and tradition, 164–65
Twentieth century, opinion of conservative thinkers on, 174–78

Universals, 37–39, 41, 44–45, 48

Values, imposing on society,
    69–70
Variety, 78, 122–23; and freedom,
    123
Viereck, Peter, 12
Virtue, 31, 59, 60–61, 77–78, 84–85,
    86, 168; aided by hierarchy,
    145–46; aim of human exist-
    ence, 89, 91, 95; and govern-
    ment, 93–94, 105–6, 113; sup-
    ported by property, 82; threat-
    ened by materialism, 119

Vivas, Eliseo, 11
Voegelin, Eric, 11
Von Mises, Ludwig, 11

Weaver, Richard M., 11
Welfare state, 82
Wilhelmsen, Frederick, 11
Will, George F., 12
Wilson, Francis, 12

Zoll, Donald Atwell, 11

About the Author

MELVIN J. THORNE is the executive editor and a member of the board of directors of the Foundation for Ancient Research and Mormon Studies, in Provo, Utah.